The Complete **RHIT** and **RHIA** Prep

A Guide for Your Certification Exam and Your Career

Payel Bhattacharya Madero, MBA, RHIT
ICD-10 AHIMA Approved Trainer – 2009
Program Chair and Instructor for Medical
    Reimbursement and Health IT
Ontario, California

JONES & BARTLETT
LEARNING

World Headquarters
Jones & Bartlett Learning
5 Wall Street
Burlington, MA 01803
978-443-5000
info@jblearning.com
www.jblearning.com

Jones & Bartlett Learning books and products are available through most bookstores and online booksellers. To contact Jones & Bartlett Learning directly, call 800-832-0034, fax 978-443-8000, or visit our website, www.jblearning.com.

Substantial discounts on bulk quantities of Jones & Bartlett Learning publications are available to corporations, professional associations, and other qualified organizations. For details and specific discount information, contact the special sales department at Jones & Bartlett Learning via the above contact information or send an email to specialsales@jblearning.com.

18666-6

Production Credits
VP, Product Management: Amanda Martin
Director of Product Management: Cathy Esperti
Product Manager: Danielle Bessette
Product Assistant: Tess Sackmann
Project Manager: Kristen Rogers
Project Specialist: John Fuller
Digital Products Manager: Jordan McKenzie
Digital Project Specialist: Angela Dooley
Senior Marketing Manager: Susanne Walker
Production Services Manager: Colleen Lamy

Manufacturing and Inventory Control Supervisor: Amy Bacus
Composition: codeMantra U.S. LLC
Project Management: codeMantra U.S. LLC
Text Design: Kristin E. Parker
Cover Design: Michael O'Donnell
Senior Media Development Editor: Shannon Sheehan
Rights Specialist: Maria Leon Maimone
Cover Image (Title Page, Part Opener, Chapter Opener):
   © Liu zishan/Shutterstock
Printing and Binding: Sheridan Books

Library of Congress Cataloging-in-Publication Data
Names: Bhattacharya, Payel Madero, author.
Title: The complete RHIT and RHIA prep : a guide for your certification exam and your career / Payel Bhattacharya Madero.
Other titles: Complete Registered Health Information Technician and Registered Health Information Administrator prep
Description: First Edition. | Burlington, Massachusetts : Jones & Bartlett Learning, 2020. | Includes bibliographical references and index.
Identifiers: LCCN 2019033968 | ISBN 9781284186666 (Paperback)
Subjects: LCSH: Medical records—Management—Examinations, questions, etc. | Information resources management—Examinations, questions, etc.
Classification: LCC RA976 .B49 2019 | DDC 651.5/04261—dc23
LC record available at https://lccn.loc.gov/2019033968

6048

Printed in the United States of America
23 22 21 20 19   10 9 8 7 6 5 4 3 2 1

Dedication

Thank you Jehovah for my life, my heart, my mind, and my soul. Every perfect present is from you. I am in awe and appreciation of all that you have done for me.

Thank you to my husband Chris who kept me laughing through every obstacle we face. I can never repay you for the joy that you shine on me. There are no perfect words that I can share that communicate how special you are to me; all I can express is thanks for joining me on this wild adventure! I love you!

Thank you Amora and Sabrina for your love, patience, and encouragement through each step of this project. To have you both proud of me brings meaning to my life. You are both my favorite blessings.

To Danielle Bessette, who saw potential in this project and believed in it every step of the way.

To all those special friends, you know who you are, who work hard to keep me deep rooted and balanced through this project's completion and facing life's challenges as they come. Thanks for believing in me and loving me every step of the way.

Contents

About the Author

Payel Bhattacharya Madero's journey into medical reimbursement began when her mom, Chandana Basu, started a medical billing service after receiving training in St Louis. Although she was just 12 at the time, she was fascinated with medical code sets and taught herself to code with coding manuals, health insurance plan manuals, and a medical dictionary. Every weekend and school break Madero worked with her mom to build the medical billing service that eventually expanded to over 20 states with a variety of medical specialties and surgery centers.

After Madero finished college she joined Basu and they took the company public. Within a year they had secured over $2 million to develop practice management software to facilitate accurate medical billing and coding for physicians' offices for which she was a software architect. However, in an effort to add credibility to the software, Madero went to graduate school to complete a master's degree in Health Services Management in 2007. After she completed her degree at Keller Graduate School she was asked to join their team as an instructor and she never went back to the corporate world.

Madero wanted to unite her passions for Health IT and Medical Reimbursement with her new love for teaching. She became an RHIT professional after completing an associate's degree in Health Information Technology at DeVry University in 2009.

Madero brought her self-taught coding strategies to the classroom to help students grasp challenging HIT and HIM concepts. She also contributed to several published textbooks, including *Insurance Handbook for the Medical Office, Thirteenth* and *Fourteenth Editions*, and *Kinn's The Medical Assistant: An Applied Approach, Thirteenth Edition*. She currently is a program chair for a growing medical coding and billing certificate program.

A New Type of Exam Prep

Teaching HIT and HIM for the past 10 years, Madero recognized a significant gap in resources for students preparing to sit for the RHIT and RHIA exams. The handful of other prep texts exist that are, in essence, large question test banks. Madero passed her exam by using these test banks repeatedly until she felt ready. However, this method did not prepare her for the HIT industry. She had studied and memorized terms, but felt ill-prepared to *apply* these concepts in the real world. She saw the need for a resource that focused on application instead of rote memorization. The ability to incorporate online interactive modules to provide the student with the opportunity to actively apply concepts was the primary inspiration for *The Complete RHIT and RHIA Prep*.

Because the HIT and HIM industry is very specialized, Madero added an extensive career planning and development chapter to this text. It provides students with HIT- and HIM-specific resources for both starting a career and then reaching career goals within the industry.

Another contributing factor to *The Complete RHIT and RHIA Prep* is that the certification exam is computerized, whereas most RHIT and RHIA prep texts are primarily print. Madero felt the current student generation required a robust online and interactive learning platform in order to feel engaged. In this edition, only the questions are in the print text; all of the online learning and exam competency prep is completed online.

Finally, there has been a need for a textbook that merges the exam competencies with the AHIMA Core Competencies found in CAHIIM-approved HIT and HIM programs. This product is the only RHIT and RHIA exam prep on the market that achieves this.

Get the Most Out of *the Complete RHIT and RHIA Prep*

The Complete RHIT and RHIA Prep contains three distinct parts to help students comprehensively prepare for the exam: the **main text**, with questions and resources; the **online test prep** to provide additional practice with the questions, including the ability to generate a self-administered mock exam; and the **online interactive modules** that allow students to listen, watch, and interact with the content so that they learn to apply concepts.

The main text contains 29 chapters, which are supplemented by the online interactive modules to provide a holistic review of the exam content using the following configuration:

Chapter 1: Introduction to the RHIT and RHIA Certification Exams
- Main text—Provides an explanation of how to qualify and register for the AHIMA-sponsored exam. Also contains test-taking tips for each exam.

Chapters 2 through 27 cover domain topics from the AHIMA Core Competencies
- Main text—Contains multiple-choice test questions
- Online interactive module—Reviews the AHIMA Core Competencies and includes interactive scenarios for experiencing concepts in action

Chapter 28: Prepping for the RHIA Exam
- Main text—Assists RHIA exam candidates to prepare for their exam

Chapter 29: Planning for a Career in HIM
- Main text—Proposes career search, development, planning, and growth strategies for recent RHIT- and RHIA-licensed professionals

There are over 500 practice exam questions covering all topics addressed by the AHIMA Core Competencies to provide practice for both RHIT and RHIA exam candidates, with hundreds more available online for qualified instructors teaching capstone or exam review courses. The main text contains a list of common healthcare statistical formulas, an extensive pharmaceutical terms supplement, the AHIMA Code of Ethics, the RHIT and RHIA Exam Competency Outlines, and a glossary with 550 HIM terms. The interactive online learning modules provide a brief review of HIT and HIM concepts that students should have learned through the CAHIIM-approved HIT/HIM educational program.

CAHIIM-approved associate's, baccalaureate, and post-baccalaureate programs require students to study computer informatics, medical terminology, anatomy and physiology, pathophysiology, and pharmacology. Exam candidates will face questions from these subjects on their RHIT/RHIA exams as well, so there will be applicable practice questions. Finally, Appendix B contains a list of common pharmaceuticals students may find in healthcare documentation; this section is valuable for practice and review.

CHAPTER 1

Introduction to the RHIT and RHIA Certification Exams

In this chapter, we explore the following:
- Confirm eligibility to take the RHIT/RHIA certification exams
- Compare the requirements to take the RHIT and RHIA certification exams
- RHIT and RHIA certification exam application process
- Prepare for exam day
- Find success with multiple-choice exams
- Obtain exam results

Confirm Eligibility to Take the RHIT/RHIA Certification Exams

If you have purchased this book, congratulations! You are close to reaching a monumental education goal. Let's take a moment to acknowledge the hard work it took for you to get here.

Students graduating from a Commission on Accreditation for Health Informatics and Information Management (CAHIIM)-approved associate's degree program in health information technology are eligible to take the Registered Health Information Technologist (RHIT) exam. Students graduating from a CAHIIM-approved bachelor's degree or post-baccalaureate program are eligible to take the Registered Health Information Administrator (RHIA) exam. To confirm that you are enrolled in a CAHIIM-approved education program, (please visit www.cahiim.org /directoryofaccredpgms/programdirectory.aspx).

Value of Certification

You have worked very hard to earn this degree. Why would it be valuable for you to earn the RHIT or RHIA credential as well? Through your education program, you have learned the daily operations of information in the healthcare facility. However, passing the certification exam proves that you are competent and proficient in your knowledge of Health Information Management (HIM). Both RHIT and RHIA certification exams provide evidence that you have met the minimum knowledge standards to effectively manage health information. In other words, the certification offers a professional step beyond earning your degree, so it can add great value to your resume.

Not all HIM programs at the associate's, baccalaureate, and/or master's level are approved by CAHIIM, so these candidates do not have the option of taking these exams. The opportunity to take these exams is a privilege that your educational institutional program worked hard to obtain for your professional benefit, so take advantage of it!

Course Mapping

Part of the process to meet CAHIIM education requirements is that all the HIM courses need to map to American Health Information Management Association (AHIMA) competencies or standards. You may have come across a document that looks similar to **TABLE 1-1**. This map is used to ensure that you have learned about all of the requirements to become a credentialed professional. This alone should give you confidence as you prepare for your exam.

Compare the Requirements for the RHIT and RHIA Exams

We will cover the requirements for both the RHIT and the RHIA exams in this one exam prep book and online modules. The RHIA exam covers the same topics for the most part, just to a deeper level, so prepping with RHIT materials provides a strong foundation for success on the RHIA exam. In Chapter 28, we will highlight topics just for RHIA candidates are not adequately covered in the RHIT exam prep 28. Download the Commission on Certification for Health Informatics and Information Management (CCHIIM) candidate guide for specific vital information on the application process; it can be found at www.ahima.org/downloads/certification/Candidate_Guide_2019_Updates.pdf.

RHIT Eligibility and Exam

RHIT applicants must meet one of the following eligibility requirements:

	Healthcare Delivery and Processes	Introduction to the Health Care Record	Information Systems in the Health Care Environment W/Lab	Healthcare Statistics W/Lab	Healthcare Data Sets and Registries	Coding I W/Lab	Coding II W/Lab	Procedural Coding W/Lab	Health Insurance Reimbursement W/Lab	Healthcare Law and Ethics	Quality and Performance Improvement	Leadership Roles, Theories and Skills	Health Information Practicum
Subdomain I.A Classification Systems													
1. Apply diagnosis/procedure codes according to current guidelines						X	X	X					
2. Evaluate the accuracy of diagnostic and procedural coding						X	X	X			X		
3. Apply diagnostic/procedural groupings						X	X	X	X		X		
4. Evaluate the accuracy of diagnostic/procedural groupings						X	X	X					
Subdomain I.B. Health Record Content and Documentation						X	X	X					
1. Analyze the documentation in the health record to ensure it supports the diagnosis and reflects the patient's progress, clinical findings, and discharge status		X											X
2. Verify the documentation in the health record is timely, complete, and accurate		X											X
3. Identify a complete health record according to, Organizational policies, external regulations, and standards		X							X	X			X
4. Differentiate the roles and responsibilities of various providers and disciplines, to support documentation requirements, throughout the continuum of healthcare	X												

TABLE 1-1 HIM map for an associate's degree program

Modified from Registered Health Information Technician (RHIT) Exam; Registered Health Information Administrator (RHIA) Examination Content Outline, AHIMA.

- Successfully complete the academic requirements, at an associate's degree level, of an HIM program accredited by CAHIIM
  OR
- Graduate from an HIM program approved by a foreign association with which AHIMA has a reciprocity agreement

The RHIT certification exam includes 150 multiple-choice questions for an exam time of 3.5 hours. Out of the 150 questions, only 130 are scored; the other 20 questions are pretest questions, which are not scored, so they cannot count for or against the final score. The passing score for the RHIT exam is 300 out of 400, which is a scaled score. When you are taking practice exams, aim for scores above 75%. For an outline of the RHIT exam, please visit Appendix A. Take a few minutes to read through the content outline and check off the competencies about which you feel more confident and circle the ones that you feel you might need to work on.

RHIA Eligibility and Exam

RHIA applicants must meet one of the following eligibility requirements:

- Successfully complete the academic requirements, at the baccalaureate level, of an HIM program accredited by CAHIIM
  OR
- Successfully complete the academic requirements, at the master's level, of an HIM program accredited by CAHIIM and following a specific set of criteria
  OR
- Graduate from an HIM program approved by a foreign association with which AHIMA has a reciprocity agreement
  OR
- Be an RHIT who meets the Proviso conditions approved by the 2017 CCHIIM

The RHIA certification exam includes 180 multiple-choice questions for an exam time of 4 hours. Out of the 180 questions, only 160 are scored; the other 20 questions are pretest questions, which are not scored, so they cannot count for or against the final score. The passing score for the RHIA exam is 300 out of 400, which is a scaled score. When you are taking practice exams, aim for scores above 75%. For an outline of the RHIA exam, please visit Appendix B. Take a few minutes to read through the content outline and check off the competencies about which you feel more confident, and circle the ones that you feel you might need to work on.

RHIT and RHIA Certification Exam Application Process

Qualified candidates should visit the AHIMA webstore to purchase the exam and to begin the online application process. Other requirements of the application include the following:

- Official college transcripts via email to CertificationTranscripts@ahima.org or mailed to AHIMA, Certification Transcripts 233 N. Michigan Ave., 21st Fl. Chicago, IL 60601

Once AHIMA has verified the transcript and confirmed that the exam fees have been paid, they will issue an authorization to test (ATT). Candidates with an approved exam application will receive the ATT letter within 5 business days. The ATT letter contains an authorization number, the eligibility period for testing, and instructions for scheduling an appointment at a testing center. Candidates may only schedule their appointment within their assigned 4-month eligibility window. The eligibility start date and end date are provided in the ATT letter.

With the ATT letter in hand, visit the Pearson Vue testing locations website. To schedule a date, provide the authorization number listed on the ATT letter. For a list of testing locations nationwide, please visit pearsonvue.com/ahima.

Be sure to note the time and location of the testing center in multiple places, including your phone and your laptop! Before the day of the examination, please be sure the address and directions to the test center are correct; map the directions to confirm driving time so that you are not late. If a candidate goes to the wrong test center on the day of the examination and cannot test, the exam fee will be forfeited and the candidate must re-apply and re-submit another application and fee.

Early Testing

Students enrolled in a CAHIIM-accredited programs for RHIT or RHIA, who are enrolled in their final term of study, are eligible to apply for and take their respective certification exam early. Eligible students include the following:

- Students currently enrolled and in their last term of study
- Students who have completed their coursework but have not yet graduated
- Graduates who are currently waiting for their official transcripts

To apply as an early tester, purchase the exam through the AHIMA webstore. When completing the online exam application, select the early testing options and upload the completed application for early testing. Please be sure to only submit your exam application with the completed application for early testing; otherwise, your application will not be approved.

Candidates who apply for early testing and successfully pass their exam will have their credential granted once official transcripts (must include graduation date) are received. The exam date will be used as the official date the credential is granted.

Appointment Changes

AHIMA's policies about changing a testing appointment are as follows:

- Candidates may cancel and reschedule the examination up to 15 days prior to the scheduled examination date at no charge.
- Any candidate who reschedules or cancels his or her appointment between 14 days and 24 hours prior to the exam date will be charged a penalty of $30 by Pearson VUE. Rescheduling and payment must be completed using a valid credit card through pearsonvue.com/ahima or by calling the Pearson VUE Call Center at (888) 524–4622.
- Candidates may not reschedule the examination less than 24 hours prior to the examination appointment.
- Candidates who do not arrive or who arrive late to their scheduled exam appointment time will be considered no-shows and will forfeit their application fee.
- Candidates who fail to appear for the scheduled appointment or who are over 15 minutes late will not be allowed to test. A new application and the full application fee must be submitted in order to test.

Prep for Exam Day

The Pearson VUE staff adheres to approved procedures to ensure the test center meets AHIMA's testing criteria. Please review the following information prior to the testing date to ensure familiarity with the procedures:

- Plan to arrive at the test center 30 minutes before the scheduled appointment. Candidates arriving at the test center 15 minutes after the scheduled appointment will not be allowed to test and will forfeit the testing fee.
- Know when and where the test will be given and be ready to be tested (no materials are allowed in the exam).

- Please ensure that both forms of your identification meet the requirements posted on pearsonvue.com/ahima under "On Examination Day."

  When arriving at the Pearson Vue test center, candidates will:

- Receive the Professional Examination Rules Agreement
- Submit two valid, correct forms of identification (ID)
- Have their digital signature captured to verify that signatures match
- Have their palm vein pattern captured
- Have a photograph taken
- Store belongings
- Show reference materials for approval (when applicable)

A dry erase board will be provided to all candidates for use during the examination. No scratch paper is allowed.

Identification Requirements

To be allowed to test, candidates must present a primary form of ID containing their signature and picture, and a second form of ID showing their signature. **The candidate's name on the primary and secondary forms of ID must match the name appearing on the ATT letter.**

Acceptable forms of primary ID must be valid and nonexpired, and feature the candidate's photograph and signature. These include:

- Government-issued driver's licenses, including temporary licenses with all required elements (refer to "Unacceptable Forms of Candidate Identification" for an exception when presented with a Texas driver's license that carries two expiration dates)
- U.S. Department of State driver's license
- U.S. learner's permit (plastic card only with photo and signature)
- National/state/country identification card
- Passport
- Passport card
- Military ID
- Military ID for spouses and dependents
- Alien registration card (green card, permanent resident visa)
- Government-issued local language ID (plastic card with photo and signature)

Acceptable forms of secondary ID must be valid and nonexpired and must feature the candidate's signature. These include:

- Social Security card
- Debit/ATM card
- Credit cards (must have a visible expiration date)
- Any form of ID on the primary list

The following are examples of unacceptable forms of ID:

- Expired driver's license or expired passport
- Library card
- Marriage certificate
- Voter's registration card
- Club membership card
- Public aid card
- Temporary driver's license without proper paperwork and photo identification
- Temporary Social Security card without signature
- Video club membership card
- Traffic citation (arrest ticket)
- Fishing or hunting license
- AHIMA membership card

Find Success with Multiple-Choice Exams

All of the questions on both the RHIT and the RHIA exam are multiple choice. This means that you can employ a few test-taking methods to deduce the correct response. Here are some tips to find success in multiple choice exams:

- Read the entire question
  At times, we may feel overconfident and answer a question prior to reading the entire question and inadvertently get it wrong! You will have almost a minute per question on either exam; it sounds like a short amount of time, but it's not!
- Answer the questions you are confident you know
  Do not spend too much time on these, but don't go too fast through them. Be sure to read through the entire question, and if you're confident, answer it and go on!
- Eliminate the obvious wrong answer
  These questions will be done on the computer, but you will be able to keep notes on a provided dry erase board. If you are unsure about a question, flag it on the computer, write out the answers that you know are wrong, and continue with the test. As you complete the rest of the test, the answer may come to you.
- Key words *always*, *never*, *sometimes*, *not*
  These words may not be highlighted or bolded, and they can be easy to miss. Be sure to read each and every question thoroughly.
- Final check!
  Use your dry erase board to keep a record of the answers you get right and the ones that you are not sure about. Before you click submit, take the time to review each question.

Types of Questions

On the RHIT and RHIA exams, there are a mix of three categories of multiple-choice questions, which include:

- **Recall questions.** These are questions that designed to test your memory. You'll be required to identify HIM terms, specific facts, data and information management procedures, and so on.
- **Application questions.** These use critical thinking skills to apply the facts that you have learned.
- **Analysis questions.** These are used to measure the depth of your knowledge and ability to apply it to various situations.

Obtain Exam Results

Once the candidate submits the exam, he or she returns to the exam proctor to collect the score report. The score report informs the candidate about whether they passed right after they completed the exam, so there is no wait time! The score report contains some valuable information, especially if the candidate did not pass. The report separates the results based on the domains listed on the exam content outlines to identify possible areas of improvement for future testing.

Candidates who pass are considered credentialed professionals from the date of the exam! Newly credentialed professionals (if authorized) will appear on AHIMA's website at secure.ahima.org/certification /newly_credentialed.aspx.

Beta Period Testing

At times, AHIMA publishes a new testing format and closes instant grading for a period of time. In this case, the results are not released after the exam, but AHIMA will mail the results to the candidates once the exam is graded. To check if your exam is scheduled during a beta period, please contact AHIMA directly to confirm.

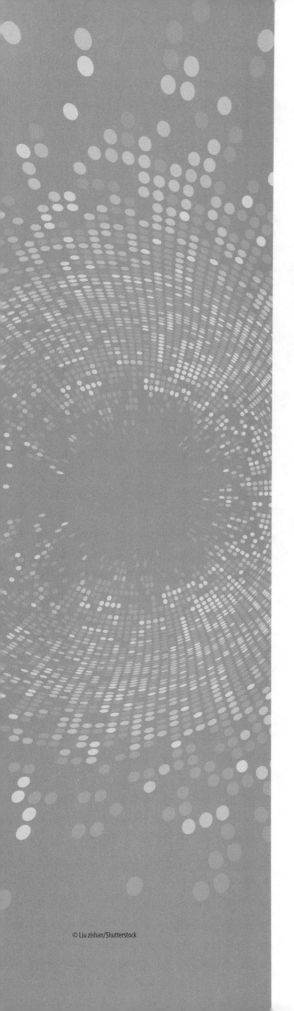

DOMAIN I

Classification Systems

CHAPTER 2

Classification Systems

In this chapter, we review the following subdomains:

- I.A.1. Apply diagnosis/procedure codes according to current guidelines
- I.A.2. Evaluate the accuracy of diagnostic and procedural coding
- I.A.3. Apply diagnostic/procedural groupings
- I.A.4. Evaluate the accuracy of diagnostic/procedural groupings

The following topics are covered in this subdomain:

- Principles of Nomenclatures
- Clinical Vocabularies
- Taxonomies
  - OASIS
  - HEDIS
  - UHDDS
  - DEEDS
- Classification Systems
  - ICD-10-CM
  - ICD-10-PCS
  - HCPCS
  - CPT
  - SNOMED
  - DSM

- Principles and applications of classification systems and audits
- Principles and applications of diagnostic and procedural groupings
  - Diagnosis Related Group (DRG)
  - Medicare Severity Diagnosis Related Group (MS-DRG)
  - Ambulatory Payment Class (APC)
  - Resource Utilization Groups (RUGs)
- Principles and applications of diagnostic and procedural groupings and audits

MAIN TERMS

APC	Data sets	Grouper
Clinical vocabularies	DEEDS	HCPCS
CPT	DSM	HEDIS

MAIN TERMS (CONTINUED)

ICD-10-CM	Nomenclature	Taxonomy
ICD-10-PCS	OASIS	UACDS
LOINC	RUGs	UHDDS
MDCs	RxNorm	
MS-DRG	SNOMED	

Practice Questions

1. Referring to the following 0CQ table, which code would be considered invalid?

Section	0	Medical and Surgical
Body System	C	Mouth and Throat
Operation	Q	Repair: Restoring, to the extent possible, a body part to its normal anatomic structure and function

Body Part	Approach	Device	Qualifier
0 Upper Lip **1** Lower Lip **2** Hard Palate **3** Soft Palate **4** Buccal Mucosa **5** Upper Gingiva **6** Lower Gingiva **7** Tongue **N** Uvula **P** Tonsils **Q** Adenoids	**0** Open **3** Percutaneous **X** External	**Z** No Device	**Z** No Qualifier
8 Parotid Gland, Right **9** Parotid Gland, Left **B** Parotid Duct, Right **C** Parotid Duct, Left **D** Sublingual Gland, Right **F** Sublingual Gland, Left **G** Submaxillary Gland, Right **H** Submaxillary Gland, Left **J** Minor Salivary Gland	**O** Open **3** Percutaneous	**Z** No Device	**Z** No Qualifier

Body Part	Approach	Device	Qualifier
M Pharynx **R** Epiglottis **S** Larynx **T** Vocal Cord, Right **V** Vocal Cord, Left	**0** Open **3** Percutaneous **4** Percutaneous Endoscopic **7** Via Natural or Artificial Opening **8** Via Natural or Artificial Opening Endoscopic	**Z** No Device	**Z** No Qualifier
W Upper Tooth **X** Lower Tooth	**0** Open **X** External	**Z** No Device	**0** Single **1** Multiple **2** All

Reproduced from ICD-10-PCS Tables, Centers for Medicare & Medicaid Services, Retrieved from https://www.njmmis.com/downloadDocuments/pcs_2018.pdf

   a. 0CQ3XZZ

   b. 0CQ80ZZ

   c. 0CQ74ZZ

   d. 0CQWXZ2

2. Which of the following CPT coding guidelines is true when a reduction of a fracture is performed with cast application?

   a. Use the terminology *immobilization* rather than *reduction*.

   b. Include external fixation in all codes.

   c. Do not use a separate code for the application of a cast separately.

   d. Do not differentiate between open and closed treatment—CPT only specifies the site of the fracture.

3. The operative report states a laparoscopic cholecystectomy was performed. A small gallstone was found and removed. What ICD-10-PCS root operation would be coded for this procedure?

   a. Excision

   b. Extirpation

   c. Resection

   d. Inspection

4. A patient is discharged from the hospital with a principal diagnosis of referred abdominal pain due to peptic ulcer, versus cholecystitis, which are <u>both equally treated</u> and well documented. Which of the following would be the correct ICD-10-CM coding and sequencing?

a. Peptic ulcer, cholecystitis, abdominal pain

b. Cholecystitis, peptic ulcer, abdominal pain

c. Abdominal pain

d. Abdominal pain, peptic ulcer, cholecystitis

---

5. A patient is discharged from the hospital with a diagnosis of abdominal pain, probable Crohn's disease. Which of the following would be the correct diagnosis sequencing and coding for this case?

a. Abdominal pain

b. Abdominal pain, Crohn's disease

c. Crohn's disease, abdominal pain

d. Crohn's disease

---

6. When coding, what is the best medical documentation source used to determine the weight of a removed malignant lesion?

a. Anesthesia report

b. Operative report

c. Pathology report

d. History and physical report

---

7. The patient was admitted from the emergency department because of chest pain. Following blood work, it was determined that the CPK and MB enzymes were elevated. Which report will show this information?

a. Pathology report

b. Laboratory report

c. Triage intake form

d. Anesthesia report

---

8. Mary works as a coder in a hospital inpatient department. She sees a lab report in a patient's health record that is positive for strep infection; however, there is no mention of strep in the physician's documentation. What should Mary do?

a. Tell her supervisor

b. Query the physician

c. Assign a code for the staph infection

d. Put a note in the chart

9. The physician has ordered calcium supplements for the patient. Which of the following would the coder expect to see as a diagnosis?

   a. Hypocalcemia
   b. Hyponatremia
   c. Hyperkalemia
   d. Hypernatremia

10. A patient is admitted to the hospital for an acute myocardial infarction. The patient also suffers from Type 2 diabetes and hypertension. While hospitalized, the patient develops hypertension, which subsequently resolves. In the DRG system, which of the following would most likely be considered a complication in this case?

    a. COPD
    b. Pneumonia
    c. Myocardial infarction
    d. Hypertension

11. A patient is admitted to the hospital with a diagnosis of pyelonephritis and anemia. The patient also has a diagnosis of COPD. While in the hospital, the patient suffers a myocardial infarction and has to undergo an angioplasty. Given this information, how many MS-DRGs would be assigned to this case?

    a. One
    b. Two
    c. Three
    d. Four

12. A patient is admitted to the hospital with back pain. The principal diagnosis is pyelonephritis. The patient also has depression, irritable bowel syndrome, and diabetes. In the inpatient prospective payment system, which of the following would determine the MDC assignment for this patient?

    a. Depression
    b. Diabetes
    c. Diverticulosis
    d. Pyelonephritis

13. A _____ is an examination of health records to determine the level of coding accuracy and to identify areas of coding problems.

    a. data quality improvement program

    b. payment error prevention program

    c. data quality review

    d. process analysis

14. In performing an internal audit to identify risk areas for coding compliance, which of the following would be suitable case selections for auditing?

    a. Outlier diagnosis and procedure codes

    b. Medical and surgical MS-DRGs by low dollar and high volume

    c. Medical and surgical MS-DRGs by high dollar and high volume

    d. Medical and surgical MS-DRGs by high dollar and low volume

15. A hospital interested in finding out background information on a physician should review data from:

    a. NPDB.

    b. OASIS.

    c. ORYX.

    d. UHDDS.

16. When a physician is appointed to the medical staff of a healthcare organization, their scope of practice is determined by their:

    a. clinical knowledge.

    b. credentials.

    c. background.

    d. hospital clincal privileges.

17. When coding in the CPT code set, the word *and* should be interpreted to mean *and* as well as:

    a. *or.*

    b. *with.*

    c. *see.*

    d. *see also.*

18. In the ICD-10-CM code set, Z code are used for all of the following, except:

    a. newborn delivery.

    b. threatened to, impending case, or late effect.

    c. ankle facture, initial encounter.

    d. admission for, history of observation, or status.

19. During the operative procedure, Mr. Hampton's blood pressure spikes, so the physician decides to discontinue the procedure. Which CPT code modifier should be assigned?

    a. −22 Increased procedural service

    b. −52 Reduced service

    c. −53 Discontinued service

    d. −57 Decision for surgery

20. In the ICD-10-CM code set, what are external causes of morbidity used to report?

    a. Factors influencing health status and contact with health status

    b. External causes of injury and poisoning

    c. Injuries and poisonings

    d. Symptoms, signs, and ill-defined conditions

21. Which of the following root operations in the ICD-10-PCS code set is used when removing the entire left breast?

    a. Removal

    b. Extirpation

    c. Resection

    d. Excision

22. Congress passed which of the following to better control Medicare costs?

    a. HEDIS

    b. CMS

    c. TEFRA

    d. OASIS

23. If the medical record documentation does not include the type of diabetes or indicate whether the patient's disease is uncontrolled, what should the coder do first?

    a. Code E10, Type 1 Diabetes Mellitus

    b. Code E11, Type 2 Diabetes Mellitus

    c. Query the physician

    d. Review physician orders for additional documentation

24. Johnny Black broke his arm 2 weeks ago and has returned to Dr. Hopper for an X-ray to ensure healing of the fracture. When coding the diagnosis for the encounter, the seventh character of the ICD-10-PCS code should be:

    a. A.

    b. D.

    c. S.

    d. The character cannot be determined from the information given.

25. Assign the correct ICD-10-PCS code using the following table for this procedure: Exchange of a malfunctioning pacemaker electrode, percutaneous.

Section	0	Medical and Surgical
Body System	2	Heart and Great Vessels
Operation	W	Revision: Correction, to the extent possible, a portion of a malfunctioning device or the position of a displaced device

Body Part	Approach	Device	Qualifier
5 Atrial Septum **M** Ventricular Septum	**0** Open **4** Percutaneous Endoscopic	**J** Synthetic Substitute	**Z** No Qualifier
A Heart	**0** Open **3** Percutaneous **4** Percutaneous Endoscopic	**2** Monitoring Device **3** Infusion Device **7** Autologous Tissue Substitute **8** Zooplastic Tissue **C** Extraluminal Device **D** Intraluminal Device **J** Synthetic Substitute	**Z** No Qualifier

Body Part	Approach	Device	Qualifier
		K Nonautologous Tissue Substitute **M** Cardiac Lead **N** Intracardiac Pacemaker **Q** Implantable Heart Assist System **Y** Other Device	
A Heart	**0** Open **3** Percutaneous **4** Percutaneous Endoscopic	**R** Short-term External Heart Assist System	**S** Biventricular **Z** No Qualifier

    a. 02WM4JZ

    b. 02WA3NZ

    c. 02WA4NZ

    d. 02WA0RS

26. Pam is a patient of the Happy Days Behavioral Health Long Term Facility. Which of the following code sets is used to code for this type of facility?

    a. CPT

    b. ICD-10-CM

    c. DSM V

    d. HCPCS

27. Which of the following information is not collected for the UHDDS?

    a. Date of birth

    b. Social Security number

    c. Diagnosis code

    d. Procedure code

28. The lipid panel (80061) in the laboratory section of CPT consists of tests for cholesterol, serum, total (82465); lipoprotein, direct measurement, high density lipoprotein (HDL) cholesterol (83718); and triglycerides (84478). If each of the codes is billed separately on the insurance claim form, this would be an example of:

    a. classifying.

    b. optimizing.

c. sequencing.

d. unbundling.

---

29. An outpatient clinic is reviewing the functionality of a health information system it is considering purchasing. Which of the following data sets should the clinic consult to ensure all of the federally required data elements for Medicare and Medicaid outpatient clinical encounters?

    a. UHDDS

    b. DEEDS

    c. UACDS

    d. OASIS

---

30. Which root operation is used in ICD-10-PCS for amputation procedures?

    a. Excision

    b. Replacement

    c. Resection

    d. Detachment

---

31. Identify the ICD-10-CM chapter in which certain signs and symptoms of gastrointestinal disease, such as Crohn's disease and gastritis, are included.

    a. Chapter 2 Neoplasms

    b. Chapter 11 Diseases of the digestive system

    c. Chapter 12 Diseases of the skin and subcutaneous tissue

    d. Chapter 14 Diseases of the genitourinary system

---

32. Which of the following ICD-10-PCS codes is correct for a cystoscopy with diagnostic bladder biopsy?

Section	**0**	Medical and Surgical
Body System	**T**	Urinary System
Operation	**B**	Excision: Cutting out or off, without replacement, a portion of a body part

Body Part	Approach	Device	Qualifier
0 Kidney, Right **1** Kidney, Left **3** Kidney Pelvis, Right	**0** Open **3** Percutaneous **4** Percutaneous Endoscopic	**Z** No Device	**X** Diagnostic **Z** No Qualifier

Body Part	Approach	Device	Qualifier
4 Kidney Pelvis, Left **6** Ureter, Right **7** Ureter, Left **B** Bladder **C** Bladder Neck	**7** Via Natural or Artificial Opening **8** Via Natural or Artificial Opening Endoscopic		
D Urethra	**0** Open **3** Percutaneous **4** Percutaneous Endoscopic **7** Via Natural or Artificial Opening **8** Via Natural or Artificial Opening Endoscopic **X** External	**Z** No Device	**X** Diagnostic **Z** No Qualifier

    a. 0TBB8ZZ

    b. 0TBB8ZX

    c. 0TBB8ZZ, 0TBB8ZX

    d. 0TBB7ZX

33. While using the CPT codeset, a repair of a laceration that includes subcutaneous tissue should be considered what type of closure?

    a. Simple

    b. Immediate

    c. Complex

    d. Not specified

34. Certified Health Information Systems use _____ for the electronic exchange of clinical health information.

    a. HEDIS

    b. SNOMED CT

    c. DEEDS

    d. UHDDS

35. The physician orders an MRI for an outpatient who presents with a fever, elevated white blood count, and a persistent cough. The physician records in the progress notes: "*Rule Out Lung Cancer.*" What should the coder report for the visit when the results have not yet been received?

    a. Lung cancer

    b. Persistent cough

    c. Fever, elevated white blood count, and persistent cough

    d. Lung cancer, fever, elevated white blood count, and persistent cough

36. A new patient comes to the office for a skin rash on the arm. The physician provides a straightforward diagnosis, and the medical decision making is simple. The collected patient history is limited. Which of the following codes should be assigned for an office visit for this case?

    a. 99201 Office or other outpatient visit for the evaluation and management of a new patient, which requires these three key components: problem-focused history and examination, straightforward medical decision

    b. 99203 Office or other outpatient visit for the evaluation and management of a new patient, which requires these three key components: detailed history and examination, low complexity medical decision

    c. 99211 Office or other outpatient visit for the evaluation and management of an established patient, which requires at least two of these three key components: problem-focused history and examination, straightforward medical decision

    d. 99212 Office or other outpatient visit for the evaluation and management of an established patient, which requires at least two of these three key components: problem-focused history and examination, straightforward medical decision

Resources

For additional resources, please review the following references:

Abdelhak, M., & Hanken, M. A. (2016). *Health Information: Management of a Strategic Resource*. St. Louis, MO: Elsevier.
  - Chapter 5: Clinical Terminologies, Classifications, and Code Systems

Oachs, P. K., & Watters, A. (2016). *Health Information Management: Concepts, Principles, and Practice*. Chicago, IL: AHIMA, American Health Information Management Association.
  - Chapter 5: Clinical Terminologies, Classifications, and Code Systems

Sayles, N. B., & Gordon, L. L. (2016). *Health Information Management Technology: An Applied Approach*. Chicago, IL: American Health Information Management Association.
  - Chapter 7: Classification Systems, Clinical Vocabularies, and Terminology

CHAPTER 3

Health Record Content and Documentation

In this chapter, we review the following subdomains:

- I.B.1. Analyze the documentation in the health record to ensure it supports the diagnosis and reflects the patient's progress, clinical findings, and discharge status
- I.B.2. Verify the documentation in the health record is timely, complete, and accurate
- I.B.3. Identify a complete health record according to organizational policies, external regulations, and standards
- I.B.4. Differentiate the roles and responsibilities of various providers and disciplines to support documentation requirements throughout the continuum of health care

The following topics are covered in this subdomain:

- Content and documentation requirements of the health record
- Documentation requirements of the health record for all record types
  - Paper, computer, web-based document imaging
  - Acute, ambulatory, long-term care, rehab, and behavioral health
- Medical staff bylaws
- The Joint Commission
- State statutes

- Legal health record
- Roles and responsibilities of healthcare providers for health information documentation
- Classification systems
- Administrative
  - Patient registration
  - Admission/discharge/transfer (ADT)
- Clinical
  - Billing
  - Lab, radiology, pharmacy

MAIN TERMS

Administrative data	Duplicate medical record number	Primary healthcare data
Alphabetic filing system	Information	Requisition
Alphanumeric filing system	Master patient index (MPI)	Secondary healthcare data
Clinical data	Middle-digit filing system	Serial numbering system
Data	Medical record number	Terminal digit filing system
Deficiency slip	Patient account number	Unit numbering system

Practice Questions

1. Dr. Thompson has fallen behind completing his medical record documentation, with 12 of her 20 medical records needing to be completed. What is her records delinquency rate?

   a. 5%

   b. 10%

   c. 40%

   d. 60%

2. When the health record technician was analyzing the patient record, the discharge order was not found. Which of the following is most likely documented in the physician's orders regarding this patient?

   a. The patient died in the hospital prior to discharge.

   b. The patient left against medical advice given.

   c. The family members requested the patient be transferred to hospice care.

   d. The patient will seek treatment on an outpatient basis.

3. How many years should the master patient index (MPI) be maintained for a healthcare facility?

   a. 5 years

   b. 10 years

   c. 20 years

   d. Indefinitely

4. Dr. Peters made an error while documenting progress notes in a patient's paper medical record. What is the first step he should take to correct the medical record?

   a. Remove the page of the medical record on which he made the error.

   b. Inform the nursing staff to ignore the error.

   c. Draw a single line through the error, and sign and date the correction.

   d. Destroy the medical record in total.

5. When a patient agrees to sign a consent for treatment, they agree to:

   a. allow the hospital to release information to his or her insurance company.

   b. accept the medical treatments and procedures suggested by the physician.

   c. take all medications prescribed.

   d. allow the hospital to dispose of his or her medical record.

6. A patient underwent an emergency appendectomy due to appendicitis. When must this operative report be completed?

   a. Immediately after surgery

   b. Within 24 hours of surgery

   c. Within 48 hours of surgery

   d. Within 15 days of discharge

7. Which of the following organizations establishes the standardization of patient records and data collection?

   a. The Joint Commission

   b. Department of Health and Human Services

   c. American Medical Association

   d. American Hospital Association

8. Which of the following users is using protected health information (PHI) for its intended purpose?

   a. A patient uses PHI to review his or her lab results.

   b. The Health Information Department uses PHI to assign medical codes.

c. An accrediting agency uses PHI to analyze the record to assure quality health care.

d. An employer reviews PHI to evaluate on-the-job injuries.

9. The _____ diagnosis underlines the purpose for the patient admission.

a. admitting

b. principal

c. preliminary

d. discharge

10. Which of the following pieces of documentation information types would be included in the discharge summary?

a. Vital signs

b. Review of body systems

c. Do not resuscitate (DNR) order

d. Instructions for patient and caregiver for continuing care

11. Which of the following is considered secondary data?

a. The patient account statement for treatment rendered

b. Documentation informing patients of their cancer status

c. Clinical documentation to improve quality of care delivery

d. Data collected for cancer research

12. A health information technician wants to review the chronological list of patients admitted to the facility during the third quarter of 20XX from Little Rock, California. Which database would the technician refer to?

a. Accession register

b. Master patient index

c. Disease index

d. Patient register

13. Richard, a 72-year-old lung cancer patient, needs palliative care. Which facility could meet his healthcare needs?

a. Skilled nursing facility

b. Hospice care

c. Acute care facility

d. Outpatient surgery center

14. Which of the following federal healthcare agencies researches communicable diseases, environmental health, and foreign quarantine activities?

    a. Centers for Medicare and Medicaid Services

    b. National Institutes of Health

    c. Health Resources and Services Administration

    d. American College of Surgeons

15. Which type of hospital provides health care to military personnel and their immediate families?

    a. Private hospital

    b. Integrated healthcare system

    c. Government hospital

    d. Not-for-profit hospital

16. Mrs. Howard had surgery early in the day and was discharged home the same day. Where did her procedure take place?

    a. Acute care facility

    b. Medical office

    c. Ambulatory surgical center

    d. Long-term care facility

17. Mr. Branson, a 78-year-old male, is unable to walk after his stroke. Although he spent 30 days in the acute care facility, he still needs continuous skilled nursing care. What type of facility should Mr. Branson be transferred to?

    a. Another acute care facility

    b. Skilled nursing facility

    c. Rehabilitation facility

    d. Home health facility

18. During the admission process, Mrs. Jones's date of birth was incorrectly recorded. An EHR audit revealed that the numbers in her date of birth were transposed. What type of error is this?

    a. Data consistency

    b. Data currency

    c. Data granularity

    d. Data comprehensiveness

19. A surgeon requests the second opinion of another surgeon, and the second surgeon reviews the patient's medical history and examines the patient. Which report should the surgeon record findings, professional impressions, and recommendations?

    a. History and physical

    b. Progress notes

    c. Consultation report

    d. Physician orders

20. Which of the following initiatives is used by the Joint Commission to collect intrahospital mortality data?

    a. DEED initiatives

    b. OASIS initiatives

    c. ORYX initiatives

    d. HEDIS initiatives

21. Which of the following paper record filing methods is considered to be the most space efficient?

    a. Terminal digit

    b. Alphabetical

    c. Alphanumeric

    d. Straight numeric

22. In progress notes using the SOAP note style, in which section will vital signs be recorded?

    a. Subjective

    b. Objective

    c. Assessment

    d. Plan

23. Dr. Harris entered the progress note in the patient record 48 hours after he visited the patient. Which data quality characteristic is lacking?

    a. Data currency

    b. Data timeliness

    c. Data completeness

    d. Data precision

24. Which of the following information is not considered clinical data?

    a. Admitting diagnosis

    b. Health insurance

    c. Admission date

    d. Vital signs

25. Gary Harman comes into the ER with a gunshot wound and is losing blood quickly. The ER physician, the lab technician, and the radiologist review the patient record simultaneously. Which data characteristic is represented here?

    a. Data comprehensiveness

    b. Data currency

    c. Data accessibility

    d. Data accuracy

26. The primary purpose of the health record is to use patient health information to:

    a. deliver quality health care.

    b. research specific health diagnoses.

    c. educate patients on how to care for their health.

    d. develop healthcare policies to support the community.

27. Which of the following healthcare facilities uses the OASIS data set?

    a. Long-term care facility

    b. Acute care facility

    c. Skilled nursing facility

    d. Home health facility

28. Delinquent records happen when the patient record is:

    a. sent to the court to act as a witness.

    b. not complete within the timeframe outlined by the medical staff bylaws.

    c. incomplete because the physician's orders are not signed.

    d. pending because the patient has yet to be discharged.

29.   How do accreditation organizations, such as the Joint Commission, use the health record?

   a.   As a source for case study information

   b.   To support an insurance health claim for reimbursement

   c.   To ensure the documentation supports the standards of quality care

   d.   To collect information about healthcare services

30.   The San Antonio Community Hospital, a long-term acute care facility, wants to participate in federal government insurance programs such as Medicare and Medicaid. What accreditation will the facility need to participate in Medicare and Medicaid insurance programs?

   a.   OASIS

   b.   CARF

   c.   AHA

   d.   The Joint Commission

31.   Which of the following terms indicates recognition by CMS as having earned deemed status?

   a.   Certification

   b.   Licensing

   c.   Credential

   d.   Accreditation

32.   Which of the following establishes the rules and regulations for a healthcare facility?

   a.   Healthcare facility committees

   b.   Medical staff bylaws

   c.   Credentialing committee

   d.   Classification systems

33.   Which healthcare facility committee oversees the development and approval of new forms used in the healthcare facility?

   a.   Clinical forms committee

   b.   Executive management committee

   c.   Quality review committee

   d.   Medical staff committee

34. Which of the following records do nurses use for documentation?

   a. Consultation report

   b. Discharge report

   c. Therapy report

   d. Medication record

35. Which characteristic of data quality excludes the collection of patient eye color?

   a. Data currency

   b. Data precision

   c. Data relevancy

   d. Data accuracy

Resources

For additional resources, please review the following references:

Abdelhak, M., & Hanken, M. A. (2016). *Health Information: Management of a Strategic Resource*. St. Louis, MO: Elsevier.
   ■ Chapter 2: Healthcare Delivery Systems

Oachs, P. K., & Watters, A. (2016). *Health Information Management: Concepts, Principles, and Practice*. Chicago, IL: AHIMA, American Health Information Management Association.
   ■ Chapter 1: The US Healthcare Delivery System

Sayles, N. B., & Gordon, L. L. (2016). *Health Information Management Technology: An Applied Approach*. Chicago, IL: American Health Information Management Association.
   ■ Chapter 1: Healthcare Systems

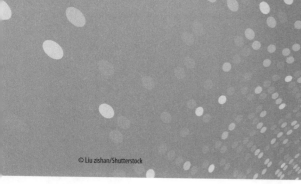

CHAPTER 4

Data Governance

In this chapter, we review the following subdomains:
- I.C.I. Apply policies and procedures to ensure the accuracy and integrity of health data.

The following topics are covered in this subdomain:
- Data stewardship and data sources for patient care
  - Management, billing reports, registries, and/or databases
- Data integrity concepts and standards
- Data interchange standards
  - Health Level 7 and X2 standards
- Medical staff bylaws
- Hospital bylaws
- Provide contracts with facilities

MAIN TERMS

Accreditation

Certification

Data governance

Data integrity

Data interchange standards

Data stewardship

Health Level Seven (HL7)

Institute of Electrical and Electronics Engineers (IEEE)

Joint Commission

Licensing

Provider credentialing

X2

Practice Questions

1. The process of standardizing medical terminology to organize data in a database is also known as:

   a. data dictionary.

   b. transaction standards.

   c. data mining.

   d. confidentiality standards.

2. Which organization has established messaging standards for electronic data interchange?

   a. X2

   b. HL7

   c. ASTM

   d. HEDIS

3. Which of the following contains the policies and procedures unique to each healthcare facility?

   a. Licensing

   b. Accreditation

   c. Classifications

   d. Bylaws

4. What can health information technicians do to ensure the authorized access of healthcare data?

   a. Identify external threats to the EHR

   b. Assign usernames and passwords

   c. Regularly conduct audit trails

   d. Limit employee access to patient information

5. The electronic interchange standard that transmits health insurance claim information between the payer and the provider is:

   a. LOINC.

   b. DEEDS.

   c. X12.

   d. SNOMED.

6. The health information department uses which of the following information systems to monitor daily hospital admissions and discharges?

    a. Enterprise information systems

    b. Management information systems

    c. Transaction processing systems

    d. Clinical decision support

7. The log created by patient record access, which includes the health provider documenter and the date and time the data is recorded in the discharge summary medical record, is an example of:

    a. data integrity.

    b. data interchange standards.

    c. interoperability.

    d. metadata.

8. Which of the following is used to establish a continuous, data-driven accreditation process that uses performance measures and data focused on quality core measures?

    a. Data aggregation

    b. ORYX initiative

    c. Data accuracy

    d. Audit trail

9. Which of the following terms defines the process of ensuring data is not altered or changed through transmission across a network?

    a. Control

    b. Extenuation

    c. Mitigation

    d. Integrity

10. Electronic information standards that provide defined descriptors of data elements are known as:

    a. metadata standards.

    b. security standards.

    c. structure and content standards.

    d. integrity standards.

11. Which of the following standards provides complete descriptions of the use of PHI in a healthcare facility?

    a. Governing board bylaws

    b. Notice of privacy practices

    c. Standard HIM policies and procedures

    d. Medical staff regulations

12. Authorization for the release of psychotherapy medical records is always required, except in case of:

    a. research-related data collection.

    b. release to the patient's health insurance company.

    c. release to the patient employer.

    d. release to the welfare office.

13. When considering an upgrade the EHR system, which of the following organizations should be consulted to ensure the EHR is certified to meet HL7 standards?

    a. Office of National Coordinator (ONC)

    b. Centers for Medicare and Medicaid Services (CMS)

    c. Health Information Exchange (HIE)

    d. Certification Commission for Health Information Technology (CCHIT)

14. A coding data analyst accidently enters the incorrect patient gender in the practice management software. What controls should be in place to prevent these types of errors?

    a. Security controls

    b. Privacy controls

    c. Validation checks

    d. Coding checks

15. All of the following are considered benefits of data exchange standards, except:

    a. to communicate within across disciplines and settings.

    b. to collect and compare health information for research purposes at regional, national, and international levels.

    c. to separate facility health data from a national database.

    d. to integrate disparate health data systems.

16. What resource should be consulted to determine who may authorize access, use, or disclosure of the health records of minors?

    a. HIPAA because it has strict rules regarding minors

    b. Hospital attorneys because they know the rules of the hospital

    c. State law because HIPAA defers to state laws on matters related to minors

    d. Federal law because HIPAA overrides state laws on matters related to minors

17. Which of the following is required of all healthcare facilities at the local and state levels?

    a. Accreditation

    b. Certification

    c. Licensing

    d. Certification

18. According to the Joint Commission, an acute care facility is required to:

    a. deliver quality care to Medicaid patients.

    b. implement performance improvement measures.

    c. ensure an RHIT or RHIA professional manages the healthcare facility's information department.

    d. evaluate organizational management policies yearly.

19. The main objective of clinical practice guidelines established by the healthcare facility board of directors is to:

    a. determine the outcomes from the delivery of patient care.

    b. standardize the content of clinical pathways.

    c. standardize the clinical decision-making process.

    d. establish accreditation standards.

20. Secondary databases are collected mostly via which of the following?

    a. Automated data entry

    b. Encoders

    c. Groupers

    d. Encryption

Resources

For additional resources, please review the following references:
Citations

Abdelhak, M., & Hanken, M. A. (2016). *Health Information: Management of a Strategic Resource*. St. Louis, MO: Elsevier.
- Chapter 6: Data Management
  - Data Governance

Oachs, P. K., & Watters, A. (2016). *Health Information Management: Concepts, Principles, and Practice*. Chicago, IL: AHIMA, American Health Information Management Association.
- Chapter 3: Data Governance and Stewardship

Sayles, N. B., & Gordon, L. L. (2016). *Health Information Management Technology: An Applied Approach*. Chicago, IL: AHIMA, American Health Information Management Association.
- Chapter 4: Health Data Concepts and Information Governance

CHAPTER 5
Data Management

In this chapter, we review the following subdomains:
- I.D.1. Collect and maintain health data
- I.D.2. Apply graphical tools for data presentations

The following topics are covered in this subdomain:
- Health data collection tools
- Data elements
- Data sets
- Databases and Indices
- Data mapping
- Data warehousing
- Graphical tools and presentations

MAIN TERMS

Bar chart	Data mart	Gannt chart
Clinical forms committee	Data mining	Line chart
Data accessibility	Data precision	Object-oriented database
Data accuracy	Data relevancy	Object-relational database
Data comprehensiveness	Data timeliness	ONC
Data consistency	Data warehouse	Pareto chart
Data currency	Database Management Systems (DBMS)	Pie chart
Data definition		Primary key
Data dictionary	EHR	Relational database
Data granularity	Flow sheets	Structured data
Data mapping	Foreign key	Unstructured data

Practice Questions

1. In an effort to assist the hospital systems analyst in creating a centralized repository of all data elements collected in the MPI database, some database definitions were provided. An example of this documentation includes: Length: 8 characters; Type: numeric; Value: XX/XX/XXXX. This resource is known as:

    a. a data warehouse.

    b. a data dictionary.

    c. a data set.

    d. data mapping.

2. The computerized provider order entry (CPOE) tool is a component of a(n):

    a. electronic health record.

    b. management information system.

    c. clinical decision support system.

    d. unified medical language system.

3. The search feature in a database is used to:

    a. find a patient medical record.

    b. alert the user that data fields are not complete and cannot be saved.

    c. delete the patient medical record.

    d. move a patient record from archive to active.

4. The Department of Health Information wants to run a query in the physician index to determine how many providers specialize in gastroenterology for the hospital group. Which computer language would be used to run this query?

    a. Java

    b. HTTP

    c. SQL

    d. XML

5. According to AHIMA, how long should the MPI be retained for any healthcare facility?

    a. 5 years

    b. 10 years

    c. 25 years

    d. Permanently

6. In the state of California, 753 deaths were reported for the month of October. Of these, 65% were from gun violence, 25% from stab wounds, 5% as a result of domestic violence, and 5% from road rage. Given the preceding data, what would be the best graphical presentation?

    a. Frequency table

    b. Bar graph

    c. Gantt chart

    d. Pie chart

7. The Director of Health Information would like to compare the coding completion rates among their five coders. Which graphical presentation would be the most appropriate?

    a. Line graph

    b. Pie chart

    c. Bar graph

    d. Frequency table

8. Which of the following charts is used in project management to display the processes that need to be completed?

    a. Bar chart

    b. Pareto chart

    c. Gannt chart

    d. Line graph

9. Which of the following is true about a primary key of the database?

    a. It is a repeating value.

    b. It is a duplicate value in the table.

    c. It is a unique value in the table.

    d. It is dependent on other values in the table.

10. A CPOE software interface in the EHR is used to:

    a. scan lab reports into the patient medical record.

    b. enter physician orders.

    c. review EGD and colonoscopy reports.

    d. alert healthcare professionals of patient allergies.

11.   In designing a form for the EHR, which of the following is a method of capturing structured data?

    a. 20-character text box

    b. Speech-to-data output

    c. Scanned document markup

    d. Drop-down menu

12.   Which of the following represents simple data?

    a. Lab result value 19

    b. Lab result value 19 is for units above the range

    c. Lab result 19 g/dL hemoglobin

    d. Lab results indicate hemochromatosis

13.   Patient last name, date of birth, and gender are all examples of:

    a. data sources.

    b. data warehouses.

    c. data mapping.

    d. data fields.

14.   The Chief Privacy Officer wants to compare the number of information breaches for each month in the last year. What type of chart would be most effective in presenting this information?

    a. Pie chart

    b. Bar chart

    c. Line chart

    d. Histogram

15.   The board of directors wants to review how many more labor and delivery patients they have admitted since the opening of the new maternity ward. What type of chart would be most effective in presenting this information?

    a. Pie chart

    b. Bar chart

    c. Line chart

    d. Histogram

16. For decades, Medicare has used which primary key for their patient ID numbers?

    a. Date of birth

    b. Last name

    c. Employer ID number

    d. Social Security number

17. The Sunrise Skilled Nursing Facility EHR does not interoperate with the Lab Information System, so their reports are scanned into the patient EHR. What type of database would they use to store the scanned lab reports?

    a. Relational database

    b. Object-oriented database

    c. Object-relational database

    d. Network database

18. When a physician is using CPOE, the EHR should use authentication to ensure that the individual who entered the data is authorized to do so. This is an example of a data:

    a. definition.

    b. accuracy.

    c. completeness.

    d. timeliness.

19. When the patient visited the ER, the triage nurse did not collect the list of medications that they are currently taking. Which data quality characteristic is missing?

    a. Completeness

    b. Timeliness

    c. Granularity

    d. Accuracy

20. The board of directors is reviewing the expenses for durable medical equipment costs over the past 5 years. Which of the following charts should they use?

    a. Gannt chart

    b. Bar chart

    c. Line chart

    d. Pareto chart

21. Which of the following charts would most effectively compare productivity of the four coders in the department for the last month?

    a. Gannt chart

    b. Bar chart

    c. Line chart

    d. Pareto chart

Resources

For additional resources, please review the following references:

Abdelhak, M., & Hanken, M. A. (2016). *Health Information: Management of a Strategic Resource*. St. Louis, MO: Elsevier.
- Chapter 6: Data Management
- Chapter 13: Research and Data Analysis
  - Presentation of Statistical Data

Oachs, P. K., & Watters, A. (2016). *Health Information Management: Concepts, Principles, and Practice*. Chicago, IL: AHIMA, American Health Information Management Association.
- Chapter 4: Health Data Concepts and Information Governance

Sayles, N. B., & Gordon, L. L. (2016). *Health Information Management Technology: An Applied Approach*. Chicago, IL: AHIMA, American Health Information Management Association.
- Chapter 6: Data Management

CHAPTER 6

Secondary Data Resources

In this chapter, we review the following subdomains:

- I.E.1. Identify and use secondary data presentations
- I.E.2. Validate the reliability and use secondary data sources

The following topics are covered in this subdomain:

- Specialized data collection systems and registries
- Purposes and applications of secondary data sources

MAIN TERMS

American College of Surgeons (ACS)

Birth defects registry

Cancer registry

Certified tumor registrar (CTR)

Clinical trials

Commission on Cancer (CoC)

Disease index

Disease registry

ICD-O-3

Immunization registry

Indices

Medicare Provider Analysis and Review file (MPAR)

National Cancer Registrars Association (NCRA)

National Provider Data Bank (NPDB)

National Vaccine Advisory Committee

North American Association of Central Cancer Registrars (NAACCR)

Operation index

Physician index

Reference date

Registries

Trauma registry

Practice Questions

1. Which of the following data is an example of secondary data collected from a structured query?

    a. Lab results dated October 1

    b. ICD-10-CM code E10 in the diagnostic index

    c. Chest X-ray record at Grove Diagnostic Center

    d. Hospital record for labor and delivery

2. The physician index contains all of the following, except:

    a. physician DEA license number.

    b. patient medical records in the healthcare facility.

    c. physician medical office name and address.

    d. physician NPI number.

3. The purpose of collecting patient data for the disease registry is to:

    a. bill for healthcare services rendered for the specific disease.

    b. educate the patient on their healthcare conditions, including any health changes they should make.

    c. analyze data to determine trends in disease management.

    d. protect the community by not informing them of the risks for disease infection.

4. A cancer registry's reference date is commonly set as:

    a. January 1 of the past year.

    b. January 1 of a given year.

    c. December 31 of the past year.

    d. December 31 of a given year.

5. Public health agencies can use secondary data for:

    a. delivery of care directly to the patient.

    b. purposes related to health insurance reimbursement.

    c. development of a patient care plan for a home health patient.

    d. education programs to prevent the spread of a communicable disease.

6. Data collected through the patient delivery process is considered:

    a. primary data.
    b. secondary data.
    c. tertiary data.
    d. live data.

7. The certification standards for Certified Tumor Registrar (CTR) are established by:

    a. Medicare Provider Analysis and Review.
    b. National Practitioner Data Bank.
    c. National Cancer Registrars Association.
    d. The Joint Commission.

8. The National Center for Health Statistics collects data on the incidences of which of the following?

    a. Deaths and herpes
    b. Divorce and viral meningitis
    c. Fetal death and cancer
    d. Deaths and divorce

9. The Master Patient Index (MPI) is considered primary patient data because it reports:

    a. diagnostic data.
    b. procedural data.
    c. patient demographic data.
    d. place of service data.

10. All of the following databases are used for clinical secondary research purposes EXCEPT:

    a. NPDB.
    b. UMLS.
    c. clinical trials database.
    d. MEDLINE.

11. San Antonio Hospital reported three colonoscopy patients who were diagnosed with a postoperative infection within 48 hours. In order to investigate the delivery of care, which facility-based index can be used to identify the provider who performed the procedure?

    a. Disease index

    b. Physician index

    c. Disease registry

    d. Physician registry

12. Which of the following collection tools manages primary data?

    a. Cancer registry

    b. Trauma registry

    c. Vital statistics

    d. Computerized order entry

13. A large number of multiple births were occurring in communities that received their drinking water from the Rio Grande. After sampling the water, it was clear there was a correlation between the water and the multiple births. What other secondary uses could this data be used for?

    a. For patient caregiver support

    b. To deliver quality care to the patient

    c. To report corporate environmental pollution

    d. For developing community policy making

14. According to the Commission on Cancer (CoC), what is the cancer patient follow-up rate for analytic cases for approved cancer registries up to 5 years?

    a. 60%

    b. 80%

    c. 85%

    d. 100%

15. The Abbreviated Injury Scale (AIS) is used to communicate the nature of the injury and the threat to life by body system. Which facility-based index uses AIS data most frequently?

    a. Birth defects index

    b. Transplant index

    c. Trauma index

    d. Immunization index

16. Which of the following national registries is required report clinical health data to *Healthy People 2020*, an initiative used to promote public health goals?

    a. Birth defects registry

    b. Transplant registry

    c. Trauma registry

    d. Immunization registry

17. To determine the effectiveness of ambulant care, which of the following patient data on diabetes management would be included in the facility-based disease index for acute care facilities?

    a. Patients taking insulin prescribed by a primary care physician

    b. Patients receiving education on how to manage diabetes from the hospital

    c. Patients admitted to the hospital for diabetes-related complications

    d. Patients transferred to skilled nursing facility for diabetes-related complications

18. Which national health organization plays an important role in managing birth defects registries?

    a. March of Dimes

    b. Susan B Komen Breast Cancer Research

    c. American Heart Association

    d. City of Hope

19. What type of data is included in a population-based registry?

    a. Facility-based clinical data

    b. Community-based clinical data

    c. State-based clinical data

    d. All of these are correct.

20. Authorized individual users of primary health data include all of the following, except:

    a. clinical investigators.

    b. health practitioners.

    c. healthcare managers.

    d. healthcare support staff.

Resources

For additional resources, please review the following references:

Abdelhak, M., & Hanken, M. A. (2016). *Health Information: Management of a Strategic Resource.* St. Louis, MO: Elsevier.
- Chapter 13: Data Analytics: Reporting Interpretation, and Use
  - Data through Medical Research

Oachs, P. K., & Watters, A. (2016). *Health Information Management: Concepts, Principles, and Practice.* Chicago, IL: AHIMA, American Health Information Management Association.
- Chapter 6: Data Management
  - Data and Data Sources
  - Healthcare Databases

Sayles, N. B., & Gordon, L. L. (2016). *Health Information Management Technology: An Applied Approach.* Chicago, IL: American Health Information Management Association.
- Chapter 7: Secondary Data Sources

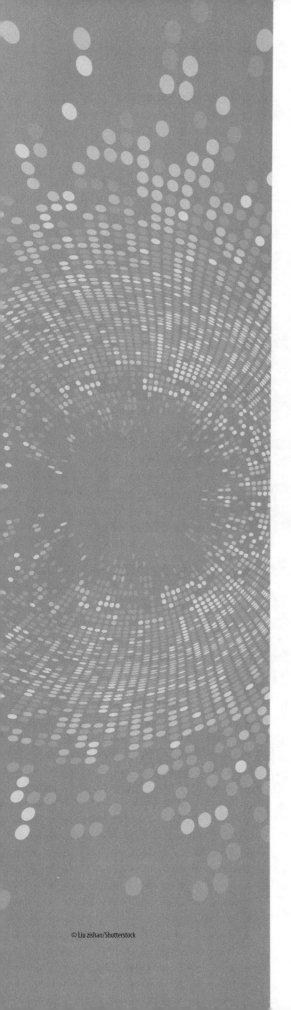

DOMAIN II

Information Protection: Access, Disclosure, Archival, Privacy, and Security

CHAPTER 7

Health Law

In this chapter, we review the following subdomains:
- II.A.1. Apply healthcare technology
- II.A.2. Identify the use of legal documents
- II.A.3. Apply legal concepts and principles to the practice of HIM

The following topics are covered in this subdomain:
- Healthcare legal terminology
- Health information/record laws
  - Consent for treatment
  - Health records retention
  - Patient privacy
  - Advocacy for patient rights
  - Health power of attorney

- Maintain a legally defensible legal record
  - Subpoena
  - Depositions
  - Court orders
  - Warrants

MAIN TERMS

Administrative law	Courts of appeal	Justice
Advanced directive	Defendant	Litigation
Advocacy	Deposition	Medicare conditions of participation
Autonomy	Disclosure and use	
Beneficence	Do not resuscitate (DNR) order	Nonmaleficense
Breach of contract	False Claims Act	Office of the Inspector General
Consent for treatment	Joint Commission	Patient amendment request
Court order	Judicial decisions	Plaintiff

MAIN TERMS *(CONTINUED)*

Power of attorney	Subpoena	Unbundling
Privacy	Subpoena *ad testificandum*	Upcoding
Records retention	Subpoena *duces tecum*	Warrant
Recovery audit contractors	Subpoena *gestae*	Whistleblowers
STARK	Supreme Court	
Statutes	Trial courts	

Practice Questions

1. A patient's health record becomes a legal record according to the court of law once which of the following conditions has been met?

    a. The patient has been discharged from the facility.

    b. The physician has signed the discharge record.

    c. The health information department has audited the record for deficiencies.

    d. All record deficiencies are resolved according to the facility bylaws.

2. In a court of law, the Director of the health information department of an accredited healthcare facility can be known as:

    a. the Director of patient records.

    b. the Manager of patient records.

    c. the Custodian of patient records.

    d. the Keeper of patient records.

3. In a court of law, the party that files a claim against another party is also known as the:

    a. plaintiff.

    b. defendant.

    c. judge.

    d. jury.

4. What is the responsibility of the health information department when a subpoena *duces tecum* is received?

 a. Contact the court clerk to clarify the request

 b. Organize and send all health records related to the patient and dates of service listed in the subpoena

 c. Inform the patient that a subpoena was requested

 d. Submit health insurance information

5. In the process of prepping the patient for bunion surgery on the left foot, the physician marks the left leg to ensure that he performs the procedure on the correct foot. The physician is exercising which ethical principle?

 a. Autonomy

 b. Beneficence

 c. Justice

 d. Nonmaleficence

6. A patient is admitted to the hospital with chest pains. After a series of tests, the physician recommends the patient undergo a triple bypass procedure because of coronary artery blockage. The patient is scared and does not want to have the procedure. The patient exercises his or her ethical right to _____ by refusing the procedure.

 a. Autonomy

 b. Beneficence

 c. Justice

 d. Nonmaleficence

7. Frances wants to write down her healthcare decisions to prepare in case she is diagnosed with an incurable disease that leaves her unable to communicate her wishes. What legal document should she use?

 a. Patient consent

 b. Advance directive

 c. Disclosure report

 d. Subpoena

8. Which of the following information must be provided for the patient to sign the informed consent form?

   a. Statistics on surgery success at the operative facility

   b. Physician error statistics

   c. An explanation of the risks and the benefits from the procedure

   d. A breakdown of all costs involved with the procedure

9. Statutes are enacted by which of the following?

   a. Federal agencies

   b. Local governments

   c. Judicial systems

   d. Legislative bodies

10. Mary lives in Connecticut and her father, George, lives in New York. George fell outside his home, which left him unconscious; the ambulance transferred him to the local hospital. What legal document would Mary need to get information about her father's health condition and to make decisions for him in his unconscious state?

    a. Advance directive

    b. Power of attorney

    c. Informed consent

    d. Patient amendment request

11. The ambulatory surgery center failed to obtain a signed patient consent form prior to surgery. How has the facility violated the patient's rights?

    a. Medical malpractice

    b. Assault and battery

    c. Libel and tort

    d. Slander and tort

12. All legal health records can be admitted as witnesses in court if:

    a. the health record meets all facility bylaws and regulations.

    b. the healthcare facility is accredited.

    c. the Director of Health Information acts as the custodian of the record.

    d. all of the above

13. AHIMA requires that health information records be maintained for a minimum of ____ years.

    a. 5

    b. 7

    c. 10

    d. This number varies based on the state's minimum requirements, if those requirements are longer than AHIMA's standard

14. Reggie Howard sued Marshall Hospital for negligence because his wife died under suspected neglect and was awarded a financial settlement in the state of Nevada. However, Marshall Hospital is appealing the decision based on not being able to present all facts of the case. Which court will accept the case?

    a. Nevada State appellate court

    b. Nevada State supreme court

    c. Federal appellate court

    d. Federal supreme court

15. When Reggie Howard sued Marshall Hospital, which legal party is Marshall Hospital considered?

    a. Plaintiff

    b. Jury

    c. Judge

    d. Defendant

16. Which document provides details on the powers of the three branches of government in the United States?

    a. Declaration of Independence

    b. Constitution

    c. Bill of Rights

    d. Acts of Congress

17. The Director of Health Information has been extremely busy and didn't send the documents requested by the subpoena on time. What will happen at the court?

    a. The court case will be postponed.

    b. A warrant for the physician will be issued.

    c. The Director of Health Information will be held in contempt.

    d. The court will issue another subpoena.

18. Statutes of limitations refer to:

    a. the maximum amount of time after an incident during which legal proceedings can be brought.

    b. a maximum amount that could be collected.

    c. the minimum standards for the delivery of care.

    d. the minimum healthcare statistics acceptable for healthcare delivery.

19. Helen was a patient with the Harmony Ambulatory Center, but she was unhappy with the care provided. She went online and slightly embellished her negative experience on several online survey websites. What legal course can the facility charge against Helen?

    a. Assault

    b. Slander

    c. Libel

    d. Tort

20. The physician–patient relationship is established when:

    a. the patient makes an appointment.

    b. the patient meets the physician.

    c. the physician bills the patient's health insurance.

    d. the physician receives payment from the health insurance.

21. The purpose of the notice of privacy practice is:

    a. to introduce the procedures and policies of the healthcare facility.

    b. to explain to the patient the fee collection process of the facility.

    c. to be given to every patient at the first encounter.

    d. to explain to the patient the facility's health information management process.

22. All of the following are sources of laws in the United States EXCEPT:

    a. administrative government agencies.

    b. the judicial system.

    c. the Constitution.

    d. the legislative system.

23. Which of the following circumstances would represent a breach of contract?

    a. A patient visiting a different specialist for a second opinion

    b. A physician refusing to treat the patient on the basis of religious differences

    c. A release of health information without patient approval

    d. A postcard sent from the physician to inform the patient of an upcoming appointment

24. What is the difference between a court order and a subpoena?

    a. The court order is a request for information.

    b. The subpoena represents the court's judgement.

    c. The subpoena is issued by the judge as the decision in the case.

    d. The court order is issued by the judge.

25. Which of the following is a significant difference between health information use and disclosure?

    a. Health information use is performed within the healthcare organization.

    b. Health information use is specifically for the purpose of direct patient care.

    c. Health information disclosure occurs when reporting vital statistics.

    d. All of the above is correct.

26. The ethical principle to ensure equal and fair patient care delivery for all patients falls under:

    a. autonomy.

    b. beneficence.

    c. justice.

    d. nonmaleficence.

Resources

For additional resources, please review the following references:

Abdelhak, M., & Hanken, M. A. (2016). *Health Information: Management of a Strategic Resource*. St. Louis, MO: Elsevier.
- Chapter 15: Privacy and Health Law
  - The Legal System

Oachs, P. K., & Watters, A. (2016). *Health Information Management: Concepts, Principles, and Practice*. Chicago, IL: AHIMA, American Health Information Management Association.
- Chapter 2: Legal Issues in Health Information Management
  - Organization of Government
  - Healthcare Causes of Action

Sayles, N. B., & Gordon, L. L. (2016). *Health Information Management Technology: An Applied Approach*. Chicago, IL: American Health Information Management Association.
- Chapter 8: Health Law
  - Basic Legal Concepts
  - Patient Rights Regarding Healthcare Decisions

CHAPTER 8

Data, Privacy, Confidentiality, and Security

In this module, we review the following subdomains:

- II.B.1. Apply confidentiality, privacy, and security measures and policies and procedures for internal and external use and exchange to protect electronic health information
- II.B.2. Apply retention and destruction policies for health information
- II.B.3. Apply system security policies according to departmental and organizational data information standards

The following topics are covered in this subdomain:

- Internal and external standards
- Regulations and initiatives
  - Federal and state privacy and security laws
- Patient verification
  - Medical identity theft
- Data security concepts, processes, and monitoring
- E-discovery
- Data storage and retrieval
- Security processes and policies
  - Data and information standards

MAIN TERMS

Access controls	Confidentiality	Privacy
Administrative Simplification	Covered entities	Protected health information
ARRA	De-identified information	Security
Audit controls	HIPAA	Statutes of limitations
Business associates	HITECH	
Business continuity plan	Medical identity theft	

Practice Questions

1. Under the HIPAA Privacy Rule, which of the following is considered a covered entity?

   a. Healthcare clearing house

   b. The Joint Commission

   c. American Medical Association

   d. Department of Health and Human Services

2. Which of the following data elements should be removed to deidentify the patient record?

   a. Principal diagnosis

   b. Place of service code

   c. Social Security number

   d. Facility NPI number

3. According to the HIPAA Privacy Rule, all of the following are considered workforce members, except:

   a. a hospital volunteer.

   b. a respiratory therapist intern.

   c. an EHR software trainee.

   d. All of the above

4. Protected health information minimum necessary standards are outlined in which of the following HIPAA regulation titles?

   a. Title I—Insurance Portability

   b. Title II—Administrative Simplification

   c. Title III—Medical Savings and Tax Deduction

   d. Title IV—Group Health Plan Provisions

5. A health information organization is an example of a(n):

   a. covered entity.

   b. business associate.

   c. workforce member.

   d. health insurance plan.

6. The purpose of the Title II Administration Simplification Provision of HIPAA is:

    a. to standardize the management of protected health information.

    b. for medical savings accounts and tax deduction for health insurance plans.

    c. to detail provisions related to group health plans.

    d. to outline protections through revenue offset.

7. Dr. Marshall is treating Becky Sharpe for cellulitis. When consulting Becky, Dr. Marshall opened the medical record of another patient with a similar diagnosis and started reviewing treatment options with Becky. Which of the following HIPAA elements was compromised?

    a. Privacy

    b. Security

    c. Confidentiality

    d. Administration Simplification

8. A dermatologist is sending patient records to the Center for Disease Control Centers for Disease Control and Prevention for further research. The records include full-face photo images. What should be done to deidentify protected health information?

    a. Send the health records without the photos

    b. Send the health records without the patient name and dates, but with the photos

    c. Send the health records without the patient name, geographic information, dates, and contact information, but with the photos

    d. Send the health records without the patient name, geographic information, dates, and contact information, and blacken across the eye area of all patients before sending the photos

9. The HIPAA Security Rule incorporates flexibility, in that the legislation allows:

    a. the covered entity to eliminate security protection measures that are not needed to manage PHI.

    b. the covered entity to adopt security protection measures that are reasonable and appropriate for the size of their organization.

    c. the business associate to eliminate security protection measures that are not needed to manage PHI.

    d. the business associate to adopt security protection measures that are reasonable and appropriate for the size of his or her organization.

10.   The administrative safeguard that prepares the covered entity for times of emergency is also known as the:

    a. security management process.

    b. security incident procedures.

    c. information access management.

    d. contingency plan.

11.   An example of a physical safeguard is:

    a. workstation security.

    b. assigned security responsibility.

    c. audit controls.

    d. integrity controls.

12.   How did HITECH expand the HIPAA Privacy Rule?

    a. Expanded the definition of covered entities

    b. Expanded the definition of business associates

    c. Expanded the definition of workforce members

    d. Expanded the definition of NPI numbers

13.   The Houston Community Hospital Health Information Department wants to move their coding department from the facility site to remote access. What steps need to be made to ensure HIPAA compliance for these remote coders?

    a. HIPAA provisions do not allow coders to work remotely.

    b. There are no HIPAA restrictions for remote coders to work out of the office.

    c. Remote access coders need to apply the same physical safeguards that are used in the facility.

    d. Remote access coders need to apply the same physical and technical safeguards that are used in the facility.

14. New York State has a minimum record retention of 10 years, while AHIMA's standards is 7 years. The Department of Veteran Services requires patient records to be retained for 75 years after the last date of service. Which of the following would be correct for a VA hospital in New York?

    a. Patient records are retained for 7 years.

    b. Patient records are retained for 10 years.

    c. Patient records are retained for 75 years.

    d. Patient records are retained forever.

15. Bobby Fisher was 12 years old when he had Eustachian tubes inserted into his ears on 11/23/17. If Bobby's date of birth is 10/2/05, how old will he be when his record is eligible to be destroyed according to standard record retention rules (7 years)?

    a. 12

    b. 18

    c. 19

    d. 22

16. When determining record retention schedules, the MPI is handled differently because:

    a. it has a shorter retention schedule than the AHIMA standard.

    b. it has a longer retention schedule than the AHIMA standard.

    c. the healthcare facility does not have to report that the MPI is retained.

    d. the MPI remains permanent and is never destroyed.

17. When destroying paper medical records, which of the following should be included?

    a. File folders with patient names and medical record numbers

    b. Medical records transferred from other providers

    c. Microfiche copies of the medical record

    d. All of these are correct.

18. The following cases are examples of when a healthcare facility will need to follow its contingency plan, except:

    a. the number of patients dropped in a given period.

    b. the power at the facility failed for 4 hours.

   c. a pipe burst on the third floor of the hospital.

   d. a power surge occurred at the facility that maintains the EHR cloud.

19. For most healthcare facilities, what can be done if the staff does not have access to the EHR while treating patients?

   a. Stop accepting patients

   b. Start medical documentation on paper forms until electronic access returns

   c. Request local facilities to accept patient transfers

   d. Stop documenting until EHR access is restored

20. Which of the following is an example of an external data threat?

   a. An employee who does not lock his or her workstation computer

   b. A hacker attempts to implant a virus in the healthcare facility cloud

   c. An intern who seeks access to celebrity medical records he or she is not approved to review

   d. A tree on the healthcare facility campus falls on the power transformer

21. Which of the following is essential to monitoring a security program?

   a. Network safeguards

   b. Facility access controls

   c. Transmission security

   d. Access controls

22. All of the following are ways to control access to health information EXCEPT:

   a. monitoring the security of data collected.

   b. protecting the privacy of data.

   c. ensuring the integrity of data.

   d. ensuring the availability of data.

23. Mrs. Johnson, the Director of Health Information for San Antonio Community Hospital, is concerned that a disgruntled fired employee may have accessed the EHR into patient records for which she was not authorized. Which of the following reports should Mrs. Johnson run to determine whether the EHR was breached?

    a. Privacy report

    b. Audit trail report

    c. Security report

    d. Confidentiality report

24. The San Antonio Community Hospital is running a contingency plan drill in which the EHR is inaccessible. Where would the employees access the medical documentation forms to replace EHR documentation?

    a. Facility board of directors

    b. Floor supervisor

    c. Facility medical bylaws

    d. Online search

25. Bob Healer visited the Care for Yourself Walk-In clinic for a medical clearance prior to starting a job as a trucker. From the examination, it was determined that Bob has COPD. If the clinic reported this diagnosis to Bob's potential employer, were Bob's rights violated?

    a. Yes, this is a violation of Bob's privacy.

    b. Yes, this is a violation of Bob's security.

    c. Yes, this is a violation of Bob's confidentiality.

    d. No, there is no violation because the purpose of the medical clearance was to determine whether the patient was fit for the job.

Resources

For additional resources, please review the following references:

Abdelhak, M., & Hanken, M. A. (2016). *Health Information: Management of a Strategic Resource*. St. Louis, MO: Elsevier.
- Chapter 5: Data Access and Retention
  - Records Retention
  - Technology in Access and Retention

Oachs, P. K., & Watters, A. (2016). *Health Information Management: Concepts, Principles, and Practice*. Chicago, IL: AHIMA, American Health Information Management Association.
- Chapter 11: Data Privacy, Confidentiality, and Security

Sayles, N. B., & Gordon, L. L. (2016). *Health Information Management Technology: An Applied Approach*. Chicago, IL: AHIMA, American Health Information Management Association.
- Chapter 9: Data Privacy and Confidentiality
  - State Laws–Privacy
  - HIPAA Privacy Rule and ARRA
- Chapter 10: Data Security
  - Components of a Security Program
  - HIPAA Security Provisions

CHAPTER 9

Release of Information

In this chapter, we review the following subdomain:

- II.C.1. Apply policies and procedures surrounding issues of access and disclosure of protected health information

The following topics are covered in this subdomain:

- Authorized users
- Access and disclosure policies and procedures

MAIN TERMS

Authorized users

Breaches

HIPAA Privacy Rule

Invalid authorizations

Need-to-know principle

Office of Civil Rights (OCR)

Penalties

Privacy officer

Protected health information (PHI)

Release of information (ROI)

Practice Questions

1. TRICARE has requested the records of patients who have been diagnosed with HIV. Can the patient records be released?

   a. No, HIV-positive patient records cannot be released.

   b. No, the record cannot be released until the patient is informed.

    c. Yes, all patient records can be released regardless of the diagnosis.

    d. Yes, the patient record can be released if a signed patient consent for release is on file.

2. Bryan Henderson moved from Idaho to Arizona and is seeking medical care for diabetes management. The clinic wants the medical record from Idaho. What will the facility need for the request?

    a. Patient medical record number

    b. Patient date of birth

    c. A signed patient consent for release of information

    d. The patient should call the clinic in Idaho to request the information

3. The fee to release information from the healthcare facility is allowed by law to cover clinic:

    a. personnel expenses.

    b. copy expenses.

    c. software expenses.

    d. facility operational expenses.

4. Stacy has an appointment with her new gastroenterologist on November 4; if she submits her written request for her records from her previous gastroenterologist on October 1, would she have access to her records prior to her appointment?

    a. She will be able to pick up her records.

    b. The records will be sent to the new gastroenterologist in time.

    c. The records will not be available within the time frame.

    d. The new gastroenterologist does not need the medical records.

5. The Privacy officer for a healthcare facility is responsible for which of the following?

    a. Developing a physical safeguard plan to protect PHI

    b. Collecting data on all inpatients through admissions

    c. Encrypting data for the electronic submission of health insurance claims

    d. Providing training on protecting patient privacy in the healthcare facility

6. Which of the following individuals can authorize the release of their PHI?

    a. A 16-year-old needing a physical exam to sign up for sports at school

    b. A 72-year-old requesting CT scan results

    c. A husband who makes medical decisions for his permanently disabled spouse

    d. A behavioral health patient who has a history of suicidal episodes

7. Sara Sampson needs to request her health record, but she forgot her purse at home. She has a picture of her driver's license on her phone and a Costco card with a photo. Can the healthcare facility accept her request?

    a. Yes; because the photo on the phone matches the Costco card, the authorization is valid.

    b. Yes, the Costco card with the photo ID is acceptable.

    c. Yes, the driver's license picture on the phone is acceptable.

    d. No, a physical copy of the driver's license should be presented when making the request.

8. A healthcare facility realized that a disgruntled employee accessed several patient records without authorization. Which healthcare facility representative should manage the health information breach?

    a. Chief Information Officer (CIO)

    b. Chief Privacy Officer (CPO)

    c. Chief Security Officer (CSO)

    d. Chief Operations Officer (COO)

9. The San Antonio Community Hospital denied the authorization release of patient information. Which of the following is a valid reason why the authorization could be denied?

    a. The authorization form was not signed.

    b. The individual making the request was not the patient.

    c. A limited description of how the information will be used was provided.

    d. The health record contains highly sensitive information.

10. According to the HIPAA Privacy Rule, which of the following is included in the administrative requirements?

    a. The use and disclosure of highly sensitive information

    b. The time limits of the authorization of the release of information

    c. Implementation of policies and procedures to ensure compliance

    d. Facility bylaws that determine the process of release of information

11. The HIPAA Privacy Rule administrative requirements protect PHI, which is also known as:

    a. protected health information.

    b. protected health insurance.

    c. private health information.

    d. private health insurance.

12. Henry submitted a complete authorization to request a copy of his medical record. However, Henry's therapist has determined that access to his PHI might endanger his life. How should the request be handled?

    a. Release the medical record to Henry

    b. Agree to release the medical record to an authorized, legally competent caregiver

    c. Accept the therapist's recommendation and deny the authorization

    d. Inform Henry on the process to appeal the decision

13. What is the penalty for violating the HIPAA Privacy Rule when willful neglect is present and cannot be corrected?

    a. $100 to $50K

    b. $1K to $50K

    c. $10K to $50K

    d. $50K

14. The PHI breach plan is a component of which of the following plans?

    a. Risk management plan

    b. Contingency plan

    c. Release of information process

    d. Facility bylaws

15. _____ is the number one defense against health information breaches.

    a. Security
    b. Confidentiality
    c. Prevention
    d. Regulation

16. San Antonio Community Hospital received an authorization to release Howard's medical record to Queen of the Mary Hospital. However, Queen of the Mary Hospital released Howard's PHI to Highland Palms Convalescent Home without obtaining a second authorization because the original had not expired. Is the Queen of the Mary Hospital authorized to release Howard's PHI?

    a. Yes, because the authorization to San Antonio Community Hospital has not expired
    b. Yes, because the PHI management standards are lower for convalescent homes
    c. Yes, because the transfer of information ensures continuity of patient care
    d. No, the authorization for the release was made from San Antonio Community Hospital to the Queen of the Mary Hospital, so a new one is needed for Highland Palms

17. Because the HIPAA Privacy Rule is a federal regulation, it:

    a. establishes the privacy guidelines for all states.
    b. requires the privacy officer to communicate with the ONC.
    c. protects the rights of the healthcare facility above the rights of the patients.
    d. reports privacy violations to health insurance plans.

18. A patient requests his medical record in electronic form. The hospital, however, maintains the patient's health record in electronic and paper form. How should the hospital deliver the record to the patient?

    a. Print out the electronic record to deliver it on paper
    b. Scan the paper record to deliver it in an electronic medium
    c. Give the record to the patient as is, as paper and electronic formats
    d. Deny the request because the record could not be given to the patient entirely in electronic form

19. What type of health records is covered by the regulations outlined by the HIPAA Privacy Rule?

    a. Health records from the hospital setting

    b. Paper health records from all healthcare facilities

    c. Electronic health records from all healthcare facilities

    d. Any health record from any healthcare facility kept in any format

20. When a hospital is served a request by the court for a release of information, the facility:

    a. can ignore the request because a signed patient authorization for release is not on file.

    b. can ignore the request if multiple facilities were requested.

    c. must comply with the court request.

    d. must request the patient signs an authorization to release the information requested.

Resources

For additional resources, please review the following references:

Abdelhak, M., & Hanken, M. A. (2016). *Health Information: Management of a Strategic Resource*. St. Louis, MO: Elsevier.
- Chapter 6: Electronic Health Record Systems
  - Release of Information

Oachs, P. K., & Watters, A. (2016). *Health Information Management: Concepts, Principles, and Practice*. Chicago, IL: AHIMA, American Health Information Management Association.
- Chapter 11: Data Privacy, Confidentiality, and Security
  - The HITECH-HIPAA Omnibus Privacy Act
  - Privacy and Security Requirements for Disclosure Management

Sayles, N. B., & Gordon, L. L. (2016). *Health Information Management Technology: An Applied Approach*. Chicago, IL: American Health Information Management Association.
- Chapter 9: Data Privacy and Confidentiality
  - Breach Notification
  - HIPAA Privacy Rule Administrative Requirements
  - Enforcement of Federal Privacy Legislation and Rules
  - Release of Information
  - Medical Identity Theft
  - Patient Verification

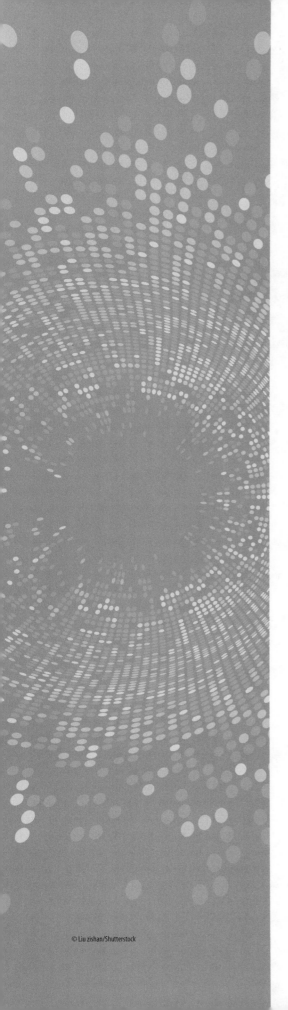

DOMAIN III

Informatics, Analytics, and Use

CHAPTER 10
Health Information Technologies

In this module, we review the following subdomains:

- III.A.1. Utilize software in the completion of HIM processes
- III.A.2. Explain policies and procedures of networks, including intranet and Internet to facilitate clinical and administrative applications

The following topics are covered in this subdomain:

- Record tracking
  - Release of information
  - Coding
  - Grouping
  - Registries
  - Billing
  - Quality improvement
  - Document imaging
- Electronic health records (EHR)

- Personal health records (PHR)
- Communication and network technologies
  - EHR
  - PHR
  - Health information exchange (HIE)
  - Portals
  - Public health standards
  - Telehealth

MAIN TERMS

Admission Discharge Transfer System (ADT) system

ANSI X12

Athena

BASIC

Clinical information system

COBOL

Computerized provider order entry (CPOE)

Connectivity system

Core clinical EHR systems

Decision support system

Digital Image and Communications in Medicine (DICOM)

MAIN TERMS (CONTINUED)

EHR

Electronic data interchange (EDI)

EPIC

Executive information system (EIS)

Expert system

Health Level 7 (HL7)

Health information exchange (HIE)

HTML

HTTP

Internet

Intranet

IP address

JAVA

Local area network (LAN)

Logical Observation Identifiers Names and Codes (LOINC)

Management information system (MIS)

Medisoft

Personal Health Record (PHR)

Picture archiving and communication system (PACS)

SNOMED CT

Source systems

Speech recognition

Structured query language (SQL)

Supporting infrastructure

TCP/IP protocol

Telehealth

Transaction processing system

Virtual private network (VPN)

Wide area network

XML

Practice Questions

1. While using a certified EHR, how are X-rays commonly stored in the patient record?

    a. In the patient's paper health record

    b. Images are reviewed by the radiologist and the report is uploaded to the EHR

    c. Scanned images of the X-ray are uploaded to the EHR

    d. Healthcare providers have to login to another portal to gain access

2. Barbara, charge nurse, was reviewing the patient record in the EHR for Sally Weston and a yellow banner alert appeared across the screen. This alert is an example of:

    a. a decision support system.

    b. a patient safety feature.

    c. clinical decision support.

    d. data mining.

3. Medisoft practice management software is an example of a(n):

    a. operating software.

    b. patient financial system application.

    c. natural language software.

    d. specialty application software.

4. As you are entering a medication order into the EHR, the system prevents it. An alert appears stating "possible drug interaction." What type of health information system are you using?

   a. Clinical information system

   b. Executive information system

   c. Expert system

   d. Clinical decision support system

5. Which of the following stakeholders manages the PHR?

   a. The provider's office

   b. The hospital

   c. The health information exchange

   d. The patient and/or caregiver

6. In performing a "what if" query to determine whether the facility should expand the neonatal intensive care unit, which of the following health information systems can be used?

   a. Executive information system

   b. Decision support system

   c. Expert system

   d. Management information system

7. During the ROI process, the patient's name, date of birth, and date of admission are used to query the EHR. What feature of the EHR is used in this process?

   a. Outguide

   b. Chart locator

   c. Admissions record

   d. Template

8. In choosing a communication standard for use in a picture archival communication system, the LEADING choice would be which of the following?

   a. HL7

   b. DICOM

   c. HTTP

   d. ANSI X12

9. Simon is visiting the dermatologist office for the first time. He did not need to request his records from the referring medical office because the dermatologist and the primary care physician are part of the same:

    a. integrated health network.
    b. Internet.
    c. clinical office repository.
    d. health information exchange.

10. Through a research query, Huntington Medical Center discovered that 13.2% of their patients are admitted for gallstones. What is the stage of data?

    a. Data
    b. Information
    c. Knowledge
    d. Cannot determine based on the information provided

11. Which of the following technologies is used for patients who are unable to physically go to the physician's office, so the encounter is performed through a secured video conference?

    a. SMART card
    b. Continuity of care record
    c. Computerized Provider Order Entry (CPOE)
    d. Telemedicine

12. The Internet is

    a. A LAN.
    b. A WAN.
    c. A combination of smaller WANs.
    d. A combination of smaller LANs and WANs.

13. The healthcare providers at the Happy Home Skilled Nursing Facility use wirelessly connected tablets for point-of-care charting. Which security protocol system would be the strongest?

    a. WPA
    b. WiFi
    c. WEP
    d. HTTP

14. An IP address is:

    a. unique to each computer on the Internet.

    b. unique to each computer on the intranet.

    c. unique to each webpage on the Internet.

    d. unique to each webpage on the intranet.

15. Which of the following EHR technologies do physicians use to enter orders into the EHR?

    a. ICD-10-CM

    b. CPOE

    c. CPT

    d. LOINC

16. PACS is an acronym for _____, which provides medical images to providers via intranet.

    a. picture archiving and communication system

    b. programming activities and communication system

    c. protocol archiving and clinical systems

    d. practice analysis and clinical systems

Resources

For additional resources, please review the following references:

Abdelhak, M., & Hanken, M. A. (2016). *Health Information: Management of a Strategic Resource*. St. Louis, MO: Elsevier.
- Chapter 6: Electronic Health Record Systems
  - What Are Electronic Health Record Systems and How Do they Work?
  - How Do Technical Infrastructure, Data Requirements, and Operations Workflow Fit in EHR Systems?

Oachs, P. K., & Watters, A. (2016). *Health Information Management: Concepts, Principles, and Practice*. Chicago, IL: AHIMA, American Health Information Management Association.
- Chapter 12: Health Information Technologies
  - EHR Functionality and Technology

Sayles, N. B., & Gordon, L. L. (2016). *Health Information Management Technology: An Applied Approach*. Chicago, IL: American Health Information Management Association.
- Chapter 11: Health Information Technologies
  - Health IT

CHAPTER 11

Information Management Strategic Planning

In this chapter, we review the following subdomains:
- III.B.1. Explain the process used in the selection and implementation of health information management systems.
- III.B.2. Utilize health information to support enterprise-wide decision support for strategic planning.

The following topics are covered in this subdomain:
- Strategic planning process
- Integration of systems
- Information management strategic plan
- Business planning
- Market share planning
- Disaster and recovery planning

MAIN TERMS

Business planning	Evaluation	Planning
Chief Medical Information Officer	Forecasting	Request for proposal
Contingency plans	Implementation	SMART goals
Design	Maintenance	

Practice Questions

1. Jennifer at the Feel Better Skilled Nursing Facility assembled the Director of Health Information, the Chief Privacy Officer, and the Nursing Manager to discuss the needed updates to the current EHR. What phase of the SDLC are they in?

    a. Planning
    b. System design
    c. Maintenance
    d. Implementation

2. A strategic plan is generally used for:

    a. short-term goals within 30 days.
    b. mid–short-term goals within 3 months.
    c. medium-term goals within 1 year.
    d. long-term goals for at least 3 years.

3. The implementation stage of the SDLC includes which of the following?

    a. Identify the need to upgrade health information systems.
    b. Specify hardware and software requirements needed for the upgrade.
    c. Install the health information system.
    d. Evaluate the health information system to ensure that initial needs are being met.

4. The planning stage of the SDLC asks what the healthcare facility needs. What question does the development stage ask?

    a. Who implements the health information system?
    b. How does the health information system meet facility needs?
    c. When will the health information system be installed?
    d. Will the health information improve the current needs?

5. A Report for Proposal (RFP) is essential to which stage in the SDLC?

    a. Planning
    b. Design
    c. Implementation
    d. Maintenance

6. In the planning stage of the Systems Development Life Cycle (SDLC), which of the following statement categories is included in SMART goals?

    a. Sustainable

    b. Measurable

    c. Reliable

    d. Testing

7. The board of directors implemented a barcode medication system for administrating medication to patients. After a few months, it seemed that some admin reports were inaccurate. When the board asked the nursing staff, they indicated that they bypassed some required components because they were not functioning properly. What stage in the strategic planning process was not emphasized in this case study?

    a. The planning stage

    b. The design stage

    c. The implementation stage

    d. The evaluation stage

8. The Family Trails Walk-in Pediatrics Facility lost power due to a tornado. Which plan should management implement?

    a. Strategic plan

    b. Contingency plan

    c. Tactical plan

    d. Implementation plan

9. Nancy, who worked for the Healthy Hearts Cardiology office, scans all laboratory results into the electronic patient record. Why wouldn't the EHR be able to directly access the patient results from the lab information system?

    a. The Healthy Hearts Cardiology Office does not use an EHR.

    b. Scanning documents is an efficient way to manage patient lab results.

    c. The lab information system is paper based.

    d. The current EHR is not interoperable with the laboratory.

10. What essential patient health information should be present in all health information systems within the enterprise system?

    a. Patient address

    b. Patient insurance information

    c. Prior admitting diagnosis

    d. Medication allergy

Resources

For additional resources, please review the following references:

Abdelhak, M., & Hanken, M. A. (2016). *Health Information: Management of a Strategic Resource*. St. Louis, MO: Elsevier.
- Chapter 9: Health Information Systems: Collaboration, Analysis, Design, Implementation and Operation

Oachs, P. K., & Watters, A. (2016). *Health Information Management: Concepts, Principles, and Practice*. Chicago, IL: AHIMA, American Health Information Management Association.
- Chapter 10: Organization Compliance and Risk
  - Business Continuity and Contingency Planning
- Chapter 13: Health Information Systems Strategic Planning

Sayles, N. B., & Gordon, L. L. (2016). *Health Information Management Technology: An Applied Approach*. Chicago, IL: AHIMA, American Health Information Management Association.
- Chapter 11: Health Information Technologies
  - Systems Development Life Cycle
- Chapter 12: Healthcare Information
  - Strategic Uses of Healthcare Information

CHAPTER 12

Analytics, Decision Support, Information Integrity, and Data Quality

In this module, we review the following subdomains:
- III.C.1. Explain analytics and decision support.
- III.C.2. Apply report generation technologies to facilitate decision-making.
- III.H.1. Apply policies and procedures to ensure the accuracy and integrity of health data both internal and external to the health system.

The following topics are covered in this subdomain:
- Analytics and decision support
  - Data visualization
  - Data dashboard
  - Data capture tools and technologies
- Organizational design
- Strategic use of patient and performance data
- Outpatient prospective payment system
- Inpatient prospective payment system
- Medical research
- Disease management process
- Quality assessment and improvement

MAIN TERMS

Analysis	Bar chart	Clinical summary
Assembly	Clinical data analytics	Data analysis
Authentication	Clinical decision support system (CDSS)	Data capture
Automated disease protocols		Data dashboard

MAIN TERMS (CONTINUED)

Data integrity

Data provisioning

Data visualization

Deficiencies

Descriptive analytics

Diagnostic analytics

Disease management process

Executive information systems

Financial data

Healthcare data analytics

Home health prospective payment system

Inpatient prospective payment system

Interoperability

Joint Commission standards for medical records

Legal analysis

Line chart

Operational data

Outpatient prospective payment system

Patient data

Performance data

Pie chart

Predictive analytics

Prescriptive analytics

Qualitative analysis

Quantitative analysis

Relational database

Skilled nursing facility prospective payment system

Practice Questions

1. The San Antonio Community Hospital had a 30% increase in childbirths last week compared to their average. Which type of analytics explains why events occurred?

    a. Descriptive analytics

    b. Diagnostic analytics

    c. Predictive analytics

    d. Prescriptive analytics

2. The Happy Life Skilled Nursing Facility has been experiencing EHR crashes more often than in the past. What type of analytics could predict the rate of EHR crashes based on reported data?

    a. Descriptive analytics

    b. Diagnostic analytics

    c. Predictive analytics

    d. Prescriptive analytics

3. Which of the following is NOT a type of data used in health data analytics?

    a. Clinical

    b. Financial

    c. Binary

    d. Operational

4. How can health data analysts ensure the capture of accurate data?

    a. Accuracy of data is insignificant.

    b. Trust that the healthcare facility collected accurate data.

    c. Communicate with the facility privacy officer to ensure capture of accurate data.

    d. Investigate the data capture procedure to ensure accurate data collection.

5. Which of the following information would be typically found in the dashboard?

    a. Allergies

    b. Patient address

    c. Health insurance ID

    d. Diagnosis code

6. Which of the following is considered to be a decision support system?

    a. Practice management system

    b. Certified electronic health record management system

    c. Executive information system

    d. Barcode medication administration system

7. The Happy Life Skilled Nursing Facility should use which of the following payment systems?

    a. OPPS

    b. IPPS

    c. HHPPS

    d. SNFPPS

8. The San Antonio Community Hospital is re-evaluating their medical records review process in order to reduce their deficiency rate. Which of the following activities will reduce the records deficiency rate?

    a. Requiring patients to complete their intake paperwork on the computer.

    b. Not allowing patients to discharge until the summary is filed.

    c. Choosing a representative from the health information department to coordinate with the lab to ensure all records are updated in the patient records daily.

    d. Measuring hospital medical records delinquency rates every 6 months instead of 3 months.

9. Which of the following is not considered part of the Joint Commission standards for medical records?

   a. The Joint Commission establishes the definition for a complete and legal health record.

   b. The healthcare facility should measure medical record delinquency every 3 months.

   c. The number of delinquent records should not exceed 50% of the number of patient discharges in 12 months.

   d. Failing the Joint Commission medical record standards will result in conditional accreditation dismissal.

10. Medicare payments for inpatient services are based on:

    a. Medicare's inpatient fee schedule.

    b. the physician's charges.

    c. the hospital's charges.

    d. the Joint Commission charges.

11. The assembly process is not done for EHR records because:

    a. it is always done for every health record.

    b. it is only used for paper health records.

    c. it is only used for retrospective review.

    d. it is the only process that is used only for concurrent review.

12. The concurrent review method of the health record is more time efficient because:

    a. it uses the electronic health record.

    b. there is no assembly or analysis process.

    c. deficiencies are resolved before patients are discharged.

    d. it uses the paper health record.

13. Which of the following would not be considered a deficiency in the health record that needs to be resolved?

    a. Physician order blood test on 11/14/XX—signature missing

    b. Physician follow-up notes on 11/15/XX—signature missing

    c. Blood test results on 11/14/XX—missing report

    d. Discharge on 11/16/XX—missing report

14. Which of the following is discovered through quantitative analysis?

    a. Authenticated discharge summary report
    b. Medication list reconciliation
    c. Detailed family history
    d. Dictated second opinion consultation report

15. Which of the following is discovered through qualitative analysis?

    a. Authenticated discharge summary
    b. Signed pathology report
    c. Preoperative anesthesia report
    d. Patient care instructions documentation

16. Dr. Harris was writing his patient discharge note in the paper record, then realized that there is a lot of empty space. What should he do?

    a. Nothing; physician orders and notes should start on the next page, regardless of space.
    b. Nothing; the patient is being discharged so it does not matter.
    c. Add the notes to the previous page and throw the additional page away.
    d. Draw a line through the additional space.

17. Dr. Harris prefers to write his physician notes in pencil. What training does he need from the department of health information?

    a. Writing in pencil is fine.
    b. Writing in pencil is determined by the facility's bylaws.
    c. Pencil is not acceptable in legal documents.
    d. Pencil is preferred because mistakes can be erased.

18. A resident physician completes and authenticates a history and physical report in the EHR. Will there be a deficiency?

    a. No, the resident physician has already authenticated the report.
    b. No, the resident physician does not have access to the EHR to completely authenticate the report, so just submitting the report is sufficient.

   c. Yes, the attending physician must also authenticate the history and physical.

   d. Yes, the resident physician is not qualified to authenticate the history and physical.

---

19. A health data analyst is reviewing the medical record for authentication. What is this common process called?

   a. Retrospective review

   b. Concurrent review

   c. Quantitative review

   d. Qualitative review

---

20. What procedure would improve the delinquency rate of San Antonio Community Hospital?

   a. Establish a one-week turnaround time for all dictated reports.

   b. Refuse to fax patient information for confidentiality purposes.

   c. Allow other departments to document in the record after the patient has been discharged.

   d. Ensure the Director of Health Information reviews all medical records daily.

Resources

For additional resources, please review the following references:

Abdelhak, M., & Hanken, M. A. (2016). *Health Information: Management of a Strategic Resource*. St. Louis, MO: Elsevier.
- Chapter 4: Health Data Concepts and Information Governance
  - Methods to Ensure Data Quality
  - Data Quality Monitoring Methods and Solutions

Demiris, G., Afrin, L. B., Speedie, S., Courtney, K. L., Sondhi, M., Vimarlund, V., … Lynch, C. (2008). Patient-centered applications: Use of information technology to promote disease management and wellness. A white paper by the AMIA knowledge in Motion Working Group. *Journal of the American Medical Informatics Association, 15*(1), 8–13. Retrieved from https://doi.org/10.1197/jamia.M2492

Oachs, P. K., & Watters, A. (2016). *Health Information Management: Concepts, Principles, and Practice*. Chicago, IL: AHIMA, American Health Information Management Association.
- Chapter 17: Healthcare Data Analytics
  - Types of Data

Sayles, N. B., & Gordon, L. L. (2016). *Health Information Management Technology: An Applied Approach.* Chicago, IL: American Health Information Management Association.

- Chapter 6: Data Management
  - Data Collection Tools
- Chapter 12: Health Information
  - Role of Data Analytics in Health Information
  - Strategic Uses of Health Information

CHAPTER 13

Healthcare Statistics

In this module, we review the following subdomains:
- III.D.1. Utilize basic descriptive, institutional, and healthcare statistics

The following topics are covered in this subdomain:
- Basic descriptive statistics
  - Mean
  - Frequency
- Healthcare statistical formulas
  - Length of stay
  - Death rates
  - Autopsy rates
  - Percentile
  - Standard deviation
  - Infection rates
  - Birth rates

MAIN TERMS

Average daily census	Gross autopsy rate	Inpatient service day (ISPD)
Average length of stay (ALOS)	Gross death rate	Measures of central tendency
Bed count	Hospital autopsy rate	Median
Bed count day	Hospital death rate	Mode
Bed turnover rate	Hospital (nosocomial) infection rate	National Vital Statistics System (NVSS)
Census		
Consultation rate	Incidence rate	Neonatal mortality rate
Crude birth rate	Infant mortality rate	Net autopsy rate
Daily inpatient census	Inferential statistics	Net death rate
Fetal autopsy rate	Inpatient discharge	Newborn autopsy rate

MAIN TERMS (CONTINUED)

Newborn death rate	Ordinal level data	Range
Nominal level data	Population based statistics	Rate
Normal distribution	Postoperative infection rate	Ratio
Notifiable disease	Prevalence rate	

Practice Questions

1. San Antonio Community Hospital reports that 19 patients were discharged between September 1 and September 15. The length of stay for each patient was 18, 5, 4, 15, 8, 4, 14, 11, 8, 9, 10, 21, 4, and 2 days. What is the median length of stay?

    a. 9 days

    b. 9.5 days

    c. 10 days

    d. 10.5 days

2. Happy Hills Long Term Care Facility has a mean length of stay of 186 days with a standard deviation of 18. How many length of stay days are 2 standard deviations below the mean?

    a. 142 days

    b. 150 days

    c. 186 days

    d. 204 days

3. The result of the data set [12,4,16,6,5,16,3,8,4,16,9,6,12,14,6] is 16. Which measure of central tendency is used?

    a. Median

    b. Mean

    c. Mode

    d. Quartile

4. Using the following data set, determine the first quartile. [12,4,16,6,5,16,3,8,4,16,9,6,12,14,6]

    a. 4

    b. 5

c. 8

d. 16

5. The standard deviation is the measurement of data variability from the mean. A larger standard deviation shows that the data samples are:

a. further from the mean.

b. closer to the mean.

c. erroneous.

d. inaccurate.

6. Which of the following measurements of central tendency formulas DOES NOT require the statistician to organize the data values from smallest to greatest?

a. Median

b. Variance

c. First quartile

d. Third quartile

7. The average range of length of stay between January and March was 4 (sample 1). The average range of length of stay between April and June was 15 (sample 2). What can we conclude from these statistics?

a. The standard deviation of the first sample will be less than the second sample.

b. The quartiles will remain the same in both samples.

c. The variance for the first sample will be more than the second sample.

d. The mode will be different for both samples.

8. How do patient deaths affect inpatient census data?

a. Deaths are not included in census data.

b. Deaths are included in some inpatient census data, but not all the time.

c. Deaths are considered discharges, so they are subtracted from inpatient census.

d. Deaths are included only in inpatient service days calculations.

9. On December 1 at San Antonio Community Hospital, there were 144 patients. On December 2, 3 patients were admitted from the Emergency Room, 2 patients were admitted after surgery, 1 patient died, and 4 patients were admitted and discharged on the same day. What is the inpatient census on December 2?

    a. 145

    b. 148

    c. 152

    d. 153

10. Diana Simpson was admitted to San Antonio Community Hospital on July 5, 20XX and was discharged on August 15, 20XX. What is her length of stay?

    a. 33 days

    b. 39 days

    c. 40 days

    d. 41 days

Use the following information for questions 11 and 12.

In the month of May, 5 adults, 2 children, and 1 newborn died at Corona Regional Hospital. A total of 189 admissions and 223 discharges for adults and children were reported for the same period. Live births for July were 190, with 2 fetal deaths recorded (1 early, 0 intermediate, and 1 late). Autopsies were performed on 2 adults, 1 child, the newborn, and 1 late fetal death case. One of the adult bodies was released to the medical examiner.

11. What is the gross death rate for the month of May?

    a. 2.45%

    b. 3.19%

    c. 3.59%

    d. 4.03%

12. What is the fetal death rate for the month of May?

    a. 0.52%

    b. 0.89%

    c. 1.10%

    d. 1.67%

13. In September, the Corona Regional Hospital had 300 beds and 25 bassinets. 873 adults and children and 243 newborns have been discharged during the same month. Calculate the bed turnover rate for adults and children.

   a. 2.91%

   b. 3.59%

   c. 9.72%

   d. 34.92%

Use the following data to answer questions 14–18.

San Antonio Community Hospital

Period—June 20XX	
Beds	283
Admissions	3,253
IPSD	7,848
Discharges	2,989
Deaths	31
Autopsies	15
Medical examiner cases	3

14. Calculate the gross hospital death rate for June 20XX.

   a. 0.40%

   b. 0.95%

   c. 1.04%

   d. 38%

15. Calculate the net autopsy rate for June 20XX.

   a. 41%

   b. 48%

   c. 54%

   d. 65%

16. Calculate the bed turnover rate for June 20XX.

    a. 10.56
    b. 11.50
    c. 12.43
    d. 27.63

17. Calculate the inpatient bed occupancy rate for June 20XX.

    a. 24.56%
    b. 35.21%
    c. 38.31%
    d. 92.44%

18. Calculate the average daily census for June 20XX.

    a. 240 days
    b. 245 days
    c. 262 days
    d. 264 days

19. The Director of Health Information wants to calculate the inpatient bed occupancy rate. The hospital is undergoing staged renovations, which affect the hospital bed count. The inpatient service days for April and May are 17,324. The bed count figures for April–May are the following:

Start Date	End Date	Beds
1-Apr	15-Apr	325
16-Apr	30-Apr	300
1-May	15-May	290
16-May	31-May	325

What is the inpatient occupancy rate for April and May?

    a. 90.1%
    b. 91.5%
    c. 95.1%
    d. 96.8%

Use the following data to answer questions 20 and 21.

Fetal Death Rate for San Antonio Community Hospital - July

Category	Value
Live births	52
Newborn Discharges	50
Fetal deaths (early)	40
Fetal deaths (intermediate)	0
Fetal deaths (late)	2
Newborn deaths	2

20. Calculate the fetal death rate.

    a. 3.70%

    b. 4.76%

    c. 5%

    d. 95.2%

21. Calculate the newborn death rate.

    a. 4%

    b. 5.2%

    c. 6.8%

    d. 9.8%

22. When calculating the hospital mortality rate, which populations are included?

    a. Adults only

    b. Adults and children only

    c. Adults, children, and newborns only

    d. Adults, children, newborns, and fetuses only

23. The census on April 30 was 293. A patient was admitted to the hospital at 1:09 AM from the ER. The patient died at 9:04 PM. How does this patient affect the census on May 1?

    a. Because the patient was admitted, the census increases.

    b. Because the patient died and was discharged, the census decreases.

    c. Because the patient was admitted through noon, the census increases.

    d. Because the patient was admitted and discharged on the same day, the census does not change.

24. San Antonio Community Hospital reports that 18 patients were discharged from June 1 to June 15. The length of stay for each patient was 5, 3, 6, 2, 7, 2, 46, 2, 1, 6, 3, 4, 2, 3, 1, 3, and 5 days. What was the average length of stay for this period?

    a. 2 days

    b. 3.6 days

    c. 4.2 days

    d. 5 days

25. Last year, San Antonio Community Hospital averaged 46 births a month with a standard deviation of 6. There were 63 births in March. How does this increase relate to the average?

    a. The increase is 2 standard deviations over the mean.

    b. The increase is within 2 standard deviations over the mean.

    c. The increase is 3 standard deviations over the mean.

    d. The increase is within 3 standard deviations over the mean.

26. In June, 167 patients were admitted to obstetrics. Of these, 159 patients delivered and 63 patients required a C-section delivery. When calculating the C-section occurrence rate, which number would be the denominator?

    a. 167

    b. 159

    c. 63

    d. 222

27. If San Antonio Community Hospital had 3,000 inpatient service days in June, what would be the average daily census during this period?

    a. 1 patient

    b. 10 patients

    c. 100 patients

    d. 1,000 patients

28. Vital statistics includes data on all of the following EXCEPT:

    a. birth.

    b. marriage.

    c. separation.

    d. death.

29. According to the CDC, an average of 130 Americans die every day from opioid overdose. This statistic is an example of:

    a. data.

    b. information.

    c. incidence.

    d. prevalence.

30. More than 100 million U.S. adults are now living with diabetes or prediabetes, according to a new report released today by the Centers for Disease Control and Prevention (CDC). The report finds that as of 2015, 30.3 million Americans —9.4% of the U.S. population—have diabetes. Another 84.1 million have prediabetes, a condition that, if not treated, often leads to type 2 diabetes within 5 years. These statistics are an example of:

    a. data.

    b. information.

    c. incidence

    d. prevalence.

Resources

For additional resources, please review the following references:

Abdelhak, M., & Hanken, M. A. (2016). *Health Information: Management of a Strategic Resource*. St. Louis, MO: Elsevier.
- Chapter: 10 Statistics and Data Presentation
  - Healthcare Statistics
  - Statistical Measures and Tests

Oachs, P. K., & Watters, A. (2016). *Health Information Management: Concepts, Principles, and Practice*. Chicago, IL: AHIMA, American Health Information Management Association.
- Chapter: 16 Healthcare Statistics

Sayles, N. B., & Gordon, L. L. (2016). *Health Information Management Technology: An Applied Approach.* Chicago, IL: AHIMA, American Health Information Management Association.

- Chapter 13: Research and Data Analysis
  - Descriptive Statistics
- Chapter 14: Healthcare Statistics

CHAPTER 14

Data Trends and Research Methods

In this module, we review the following subdomains:
- III.D.2. Analyze data to identify trends
- III.E.1. Explain common research methodologies and why they are used in health care

The following topics are covered in this subdomain:
- Structure and use of health information and healthcare outcomes
  - Comparative analytics
  - Aggregate analytics
- Quality
- Safety
- Effectiveness of health care
- Research methodologies
  - Quantitative
  - Qualitative
  - Mixed methods
- Institutional review board (IRB)

MAIN TERMS

Agency for Healthcare Research and Quality (AHRQ)

Aggregate data

American Health Information Management Association (AHIMA)

Centers for Disease Control (CDC)

Comparative data

Correlation coefficient

Correlational studies

Dependent variable

Descriptive studies

Effectiveness of health care

Epidemiologist

Ethnography

Experimental studies

Grounded theory

Healthcare Effectiveness Data and Information Set (HEDIS)

Independent variable

Individual data

International review board (IRB)

Meaningful use (MU)

Mixed methods

MAIN TERMS *(CONTINUED)*

National Committee for Quality Assurance (NCQA)

National Institutional Health Office of Behavioral and Social Science Research

Odds ratio

Paired T-test

Patient-Centered Outcomes Research Organization (PCORI)

Pay-for-reporting

Pearson correlation coefficient

Prospective studies

Qualitative research

Quantitative research

Quasi-experimental studies

Retrospective studies

Spearman correlation coefficient

World Health Organization (WHO)

Practice Questions

1. Delivering quality health care to improve the quality of patient health is essential. How are the quality and effectiveness of healthcare delivery measured?

   a. Patient satisfaction

   b. Healthcare outcomes

   c. Survival rates

   d. Data analysis

2. John Parker, the Director of Health Information, wants to review the Conditions of Participation for their accreditation status. What organization does he need to reach out to?

   a. The Joint Commission

   b. National Commission on Quality Assurance (NCQA)

   c. Agency for Healthcare Research and Quality (AHRQ)

   d. American Health Information Management Association (AHIMA)

3. Data collected on large populations that are used to make conclusions are referred to as:

   a. descriptive statistics.

   b. measures of central tendency.

   c. aggregate data.

   d. probability.

4. Data that are used to delivery direct care to the patient are also known as:

   a. comparative data.

   b. individual data.

   c. aggregate data.

   d. healthcare information.

5. The number of nosocomial infections occurring within 48 hours of colonoscopy has been increasing steadily over the past 3 months. What type of research study could be employed to determine the cause?

   a. Descriptive study

   b. Correlation study

   c. Prospective study

   d. Retrospective study

6. According to the WHO, the correlation coefficient for populations that do not have access to fresh drinking water and are more likely to develop gastrointestinal infections is +0.88. This means:

   a. these populations are most likely going to develop gastrointestinal infections.

   b. these populations are not most likely to develop gastrointestinal infections.

   c. the type of coefficient is needed to determine the likelihood of gastrointestinal infection.

   d. More information is needed to make a determination.

Use the following table for Questions 7 and 8.

Independent Variable	Dependent Variable—Bone Loss		
Radiation Exposure	Diarrhea	No Diarrhea	Total
Radiation	80 (A)	20 (B)	100
No Radiation	15 (C)	85 (D)	100
Total	95	105	a

7. What are the odds of developing diarrhea for patients who have been exposed to radiation?

   a. 0.044

   b. 0.798

   c. 1.256

   d. 22.667

8. What does the odds ratio result mean for patients exposed to radiation?

   a. All patients exposed to radiation have diarrhea.

   b. All patients not exposed to radiation do not have diarrhea.

   c. The patients exposed to radiation are more likely to develop diarrhea.

   d. The patients not exposed to radiation are not likely to develop diarrhea.

9. Participants in a prospective study:

   a. have the risk factor for the disease, and the disease has manifested.

   b. have the risk factor for the disease, but the disease has not manifested.

   c. do not have the risk factor for the disease, and the disease has not manifested.

   d. do not have the risk factor for the disease, and the disease has manifested.

10. Dr. Steven Carol has noticed an alarming trend at his dermatology practice. It seems that patients with confirmed celiac disease have been seeking medical care for facial and body acne. Dr. Carol would like to conduct a clinical trial for these patients in which he prescribes a strict gluten-free diet for the experimental group and a regular diet for the control group. Dr. Carol would like to set up patient interviews and collect blood samples for all participants. What would Dr. Carol need to do prior to conducting his experiment?

    a. Create interview questions for study participants.

    b. Determine the research methodology that would best suit the experiment.

    c. Research current case studies on celiac disease.

    d. Consult the IRB to conduct the research study.

11. The National Committee for Quality Assurance (NCQA) publishes data on the adolescent immunization rate classified by health insurance types in which of the following reports?

    a. UHDDS

    b. HEDIS

    c. PCMH

    d. ORYX

12. San Antonio Community Hospital is experiencing an increase in the postsurgical infection rate. To determine the possible source of infection, data relating to the providers, surgical rooms, and equipment audit logs are analyzed. What level of data analytics does this represent?

    a. Personal

    b. Individual

    c. Comparative

    d. Aggregate

13. Corona General Hospital is promoting a healing hands study for their cancer patients in an effort to increase patient satisfaction and improve quality of health. They hired two trained masseuses who specialize in palliative massage; these professionals offer 30-minute massages to all admitted cancer patients. After 3 months of the pilot program, the hospital realized a 30% increase in patient satisfaction directly from the healing hands program. From this case study, we can conclude that the increase in patient satisfaction is:

    a. the dependent variable of the healing hands program.

    b. the dependent variable of Corona General Hospital.

    c. the independent variable of the healing hands program.

    d. the independent variable of Corona General Hospital.

14. What is the main difference between descriptive studies and correlation studies?

    a. Descriptive studies have more than one variable.

    b. Descriptive studies use only case studies.

    c. Correlation studies have more than one variable.

    d. Correlation studies use case studies and interviews.

15. Researchers are analyzing the impact of radioactive exposure on the west coast of North America after a damaging earthquake affected the nuclear facility in Fukushima, Japan in March 2011. The goal of the study is to determine the possible future risk of radioactive exposure. This type of study is also known as a(n):

    a. retrospective study.

    b. prospective study.

    c. experimental study.

    d. qualitative study.

Resources

For additional resources, please review the following references:

Abdelhak, M., & Hanken, M. A. (2016). *Health Information: Management of a Strategic Resource*. St. Louis, MO: Elsevier.

- Chapter 10: Statistics and Data Presentation
  - Healthcare Statistics
  - Statistical Measures and Tests

Oachs, P. K., & Watters, A. (2016). *Health Information Management: Concepts, Principles, and Practice*. Chicago, IL: AHIMA, American Health Information Management Association.

- Chapter 19: Research Methods

Sayles, N. B., & Gordon, L. L. (2016). *Health Information Management Technology: An Applied Approach*. Chicago, IL: AHIMA, American Health Information Management Association.

- Chapter 13: Research and Data Analysis
  - Research Methodologies
  - Healthcare Research Organizations

CHAPTER 15

Consumer Informatics and Health Information Exchange

In this module, we review the following subdomains:
- III.F.1. Explain usability and accessibility of health information by patients, including current trends and future challenges.
- III.G.1. Explain current trends and future challenges in health information exchange.

The following topics are covered in this subdomain:
- Consumer engagement activities
  - Assessing patient engagement
  - Patient portal management
  - Health literacy
- Use of personal health records
- Analyzing consumer informatics
- Ensuring patient safety
- Exchange/sharing of health information

MAIN TERMS

Connected personal health record

Consumer informatics

Consumer mediated exchange

Detached personal health record

Direct exchange

Health informatics

Health information exchange

Interchange

Interoperability

Meaningful use (MU)

Patient-generated health data (PGHD)

Patient portals

Personal health record

Query-based exchange

Practice Questions

1. Health informatics includes the management of data and information through which of the following?

   a. Networks

   b. Applications

   c. Hardware

   d. Peripherals

2. PHR is managed by:

   a. the healthcare facility.

   b. the physician.

   c. the patient.

   d. the health information exchange.

3. Which of the following mobile technologies can the patient use to share their personal health information with the physician?

   a. CPOE

   b. Barcode Medication Administration

   c. Clinical decision support system

   d. Patient portal

4. Which of the following would be an example of a wireless mobile technology used in collecting patient data?

   a. Smart glucose monitor

   b. Patient portal

   c. Online medical library

   d. Standard glucose monitor

5. How is patient-generated health data (PGHD) collected?

   a. Through a mobile technology or healthcare application

   b. Through the physician-patient encounter

   c. Through the electronic health record

   d. Through the patient encounter with the allied health professional

6. Mary Carpenter collected her personal health record through the physician portal. The type of personal health record she has is a:

   a. physician-sponsored health record.

   b. detached personal health record.

   c. connected personal health record.

   d. connected physician health record.

7. Should a detached personal health record be maintained according to accreditation standards such as the Joint Commission?

   a. Yes, the personal health record should be maintained according to the facility's accreditation standards.

   b. Yes, the personal health record should be maintained according to specific accreditations established by the Joint Commission.

   c. No, the personal health record should be issued by the facility, so it is maintained by their standards.

   d. No; because the personal health record is maintained by the patient, they can choose how the record is maintained.

8. Health information exchange is a feature supported by which stage of meaningful use?

   a. Preparation stage

   b. Stage I

   c. Stage II

   d. Stage III

9. Which of the following cases would be an example of health information interoperability?

   a. San Antonio Community Hospital reports vital birth statistics to the state.

   b. A physician from San Antonio Community Hospital accesses the patient record from Riverside Medical Clinic to treat a jaundice patient.

   c. A physician from the Riverside Hospital accesses the patient record from the Riverside Medical Clinical that is in the same network.

   d. A physician reviews the health record updated by the patient from the portal.

10. While most healthcare facilities use a certified EHR, why can they not communicate directly?

    a. If the systems cannot communicate, then they are not using a certified EHR.

    b. Certified EHR that meets Meaningful Use standards may maintain differing data dictionaries.

    c. Part of Meaningful Use standards is to use health information exchange organizations.

    d. No certified EHR systems can communicate between facilities.

11. Which of the following is NOT considered to be a benefit to using health information exchange?

    a. Fewer medical errors

    b. Increased patient safety through healthcare delivery

    c. Enhanced public health data and information reporting

    d. Increased costs of maintaining the volume of patient data

12. Dr. Harris has been searching for the patient John Smith through the health information exchange for the Southern California area. The query provided 1,423 results. What data element should be used to narrow the results?

    a. Middle name

    b. Date of service

    c. Date of birth

    d. Address

13. Patient generated data include all of the following, EXCEPT:

    a. X-ray results.

    b. lab results.

    c. problem list.

    d. pathology results.

14. Which organization maintains standards of secure electronic correspondence between the physician and the patient?

    a. ONC

    b. Health Level 7

    c. HITECH

    d. ARRA

15. Which of the following is NOT a type of health information exchange?

    a. Direct exchange

    b. Order-based exchange

    c. Query-based exchange

    d. Consumer-mediated exchange

Resources

For additional resources, please review the following references:

Oachs, P. K., & Watters, A. (2016). *Health Information Management: Concepts, Principles, and Practice.* Chicago, IL: AHIMA, American Health Information Management Association.
- Chapter 14: Consumer Health Informatics
- Chapter 15: Health Information Exchange

Sayles, N. B., & Gordon, L. L. (2016). *Health Information Management Technology: An Applied Approach.* Chicago, IL: AHIMA, American Health Information Management Association.
- Chapter 12: Healthcare Information
  - Consumers and Health Information
  - Health Information Exchange

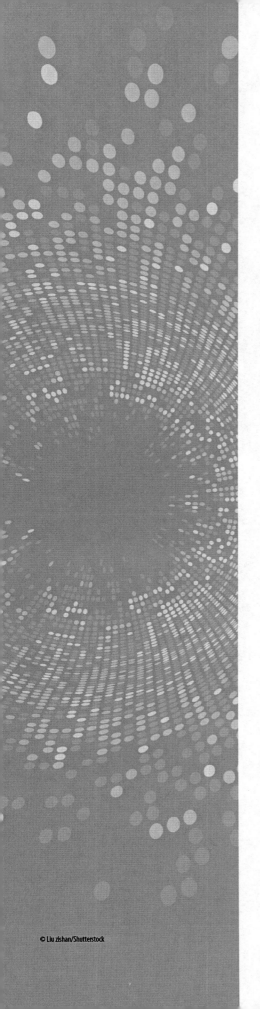

DOMAIN IV

Revenue Management

CHAPTER 16

Reimbursement

In this module, we review the following subdomains:
- IV.A.1. Apply policies and procedures for the use of data required in healthcare reimbursement

The following topics are covered in this subdomain:
- Payment methodologies and systems
  - Capitation
  - Prospective payment systems (PPS)
  - Resource-based relative value scale (RBRVS)
- Case-mix index
- MS-DRGs
- Health insurance
- Accountable care organizations

MAIN TERMS

Accountable care organizations (ACO)

Adjustments

Affordable Care Act (ACA)

Capitation

Case-mix index

ChampVA

Children's Health Insurance Program (CHIP)

Coinsurance

Medicare

Medigap

MS-DRG

National Provider Database (NPDB)

Office of the Inspector General (OIG)

Participating provider

Preferred provider organization (PPO)

Practice Questions

1. In order to become a Medicare-participating provider, the Conditions of Participation must be met through:

    a. Medicare.

    b. the Joint Commission.

    c. the Department of Human and Health Services.

    d. the Office of the National Coordinator.

2. Lucy is 3 years old. Her parents qualify for welfare payments and food stamps. Which health insurance would Lucy most likely qualify for?

    a. Medicare

    b. CHIP

    c. Blue Shield

    d. Medicaid

3. The physician charged the patient $125 for an office visit. The patient paid the physician $25 at the time of service and the patient's insurance company paid the physician $100. The patient's portion of the payment is the:

    a. copayment.

    b. discounted fee for service.

    c. coinsurance.

    d. deductible.

4. Title XVIII is the amendment to the Social Security Act that established which government-sponsored program?

    a. CHIP

    b. Medicaid

    c. Managed Care

    d. Medicare

5. Carrie Fisher was admitted to the hospital for congestive heart failure. She stayed in the facility for 4 nights. The actual charges incurred were $8,000. The PPS rate is $5,800. The per diem rate is $1,500 per day. Using the PPS, what will Medicare allow?

    a. $4,500

    b. $5,800

c. $6,000

d. $8,000

---

6. Under normal circumstances, prospective payment systems consider all of the following factors, EXCEPT:

   a. physician's charges.

   b. diagnosis codes.

   c. average charges for the geographic area.

   d. procedures codes.

---

7. While PPO and HMO are both considered managed care plans, what is the major difference?

   a. PPO plans have higher premiums.

   b. HMO plans have higher premiums.

   c. PPO plans require a gatekeeper.

   d. HMO plans require a gatekeeper.

---

8. Patients who are assigned the same DRG have all of the following comparable criteria, EXCEPT:

   a. diagnosis code.

   b. healthcare protocol.

   c. length of stay.

   d. utilization management.

---

9. The method used to calculate the hospital case mix is as follows:

   a. organizing each DRG relative weight by rank, with the patients in the most frequently occurring DRG listed as #1, and so forth.

   b. sum up all DRG relative weights in a period and then divide by the total number of cases discharged in a given time period.

   c. case mix as assigned by the Centers for Medicare and Medicaid Services (CMS).

   d. the standard deviation of all DRG relative weights.

10. Harry Windsor visited his primary care physician because he was suffering from the flu. He paid the physician's office his $30 copay for services, but the physician's office did not submit a health insurance claim for the office visit. What could explain this scenario?

    a. Harry Windsor did not have insurance.

    b. The physician's total charges for the office visit were $30, so there was no need to file a health insurance claim.

    c. The physician's office has a capitation agreement with Harry Windsor's managed care plan.

    d. Office visits are not typically billed.

11. For a provider who has a fee-for-service payment arrangement, what action should be taken after the respective diagnosis and procedure codes have been assigned?

    a. Percent discount for each procedure service

    b. Fee for bundled services

    c. Send fee schedule to third party payer

    d. Assign a fee to each procedure code

12. A health insurance plan that reimburses patients for medical expenses up to a specified amount is known as a(*n*):

    a. major medical plan.

    b. managed care plan.

    c. indemnity plan.

    d. preferred provider organization plan.

13. Tammy Harris has Medicare Part A only. Which of the following services is she covered for?

    a. Hospital stays

    b. Office visits

    c. Dental services

    d. Pharmaceuticals

14. From which prospective payment system does Medicare pay for outpatient hospital labs?

    a. MS-DRG

    b. APC

c. DEEDS

d. OPPS

---

15. Sally Stimpson is 67 years old and has Medicare. She accesses health care from Kaiser Permanente, which is an HMO provider that provides inpatient, outpatient, and prescription services. This must mean that Sally has:

    a. Medicare Part A.

    b. Medicare Part B.

    c. Medicare Part C.

    d. Medicare Part D.

---

16. The amount charged by the provider's office for the medical services rendered on the health insurance claim form is taken from:

    a. the hospital fee schedule.

    b. the provider fee schedule.

    c. the health insurance fee schedule.

    d. the Medicare fee schedule.

---

17. If the provider is a Medicare-participating provider, the balance between the amount charged for a service and the amount Medicare allows is:

    a. adjusted off from the patient account.

    b. charged to the patient.

    c. billed to the secondary insurance.

    d. The health insurance claim should be rebilled for higher reimbursement.

---

18. Sally visited Dr. Mukesh's office for migraines. It was a straightforward returning patient visit, so it was assigned the 99212 code, for which Dr. Mukesh charged $185. Sally has two insurance coverages, Medicare and Secure Horizons. Medicare fee schedule allowable for 99212 is $120. How much should Secure Horizons pay once Medicare processes and pays this claim?

    a. $13

    b. $24

    c. $37

    d. $45

---

19. Herman Henderson works part time, so he pays for his own insurance. While he works part time, his income is above the state poverty level. What type of insurance does he most likely have?

a. Affordable Care Act

b. COBRA

c. Medicaid

d. CHIP

20. Sandra Rivera currently has Medicare for primary insurance and Medicaid for secondary insurance. The hospital billed $2,500 for a colonoscopy; Medicare allowed $950 and paid $760. The Medicaid-allowed amount for the colonoscopy is $750. What amount should Medicaid reimburse as the secondary payer?

a. $19

b. $150

c. $190

d. Nothing

21. Jose visits the Riverside Medical Clinic IPA with his Blue Shield HMO benefits. The office charges $125 per office visit, and his copay is $25 for the office visit. How much will the Riverside Medical Clinic IPA charge Blue Shield HMO if they have a capitation agreement?

a. $0

b. $75

c. $100

d. $125

22. David was at work when he fell off a ladder and broke his wrist. What type of insurance would he most likely use for the work injury?

a. CHAMPUS

b. Workers' compensation

c. CHIP

d. Medicaid

23. David has Blue Cross insurance. He can choose whichever provider he wants, even specialists, but he does have a high deductible. David most likely has a(*n*):

a. HMO.

b. POS.

    c. PPO.

    d. EPO.

24. The Affordable Care Act has been amended and updated several times since it was enacted into law in 2010. However, which feature has remained until today?

    a. Expanded public health programs and coverage.

    b. Federally sponsored health insurance premiums.

    c. All private health insurance plans are mandated to participate.

    d. Children can be considered dependents until age 26.

25. Which of the following resources is NOT used during the physician credentialing process?

    a. Agency for Healthcare Research and Quality (AHRQ)

    b. State medical licensing board

    c. National Practitioner Data Bank (NPDB)

    d. Drug Enforcement Agency (DEA)

26. The Department of Health and Human Services administers Medicare and Medicaid programs. Medicare is a federally funded and managed program, whereas Medicaid is a federally funded, state-managed program. As such, who establishes the Medicaid eligibility standards?

    a. Department of Health and Human Services

    b. Federal government

    c. Specific state government

    d. The Joint Commission

27. Marcia is scheduled for a bunionectomy. She has Aetna HMO insurance and has seen the podiatrist for the presurgical appointment. After the procedure, the Aetna HMO insurance denies the claim for medical necessity. After reviewing the notes, the medical biller discovers that a surgical authorization from the HMO was never obtained. How will this claim be resolved?

    a. The physician bills the patient because the insurance denied payment.

    b. The patient contacts Aetna HMO to authorize the reimbursement.

    c. The physician requests the patient for secondary insurance information.

    d. The physician is at risk of not getting paid for the procedure.

28. All of the following healthcare facilities use MS-DRGs for reimbursement, EXCEPT:

    a. birthing centers.

    b. cancer hospitals.

    c. pediatric hospitals.

    d. religious-affiliated hospitals.

29. The DRG payment system is organized by classifying patients by:

    a. CPT codes.

    b. ICD-10-CM codes.

    c. ICD-10-PCS codes.

    d. HCPCS codes.

30. Review the following MS-DRG table and choose the most correct statement:

MS-DRG	Description	Weight
192	Chronic obstructive pulmonary disease w/o CC/MCC	0.712
193	Simple pneumonia w MCC	1.455

    a. MS-DRG 192 does not include CC or MCC, so fewer healthcare resources are required.

    b. MS-DRG 193 includes MCC, so more healthcare resources are needed.

    c. The higher the MS-DRG weight, the more healthcare resources are required.

    d. The lower the MS-DRG weight, the fewer healthcare resources are required.

31. Each MS-DRG is assigned a 3-digit number, which includes the category description and all of the following, EXCEPT:

    a. ICD-10-CM code.

    b. relative weight.

    c. geometric length of stay.

    d. average length of stay.

32. The Resource Based Relative Value Scale (RBRVS) is used by Medicare Part B and is based on which medical code set?

    a. ICD-10-CM

    b. ICD-10-PCS

    c. DSM-V

    d. CPT

33. Which of the following is a benefit of becoming an in-network participating provider for a health insurance plan?

    a. Lower health plan provider fee schedules

    b. An increase in patient referrals

    c. Quicker health insurance claims processing

    d. Payments are sent directly to the physician instead of to the patient

34. Which of the following federal agencies coordinates resources among federal, state, and local enforcement to prevent fraud in medical billing and coding?

    a. National Practitioner Data Bank (NPDB)

    b. National Provider Identifier (NPI)

    c. Office of the National Coordinator (ONC)

    d. Department of Human and Health Services (DHSS)

35. Diane has a Cigna HMO plan. She is suffering with adult acne and would like to see a dermatologist. What is her first step?

    a. Call a dermatologist in her local area to make an appointment.

    b. Contact the insurance plan member services to find a dermatologist that takes her insurance.

    c. Make an appointment with her primary care physician and share her adult acne concerns.

    d. HMO plans do not cover specialist-based health care.

Use the following information to answer questions 36–40.

Edna has a PPO plan with a $25 copay for primary physicians and a $50 copay for specialists. She also has a $3,500 deductible and a 20% coinsurance up to $5,000. In the past year she had knee arthroscopic surgery in March ($1,000) and a colonoscopy in May ($950), where it was determined she had Stage 1 colon cancer. Since June, she has visited her gastroenterologist every month and her oncologist every 2 weeks. Edna's cost for her chemotherapy infusions is $1,250 each; she has a treatment every 2 weeks, starting in June.

36. How much does Edna pay in copayments for her gastroenterology and oncology appointments in September?

 a. $100

 b. $150

 c. $250

 d. $300

37. If Edna starts her chemotherapy in June, when will she reach her full deductible?

 a. July

 b. August

 c. September

 d. October

38. If Edna starts her chemotherapy in July, when will she reach her coinsurance maximum?

 a. July

 b. August

 c. September

 d. October

39. Would Edna still need to pay her office visit copayment even if she has met her deductible and coinsurance limits for the year?

 a. No, Edna would not pay anything out of pocket after she meets her maximums.

 b. No, Edna would not pay anything out of pocket after she meets her maximum coinsurance.

 c. Yes, copayments do not add or subtract from deductibles and/or coinsurances.

 d. Yes, but copayments are applied to the following year deductibles and coinsurances.

40. Edna is still undergoing chemotherapy the following January. How much would she pay for her first chemotherapy session?

 a. Nothing, because she met the deductible and coinsurance minimums.

 b. $1,250, because the new year started.

 c. $3,500, because she needs to meet the deductible minimum.

 d. $5,000, because she needs to meet the coinsurance minimum.

Resources

For additional resources, please review the following references:

Abdelhak, M., & Hanken, M. A. (2016). *Health Information: Management of a Strategic Resource*. St. Louis, MO: Elsevier.
- Chapter 18: Revenue Cycle and Financial Management
  - Managing the Revenue Cycle

Oachs, P. K., & Watters, A. (2016). *Health Information Management: Concepts, Principles, and Practice*. Chicago, IL: AHIMA, American Health Information Management Association.
- Chapter 7: Reimbursement Methodologies

Sayles, N. B., & Gordon, L. L. (2016). *Health Information Management Technology: An Applied Approach*. Chicago, IL: AHIMA, American Health Information Management Association.
- Chapter 15: Revenue Management and Reimbursement
  - Healthcare Insurers
  - Healthcare Reimbursement Methodologies

CHAPTER 17

Revenue Cycle

In this module, we review the following subdomains:
- IV.A.2. Evaluate the revenue cycle management processes

The following topics are covered in this subdomain:
- Billing processes and procedures for hospitals, ambulatory settings and other delivery settings
  - Health insurance claims
  - Explanation of benefits (EOBs)
  - Advanced beneficiary notices (ABN)
  - Electronic data interchange (EDI)
  - Medical coding
  - Chargemaster
  - Bill reconciliation process
- Utilization management
- Case management/coordination

MAIN TERMS

Advanced beneficiary notice (ABN)

Appeals

Case management

Chargemaster

Chargemaster description

Claim denials

Clearinghouse

Concurrent review

Conditions of participation

Coordination of benefits

Electronic data interchange (EDI)

Explanation of benefits (EOBs)

HIPAA X12 837I

HIPAA X12 837P

Insurance verification

Medical necessity

National Committee of Quality Assurance (NCQA)

National Correct Coding Initiative (NCCI)

Preauthorization

Prospective review

Reconsideration

Redetermination

Retrospective review

Social Security Act

Unbundling

Utilization management (UM)

Practice Questions

1. Which of the following data fields is not commonly found on both the CMS-1500 and the UB-04 health insurance claim forms?

   a. Revenue code

   b. Subscriber employer

   c. Facility NPI

   d. Diagnosis pointer

2. A patient presented to his primary care physician three times in one month. One visit was for a throat culture in the clinic, one visit was to treat eye conjunctivitis, and one visit was to follow-up on a blood test. If the primary care physician was in a capitation agreement with the patient's health plan, then how many health insurance claims would be submitted?

   a. One claim at the end of the month totaling all charges for every date of service in one claim

   b. A separate claim per each healthcare encounter

   c. A separate claim for each healthcare encounter and medical service delivered

   d. No claims because these routine processes should be included in the capitation contract

3. Aetna sent an EOB that contained three claims. Two of the claims were paid according to the fee schedule, but the third claim was not paid. By reviewing the EOB, what informs the medical biller the reason for denial?

   a. Aetna account number

   b. Patient health insurance ID number

   c. Reason code

   d. Allowed amount

4. Mary Lassiter is new to coding. She reviewed an operative report to repair carpal tunnel syndrome in the left arm. Mary assigned the diagnosis code for right arm carpal tunnel syndrome, but used the RT modifier for the CPT code. Will the claim be paid?

   a. Yes, the insurance company will understand Mary's intention, correct the claim, and send the payment.

   b. Yes, it is not essential for the CPT modifier to match the diagnosis code.

    c. No, the claim will be denied for medical necessity.

    d. No, the claim will be denied and the patient will be responsible.

5. Which of the following data fields is not found on either the CMS-1500 or the UB-04 form?

    a. Social Security number

    b. Subscriber date of birth

    c. Procedure code description

    d. Both a and c

6. The amount difference between the charged amount and the allowed amount listed on an explanation of benefits is:

    a. adjusted off the patient account.

    b. billed to the patient directly.

    c. billed to the secondary insurance.

    d. resubmitted by the medical biller as an insurance claim for higher reimbursement.

7. Sally Fields is a Medicare patient. She was recommended by her doctor to have B12 shots, but they are not covered by her insurance. What would she need to sign?

    a. Explanation of benefits

    b. Advanced beneficiary notice

    c. Fee waiver

    d. Letter of redetermination

8. The CMS-1500 form is based on which of the following data sets?

    a. UHDDS

    b. UACDS

    c. DEEDS

    d. HEDIS

9. Both the CMS-1500 and the UB-04 forms use ICD-10-CM codes for reporting diagnosis. However, the primary diagnosis code for the CMS-1500 form is known as _____ and the UB-04 form is known as _____.

    a. reason for encounter; admitting diagnosis

    b. primary diagnosis; secondary diagnosis

    c. admitting diagnosis; reason for encounter

    d. reason for encounter; primary diagnosis

10. Which of the following code sets is used for both the CMS-1500 and the UB-04 form?

    a. ICD-10-PCS

    b. ICD-10-CM

    c. HCPCS

    d. Both b and c

11. The place of service codes can be found in which code set manual?

    a. ICD-10-PCS

    b. CPT

    c. HCPCS

    d. ICD-10-CM

12. The chargemaster is maintained by:

    a. the health insurance company.

    b. the patient.

    c. the healthcare facility.

    d. the electronic clearinghouse.

13. Harry Bleating was preauthorized for gallstone removal surgery on February 1. When the surgeon billed his insurance company, the claim was denied because Harry did not maintain monthly premiums and the coverage lapsed. Who is financially responsible for the surgeon's bill?

    a. The health insurance company because they preauthorized the surgery.

    b. The health insurance company because it is unethical for them to drop coverage during a fiscal year because of nonpayment.

    c. The surgeon because he should have confirmed coverage on the date of service.

    d. The patient because the coverage has lapsed.

14. Mary Lassiter assigned the code 99213 with modifier 50. Where can Mary check to see whether this modifier can accompany 99213?

    a. Encoder software

    b. NCCI edit table

    c. Medical necessity index

    d. Crosswalk

15. The physician was reimbursed $1,500 for a procedure for which he was contracted with the insurance company for $2,000. What can the physician's office do?

    a. Rebill the original claim for the higher reimbursement

    b. Accept the lower payment as payment in full

    c. Bill the difference to the patient

    d. Send an appeal letter to the health insurance company for the higher payment

16. When a Medicare patient has a secondary insurance plan that is listed on the remittance advice:

    a. the medical biller should bill the secondary insurance.

    b. Medicare will send the remittance advice to the secondary insurance.

    c. the patient should be notified to bill the secondary insurance.

    d. the medical biller should contact the secondary insurance to confirm.

17. The physician billed Aetna Healthcare $2,800 to surgically repair a broken finger. The reimbursement check was sent to the patient in full. Why would a health insurance company send the check to the patient and not the physician?

    a. The physician must have included the patient's address in the wrong data field.

    b. The patient requested the payment be sent to them first.

    c. The physician is not an in-network with the health insurance plan.

    d. The health insurance company sent the check to the patient by mistake.

18. Successful reimbursement begins in admitting. Why is this statement true?

    a. Admitting clerks collect all required information at the encounter.

    b. Admitting clerks are always friendly and know how to determine if the patient attempts to engage in unethical practices.

    c. Admitting clerks are responsible to code all scheduled medical care accurately.

    d. Admitting clerks communicate with the physician's offices to ensure patients are scheduled correctly.

19.   When does aging start on a patient account?

    a. The date the patient makes the appointment

    b. The date of service

    c. The date the medical bill is sent out

    d. The date of the explanation of benefits

20.   Cynthia is coding an operative report for a lumbar laminectomy. She assigns three procedure codes: one for starting the IV, another for the incision, and one more for the lumbar laminectomy procedure. Cynthia is:

    a. accurately coding.

    b. bundling codes.

    c. coding to specificity.

    d. unbundling codes.

21.   Ally Berman was a patient of the pain management practice. On 2/27/XX, she had a three-level bilateral facet procedure on her lumbar spine. The facility billed three procedure codes with a bilateral modifier for each code. The health insurance explanation of benefits showed only two procedure codes with bilateral modifier. Where can the biller confirm that actually three levels should have been billed and processed by the health insurance company?

    a. The chargemaster

    b. The electronic claims submission report

    c. The aging account report

    d. The patient account ledger

22.   Patient verification is completed in which stage of the revenue cycle?

    a. Front end cycle

    b. Mid cycle

    c. Back end cycle

    d. Every cycle stage

23. Tommy was admitted to the hospital unable to breathe. He was diagnosed with asthma in the ER. A case manager called his family the next day to provide additional community resources to provide support. This is an example of:

    a. case management.

    b. utilization management.

    c. coordination.

    d. patient verification.

24. Sally Hansen presents to the dermatology office with two insurance coverages, Blue Shield and Medicare. Can the admitting clerk assume that Medicare is primary and Blue Shield is secondary?

    a. Yes, Medicare is always a primary insurance.

    b. Yes, if the patient 65 years or older.

    c. No, the admitting clerk always confirms coordination of benefits.

    d. No, Blue Shield cannot be a secondary insurance.

25. The medical biller is submitting an electronic health insurance claim for the anesthesiologist. Which of the following claims would they submit?

    a. CMS-1500

    b. HIPAA X12 837P

    c. UB-04

    d. HIPAA X12 837I

26. In order to be a participating provider with Medicare and Medicaid, the healthcare facility must have a(n) _____ plan as a condition of participation.

    a. OASIS

    b. DEEDS

    c. UM

    d. HEDIS

27. A new general practice medical clinic opens in Cleveland, Ohio. The provider is a Medicare participating provider. For each Medicare patient, the clinic requires that they sign an advanced beneficiary notice because they want to be able to bill the patient the amount Medicare writes off. Is this a legal practice?

a. Yes, the physician has the right to collect the entire charged amount.

b. Yes, the patient should accept financial responsibility for amounts above Medicare allowance.

c. No, the advanced beneficiary notice is used to confirm patient financial responsibility for services not covered at all by Medicare.

d. No, advanced beneficiary notices are not used for Medicare patients.

28. Janice is a Medicare patient who has a secondary insurance plan through Aetna. In January, she had a cataract procedure for which Medicare paid the surgeon $360, and the Aetna secondary plan should have paid $40. Aetna denied the claim, stating medical necessity. Where should the appeal letter be sent?

a. Medicare

b. Aetna

c. Janice

d. The surgeon should accept the Medicare payment and write-off the balance

29. Utilization management evaluation is based on the following, EXCEPT:

a. projected length of stay.

b. actual length of stay.

c. type of healthcare facility.

d. patient diagnosis.

30. What is the most common cause of claims denials?

a. Medical necessity

b. NCCI edits

c. Inaccurate data collection at patient registration

d. Patient coverage lapse

31. Which of the following charges is not found on the chargemaster for a home healthcare facility?

a. Operative room charges

b. Room and board

c. Occupational therapy

d. Pharmacy

32. Which organization requires a utilization management review for managed care plans?

    a. Centers for Medicare and Medicaid Services

    b. State insurance board

    c. National Committee of Quality Assurance

    d. The Joint Commission

33. The Happy Pregnancy Obstetrics Center purchased a 4-D ultrasound machine for $20,000. They offer the service to their patients, but inform them that although the service is not covered by their insurance plan, they can pay $450 to have the service. The medical center has had the machine for a year, and it has been used only four times and has not covered the monthly lease payment for the equipment. What would the utilization review plan recommend for this machine?

    a. Reduce the price of the service in an effort to increase use.

    b. Sell the machine and use the room as an additional treatment room.

    c. Contact insurance plans to determine if private insurance will pay for use.

    d. Leave the machine as demand for the service may increase.

34. Appeal letter should include which of the following information?

    a. Code descriptions

    b. NPI numbers

    c. Insurance account number

    d. Patient Social Security number

35. An advanced beneficiary notice (ABN) is issued when:

    a. Medicare covers the procedure and/or service.

    b. Medicare covers only a percentage of the procedure and/or service.

    c. the secondary insurance pays the primary amount on the procedure and/or service.

    d. the patient is financially responsible for the procedure and/or service.

Resources

For additional resources, please review the following references:

Abdelhak, M., & Hanken, M. A. (2016). *Health Information: Management of a Strategic Resource*. St. Louis, MO: Elsevier.
- Chapter 18: Revenue Cycle and Financial Management
  - Managing the Revenue Cycle

Oachs, P. K., & Watters, A. (2016). *Health Information Management: Concepts, Principles, and Practice*. Chicago, IL: AHIMA, American Health Information Management Association.
- Chapter 8: Revenue Cycle Management

Sayles, N. B., & Gordon, L. L. (2016). *Health Information Management Technology: An Applied Approach*. Chicago, IL: AHIMA, American Health Information Management Association.
- Chapter 15: Revenue Management and Reimbursement
  - Revenue Cycle Management
  - Utilization Management
  - Case Management

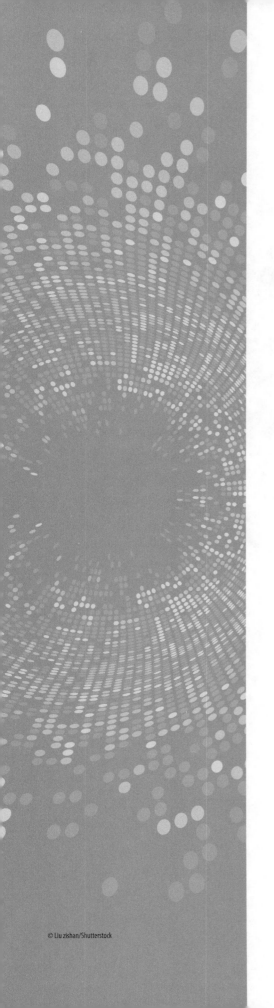

DOMAIN V
Compliance

CHAPTER 18

Regulatory Compliance

In this module, we review the following subdomains:

- V.A.1. Analyze policies and procedures to ensure organizational compliance with regulations and standards
- V.A.2. Collaborate with staff in preparing the organization for accreditation, licensure, and/or certification
- V.A.3. Adhere to the legal and regulatory requirements related to health information management

The following topics are covered in this subdomain:

- Internal and external standards, regulations, and initiatives
  - Health Insurance Portability and Accountability Act (HIPAA)
  - The Joint Commission
  - Quality integrity organizations (QIOs)
  - Meaningful use (MU)
  - Risk management
  - Patient safety
- Deeming authorities
  - Accreditation
  - Licensure
  - Certification (EHRs)
- Legislative and regulatory processes
  - Coding quality monitoring
  - Compliance strategies
  - Reporting

MAIN TERMS

Abuse	Deeming authorities	HIPAA
Accreditations	Department of Health and Human Services (DHHS)	HITECH
Benchmarking		Incident report
Certification	Fraud	Licensing
Compliance	Health Care Finance Administration (HCFA)	Meaningful use (MU)

MAIN TERMS *(CONTINUED)*

Medical peer review	Quality integrity organizations (QIOs)	Sentinel event
Outlier cases	Regulations	The Joint Commission
Quality indicators	Risk management	Waste

Practice Questions

1. Once a healthcare facility is accredited by the Joint Commission, the accreditation lasts for a maximum of _____ months.

    a. 6

    b. 12

    c. 24

    d. 36

2. When becoming a Medicare-participating provider, the difference between accreditation and certification is that accreditation is _____ and certification is _____.

    a. required; not required

    b. required; voluntary

    c. not required; required

    d. voluntary; required

3. All of the following are considered conditions of participation to earn deemed status to become a Medicare participating provider, EXCEPT:

    a. utilization management plan.

    b. quality improvement organization review.

    c. Joint Commission accreditation.

    d. National Provider Database.

4. While all healthcare professionals are vetted through the credentialing process, which management group grants clinical privileges for the facility?

    a. Board of governors

    b. Executive committee

    c. Credentialing specialist

    d. Operative committee

5. All activities involved in reducing potential and prospective liability are known as:

    a. utilization management.

    b. risk management.

    c. compliance.

    d. quality improvement.

6. According to the Joint Commission standard, the history and physical exam report should be documented into the patient record within _____ of admission.

    a. 6 hours

    b. 12 hours

    c. 24 hours

    d. 36 hours

7. Which of the following organizations reviews the patient record to ensure that standards of patient safety and quality of care delivered?

    a. Medicare

    b. The Joint Commission

    c. American Hospital Association

    d. Medicaid

8. Which of the following healthcare facilities does not need to meet Conditions of Participation standards?

    a. Medical clinics and offices

    b. Skilled nursing facilities

    c. Hospitals

    d. Home healthcare facilities

9. Which of the following challenges is not found when using electronic health records?

    a. System hacking

    b. Breach of data security

    c. Interpreting hand written orders

    d. Duplicate patient records

10. Dr. Mason accidently operated on Mrs. Stimple's right foot instead of her left foot. As a result, Mrs. Stimple needs to use a wheelchair on a regular basis. According to the Joint Commission, this is an example of:

    a. a medical error.

    b. a sentinel event.

    c. negligence.

    d. nonmalfeasance.

11. Which stage of meaningful use (MU) focuses on the evaluation of coordination of care in the delivery of quality patient care?

    a. Stage I

    b. Stage II

    c. Stage III

    d. All stages are included

12. A Medicare-sponsored group requested information from San Antonio Community Hospital's health information department to determine the level of care provided to their Medicare patient. Which organization is making this request?

    a. Medicare

    b. Medicaid

    c. RAC

    d. QIO

13. Which of the following associations/organizations meets Medicare's Conditions of Participation requirement for participating facilities?

    a. American Association for Accreditation of Ambulatory Surgery Facilities (AAAASF)

    b. American Hospital Association (AHA)

    c. Agency for Healthcare Research and Quality (AHRQ)

    d. Department of Health and Human Services (DHHS)

14. The Ontario Surgery Center is seeking accreditation to meet the conditions of participation established by Medicare. Which organization could accredit a surgery center?

    a. Accreditation Commission for Health Care (ACHC)

    b. The Joint Commission

    c. Center for Improvement in Healthcare Quality (CIHQ)

    d. Centers for Medicare and Medicaid Services (CMS)

15. The Health Care Financing Administration (HCFA) and the Office of the Inspector General are working together to prevent fraud. Which of the following is NOT included in their plan to prevent fraud and abuse?

    a. Increase in the number of prepayment reviews

    b. Decrease in the review of evaluation and management health insurance claims

    c. Increased request in medical records documentation

    d. Increase in overpayment recovery efforts

16. According to the hospital's compliance program, discharge reports need to be uploaded to the patient EHR within 24 hours of leaving the hospital; however, there are two physicians who have been noncompliant. Who should the complaints be reported to?

    a. The Director of Health Information

    b. The privacy officer

    c. The manager defined in the compliance program

    d. The board of directors

17. The Joint Commission's responsibilities include all of the following, EXCEPT:

    a. facility accreditation.

    b. sentinel event monitoring.

    c. health insurance claim evaluations.

    d. establishing quality indicators.

18. The San Antonio Community Hospital overcoded $450 for 50 patients. According to HIPAA civil monetary penalties, what will the hospital need to pay back?

    a. $22,500

    b. $32,500

    c. $67,500

    d. $77,500

19. Sally Fields is a patient at San Antonio Community Hospital. She was recovering from hip replacement surgery when she slipped on some liquid that was left on the floor of her room. What should the hospital staff do?

    a. Complete an incident report and record the incident in the patient record.

    b. Complete an incident report and do not record the incident on the patient medical record.

    c. Complete a compliance report and record the incident in the patient record.

    d. Complete a compliance report and do not record the incident in the patient record.

20. Dr. Simon Chu has decided not to make the information system upgrades to meet meaningful use standards. According to HITECH, the implementation-by date has since passed. If Dr. Chu would like to remain a Medicare participating provider despite not meeting the meaningful use standards, what would happen?

    a. Dr. Chu forfeited his Medicare participating provider status when he didn't make the information technology upgrades.

    b. Dr. Chu still remains a Medicare participating provider, but he will be reimbursed at a rate lower than the Medicare fee schedule because he did not make the information technology upgrades.

    c. Dr. Chu misses out on the financial incentives to make the information technology upgrades, but he still remains a Medicare participating provider.

    d. Dr. Chu needs to join a separate healthcare group that meets meaningful use standards in order to keep his Medicare participating provider status.

Resources

For additional resources, please review the following references:

Abdelhak, M., & Hanken, M. A. (2016). *Health Information: Management of a Strategic Resource*. St. Louis, MO: Elsevier.
- Chapter 12: Performance Management and Patient Safety
  - Risk Management

Oachs, P. K., & Watters, A. (2016). *Health Information Management: Concepts, Principles, and Practice*. Chicago, IL: AHIMA, American Health Information Management Association.
- Chapter 10: Organizational Compliance and Risk

Sayles, N. B., & Gordon, L. L. (2016). *Health Information Management Technology: An Applied Approach*. Chicago, IL: AHIMA, American Health Information Management Association.
- Chapter 17: Fraud and Abuse Compliance
  - Compliance Program

CHAPTER 19

CDI and Coding Compliance

In this module, we review the following subdomains:

- V.B.1. Analyze current regulations and established guidelines in clinical classification systems.
- V.B.2. Determine accuracy of computer-assisted coding assignments and recommend corrective action.
- V.D.1. Identify discrepancies between supporting documentation and coded data.
- V.D.2. Develop appropriate physician queries to resolve data and coding discrepancies.

The following topics are covered in this subdomain:

- Severity of illness systems
  - Present on admission
  - Hospital-acquired conditions
- Coding specialty systems
- Computer-assisted coding technology

- Clinical outcome measures and monitoring
- Clinical documentation improvement (CDI)
  - Professional communication skills
  - Roles of physicians in HIM and CDI

MAIN TERMS

Agency for Healthcare Research and Quality (AHRQ)

AHIMA CDI toolkit

Benchmarking

CDI metrics

Clinical documentation improvement (CDI)

Coding compliance plan

Computer-assisted technology

Hospital acquired conditions (HAC)

Overcoding

Physician query

Post-surgical activities

Present on admission (POA)

Pre-surgical activities

Procedural statement

Risk of mortality score (ROM)

Severity of illness (SOI)

Practice Questions

1. While auditing inpatient coding compliance programs, which medical coding systems are reviewed?

   a. ICD-10-CM and CPT

   b. ICD-10-CM and ICD-10-PCS

   c. CPT and ICD-10-PCS

   d. LOINC and ICD-10-PCS

2. What is the main goal of a coding compliance program?

   a. To shorten reimbursement times

   b. To efficiently report codes for public health purposes

   c. To prevent fraudulent coding practices

   d. To update coding functions with every code set update

3. Debra Bravo has a tracheostomy. During her hospital stay, she needs a spinal tap for meningitis. When coding for the principal diagnosis, meningitis, which indicator is reported for the tracheostomy?

   a. Hospital-acquired condition code

   b. Present on admission code

   c. Admitting diagnosis code

   d. First listed diagnosis code

4. Edna Turnbow was admitted to the hospital with pancreatitis. After 4 days of admission, the patient exhibited signs of sepsis, so antibiotics were started, and the symptoms were resolved within 3 days after antibiotic administration. How is the coder required to report the infection on the UB-04 form?

   a. Hospital-acquired condition code

   b. Present on admission code

   c. Admitting diagnosis code

   d. First listed diagnosis code

5. Mary is reviewing the operative report and wonders if she should code the incision separate from the procedure. What do you think?

   a. No; the incision is part of the pre-procedural surgical activities, so it should not be coded separately.

   b. Maybe; Mary should research how the incision was performed before assigning a separate code.

    c. Yes; because the incision is a procedure, it should be coded separately.

    d. Yes if Mary is coding for the surgeon, but not for hospital facility fee coding.

6. After birth, a newborn presents with a congenital heart valve defect. The medical documentation indicates that the patient has an APR-DRG level 3. What is the risk of mortality level?

    a. Minor

    b. Moderate

    c. Major

    d. Extreme

7. After an audit of respiratory therapist documentation in the hospital EHR, it was determined that the staff are commonly copying and pasting the documentation from one patient record into another in an effort to save time. This practice can ultimately cause all of the following, EXCEPT:

    a. reducing reimbursements.

    b. forcing medical coders to assign a more generalized code.

    c. failing to reflect the goals of the facility's coding compliance plan.

    d. increasing the number of patient cases.

8. The DSM V code set is used for encounters involved with:

    a. home healthcare patients.

    b. mental health patients.

    c. respiratory health patients.

    d. pharmacists.

9. A facility's coding compliance plan should include all of the following, EXCEPT:

    a. a clinical documentation improvement plan.

    b. an emphasis on coding accuracy instead of timeliness.

    c. measures to prevent fraudulent coding practices.

    d. ongoing staff training to support optimal coding assignment.

10. Michael Moore was admitted to the San Antonio Community Hospital on March 3 with a bowel instruction. Michael also has uncontrolled diabetes and is morbidly obese. The MS-DRG assigned was 388 G.I. Obstruction w/MCC. On March 5, a procedure was performed to remove the obstruction. On March 7, it was discovered that a surgical clamp was mistakenly left in the surgical site after incision closure. Which key indicator should be reported to Medicare?

    a. ROM

    b. SOI

    c. HAC

    d. POA

11. Corona Regional Hospital is a 250-bed community hospital. This facility has a case-mix index of 1.3 for the month of June. Which of the following facilities can Corona Regional Hospital use to benchmark?

    a. A 20-bed home healthcare facility

    b. A 275-bed community hospital

    c. A 250-bed military hospital

    d. A 250-bed privately owned hospital

12. The clinical documentation improvement process begins:

    a. when training facility staff.

    b. at the preadmission process.

    c. the day after patient admission.

    d. right after discharge.

13. The standards and criteria for a clinical documentation improvement program DOES NOT come from:

    a. Centers for Medicare and Medicaid Services.

    b. hospital bylaws, rules, and regulations.

    c. AHIMA standards of documentation.

    d. American Medical Association.

14. Who in the healthcare facility is responsible for training medical professionals on appropriate and required documentation standards?

    a. Physicians and healthcare providers

    b. Health information management professionals

    c. Medical coders

    d. Facility administration

15. Mary is coding for septal defect repair. While the report does not indicate any comorbidities, she did notice that the lab results indicate the patient may have diabetes. What should Mary do?

    a. Add the comorbidity in the DRG assignment because of the lab results.

    b. Report the case to the Director of Health Information to add the topic to a future training, but code the case as-is.

    c. Because the medical documentation does not indicate diabetes, no comorbidities should be added.

    d. Query the physician to have the documentation clarified and updated, including the review of the lab results, to include the comorbidity.

Resources

For additional resources, please review the following references:

Abdelhak, M., & Hanken, M. A. (2016). *Health Information: Management of a Strategic Resource*. St. Louis, MO: Elsevier.
- Chapter 4: Health Data Concepts and Information Governance
  - Outcome Indicators
  - Outcomes and Coding Issues
- Chapter 13: Data Analytics: Reporting, Interpretation and Use
  - Clinical Documentation Improvement

Oachs, P. K., & Watters, A. (2016). *Health Information Management: Concepts, Principles, and Practice*. Chicago, IL: AHIMA, American Health Information Management Association.
- Chapter 9: Clinical Documentation Improvement and Coding Compliance

Sayles, N. B., & Gordon, L. L. (2016). *Health Information Management Technology: An Applied Approach*. Chicago, IL: AHIMA, American Health Information Management Association.
- Chapter 15: Fraud and Abuse Compliance
  - Coding and Fraud and Abuse
  - Clinical Documentation Improvement

CHAPTER 20

Fraud Surveillance

In this module, we review the following subdomains:
- V.C.1. Identify potential abuse or fraudulent trends through data analysis

The following topics are covered in this subdomain:
- False Claims Act
- Stark Law
- Anti-Kickback Statute
- Whistleblower Protection Act
- Role of Office of Inspector General (OIG)
- Role of recovery audit contractor
- Unbundling and upcoding

MAIN TERMS

Abuse

Additional document request (ADR)

Anti-Kickback Statute

Balanced Budget Act

False Claims Act

Fraud

Fraud surveillance

Health Care Fraud Prevention and Enforcement Action Team (HEAT)

Office of the Inspector General (OIG)

Office of the Special Counsel (OSC)

Overcoding

Penalties

Qui tam

Recovery audit contractor (RAC)

Unbundling

Upcoding

Practice Questions

1. Henry Harris's medical record at San Antonio Community Hospital was requested by RACs for an audit. In this operative case, Henry went into shock during the procedure, so the routine laparoscopic gallbladder removal surgery turned into an open procedure. After the RAC audit, additional payment for the open procedure was taken back. What is the first step the hospital can take to appeal Medicare's decision?

   a. Redetermination

   b. Reconsideration

   c. Appeals council review

   d. Final judicial review

2. Medical necessity definitions are determined by which of the following, according to Medicare Administrative Contractors (MACs)?

   a. Recover audit contractors

   b. Local coverage determinations

   c. National coverage determinations

   d. Healthcare fraud prevention agents

3. According to the Office of the Inspector General (OIG), which of the following is the most common error found on health insurance claims?

   a. Missing documentation

   b. Unbundling

   c. Overcoding

   d. Upcoding

4. The Director of Health Information noticed that their department was experiencing higher additional documentation requests (ADR) from RACs. What steps can they take to reduce the ADRs in the coming quarters?

   a. Utilization management plan and review

   b. Internal coding audit

   c. Quality improvement plan

   d. Performance improvement plan

5. Dr. Johnson has been given participating provider status after Medicare charged him with upcoding 10 years ago. What would Medicare do if he was convicted of billing coding and fraud again?

    a. Dr. Johnson cannot be tried for the same crime again.

    b. Dr. Johnson would be suspended as a participating provider for another 10 years.

    c. Dr. Johnson would be suspended as a participating provider for another 15 years.

    d. Dr. Johnson would be suspended as a participating provider permanently.

6. A physician decides to code for a venipuncture for every office visit even though the procedure may not be performed every time. This is an example of:

    a. abuse.

    b. fraud.

    c. waste.

    d. medical necessity.

7. Dr. Trees went to a medical conference at which he purchased for his practice 10,000 wrapped tongue depressors, which would expire in 2 years. At the end of 2 years, 2,000 remaining tongue depressors needed to be discarded because of the expiration date. This is an example of:

    a. abuse.

    b. fraud.

    c. waste.

    d. medical necessity.

8. The Happy Hills Skilled Nursing Facility received a message from RACs that their payment was revoked, specifically because an audit of Dr. Trees's patient accounts showed patients were being charged for additional fees that were not medically necessary. When the Director of Health Information approached Dr. Trees about these charges, he stated that he did not document these services and was unaware of why they were billed. How can the director of HIM determine who is responsible for the upcoding?

    a. Audit Dr. Trees's patient records.

    b. Review the RAC review.

   c. Utilization management review

   d. Respond to the RAC review with a Medicare appeal.

9.   Which of the following is required by HIPAA legislation for all healthcare entities?

   a. Access controls

   b. Contingency plans

   c. Security plan

   d. All of these are required HIPAA elements.

10.   Dr. Walters wants to increase the number of new patients for his dermatology practice, so he hands out gift cards to primary care physicians who recommend patients to his practice. This is an example of:

   a. fraud.

   b. abuse.

   c. kickbacks.

   d. waste.

11.   Qui tam is used to protect the:

   a. Director of Health Information.

   b. whistleblower.

   c. inpatient medical coder.

   d. privacy officer.

12.   Dr. Jackson is visiting patients at the dialysis center for straightforward decision-making patient evaluations every week. However, he coded for a medium decision-making evaluation and management CPT code. This is an example of:

   a. fraud.

   b. abuse.

   c. waste.

   d. upcoding.

13.   The False Claims Act issues penalties to healthcare facilities that _____ submitted fraudulent claims.

   a. mistakenly

   b. purposely

   c. falsely

   d. knowingly

14. Dr. Goddard has an outpatient pain clinic. After a few years of practice, he realizes that many of his Medicare patients do not have transportation to his clinic. Dr. Goddard purchases a limousine service to transport his patients to the clinic for pain management procedures and bills Medicare for the transportation service. This practice is a violation of the:

    a. Anti-Kickback Statute.

    b. False Claims Act.

    c. Stark Law.

    d. Whistleblower Act.

15. The Whistleblower Protection Act protects which individuals who report against government fraud and abuse?

    a. Healthcare facilities

    b. Providers

    c. Federal employees

    d. Patients and their caregivers

16. According to the Whistleblower Protection Act, where can misconduct and offenses be reported?

    a. Office of the Inspector General

    b. Office of the Special Counsel

    c. Office of the National Coordinator

    d. Office of Medicare and Medicaid Services

17. Which of the following federal offices represents the largest team of auditors and leading healthcare law enforcement agencies in the United States?

    a. Office of the Inspector General

    b. Office of the Special Counsel

    c. Office of the National Coordinator

    d. Centers for Medicare and Medicaid Services

18. While the Recover Audit Contractor program through Medicare has recovered millions in misbilled medical procedures and services, it has increased the workload on the healthcare information departments everywhere because of:

    a. applied additional regulatory standards for medical billing and coding.

    b. RAC being a service available only to participating Medicare providers.

c. increased requests of information to review more Medicare patient medical records.

d. reductions to the standard reimbursement for services paid by Medicare.

19. What can health information departments do to reduce ADR rates?

a. Reduce Medicare denial rate

b. Reduce Medicare reimbursement rate

c. Increase Medicare accuracy coding rate

d. Increase the number of Medicare patients

20. Dr. Tate performed a laparoscopic appendectomy, but the procedure was coded as an open appendectomy procedure. This is an example of what type of fraud?

a. Overcoding

b. Upcoding

c. Unbundling

d. Bundling

Resources

For additional resources, please review the following references:

Abdelhak, M., & Hanken, M. A. (2016). *Health Information: Management of a Strategic Resource*. St. Louis, MO: Elsevier.
- Chapter 18: Revenue Cycle and Financial Management
  - Financial Aspects of Fraud and Abuse Compliance

Oachs, P. K., & Watters, A. (2016). *Health Information Management: Concepts, Principles, and Practice*. Chicago, IL: AHIMA, American Health Information Management Association.
- Chapter 10: Organizational Compliance and Risk

Sayles, N. B., & Gordon, L. L. (2016). *Health Information Management Technology: An Applied Approach*. Chicago, IL: AHIMA, American Health Information Management Association.
- Chapter 16: Fraud and Abuse Compliance
  - Federal Regulations and Initiatives

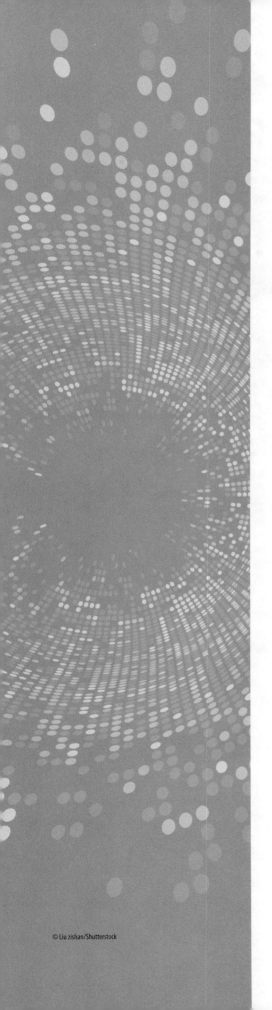

DOMAIN VI

Leadership

CHAPTER 21
Leadership Roles

In this chapter, we review the following subdomain:
- VI.A.1. Summarize health-information–related roles
- VI.A.2. Apply the fundamentals of team leadership
- VI.A.3. Organize and facilitate team meetings

The following topics are covered in this subdomain:
- Healthcare providers, including administrators
- Team leadership concepts and techniques
- Roles and functions of teams and committees
  - Communication, including interpersonal and critical thinking

MAIN TERMS

Agenda	Chief Information Officer (CIO)	Middle management
Authoritarian leadership	C-Suite Executives	Mission statement
Behavior theory	Executive management	Organization chart
Brainstorming	Laissez-faire leadership	Power and influence theory
Chief Executive Officer (CEO)	Leadership	
Chief Financial Officer (CFO)	Meeting minutes	

Practice Questions

1. Facility bylaws, policies, and procedures are based on federal, state, local documentation standards AND:

    a. mission and vision statements.

    b. the C-Suite.

    c. organizational chart.

    d. committee minutes.

2. What level of management is the Director of Health Information considered?

    a. First-level management

    b. Executive-level management

    c. Middle-level management

    d. Supervisory-level management

3. Which of the following executives is considered the head of the board of directors?

    a. Chief Information Officer (CIO)

    b. Chief Operations Officer (COO)

    c. Chief Financial Officer (CFO)

    d. Chief Executive Officer (CEO)

4. The leadership theory that states a leader's effectiveness, such as a monarch's, is dependent on the circumstances he or she is in is:

    a. trait theory.

    b. behavior theory.

    c. contingency theory.

    d. power and influence theory.

5. Anna Wintour, the successful editor and chief of *Vogue* magazine, completed high school but did not complete any further education in fashion. Which leadership theory explains her professional leadership success?

    a. Trait theory

    b. Behavior theory

    c. Contingency theory

    d. Power and influence theory

6. Leadership is one of four essential management functions. Which of the following is NOT considered an essential management function?

   a. Planning

   b. Evaluation

   c. Controlling

   d. Organizing

7. Alice is the coding supervisor for the San Antonio Community Hospital. She requires all medical coders to send in their codes for her to review before health insurance claims are submitted. What type of leadership style is this?

   a. Trait leadership

   b. Laissez-faire leadership

   c. Authoritarian leadership

   d. Democratic leadership

8. The San Antonio Community Hospital has a president and a CEO. The president is focused on marketing efforts for the facility, whereas the CEO handles all of the strategic planning responsibilities. The president takes a laid-back outlook on strategic responsibilities, so his leadership style is:

   a. contingent.

   b. laissez faire.

   c. authoritarian.

   d. democratic.

9. Which executive manages the responsibility of planning, maintaining, and managing the information systems for a healthcare facility?

   a. Chief Information Officer (CIO)

   b. Chief Operations Officer (COO)

   c. Chief Financial Officer (CFO)

   d. Chief Executive Officer (CEO)

10. Which of the following characteristics is NOT essential for effective team leaders?

    a. Respectfulness

    b. Authoritarianism

c. Integrity

d. Delegating

11. The team assembled to assist San Antonio Community Hospital transition into a new, certified EHR system includes the Director of Health Information, the Privacy Officer, the Security Officer, and the Chief Information Officer. They meet the first Monday of every month to review the progress of implementation. What team document includes a list of all team members and their respective responsibilities?

a. Meeting agenda

b. Team charter

c. Meeting minutes

d. Organization chart

12. Successful meetings include all of the following, EXCEPT:

a. starting the meeting on time.

b. asking each team member to confirm their agreement with proposals.

c. agenda are sent to team members ahead of scheduled meeting times.

d. team members are accountable for their project contributions.

13. Brainstorming is what type of team building and communication process?

a. Authoritative

b. Democratic

c. Critical thinking

d. Laissez-faire

14. There was a 14% increase in infection for gastroenterology patients in the month of June. What critical-thinking tool should be used to explain the reason for the increase?

a. Root-cause analysis

b. Team charter

c. Organization chart

d. Meeting minutes

15. Which of the following team members releases the meeting agenda?

    a. Board of directors

    b. Team leader

    c. Director of health information

    d. Chief executive officer

Resources

For additional resources, please review the following references:

Abdelhak, M., & Hanken, M. A. (2016). *Health Information: Management of a Strategic Resource*. St. Louis, MO: Elsevier.
- Chapter 17: Operational Management
  - Systems and Organizational Level (Midlevel)
  - Strategic Management

Oachs, P. K., & Watters, A. (2016). *Health Information Management: Concepts, Principles, and Practice*. Chicago, IL: AHIMA, American Health Information Management Association.
- Chapter 22: Managing and Leading During Organization Change
  - Trends in Leadership Theory

Sayles, N. B., & Gordon, L. L. (2016). *Health Information Management Technology: An Applied Approach*. Chicago, IL: AHIMA, American Health Information Management Association.
- Chapter 17: Leadership
- Chapter 19: Management
  - Organizational Structure

CHAPTER 22

Process Improvement and Change Management

In this chapter, we review the following subdomains:

- VI.B.1. Recognize the impact of change management on processes, people, and systems
- VI.C.1. Utilize tools and techniques to monitor, report, and improve processes
- VI.C.2. Identify cost-saving and efficient means of achieving work processes and goals
- VI.C.3. Utilize data for facility wide outcomes reporting for quality management and performance improvement

The following topics are covered in this subdomain:

- Organization mergers
- New systems and processes implementation
- Tools and techniques for performance improvement
- Incident response
- Medical record reconciliation
- Sentinel events
- Data for outcomes reporting
- Continuous Quality Improvement (CQI)

MAIN TERMS

Affinity grouping

Continuous Quality Improvement (CQI)

External force

Fishbone diagram

Histogram

Internal force

Medical record reconciliation

Movement diagram

Organization mergers

Outcome indicator

Outcomes reporting

Pareto chart

Process indicator

Quality indicator

Scatter diagram

Sentinel events

Practice Questions

1. The EHR implementation team has several important priorities to accomplish, but the team is divided on what should be most important. Which of the following tools or techniques can be used to rank the first priority?

   a. Nominal group technique

   b. Histogram

   c. Fishbone diagram

   d. Quality indicators

2. Christus Santa Rosa Hospital in Texas is merging with Saddletown Community Hospital in Oklahoma. Christus Santa Rosa Hospital has met the Medicare conditions of participation and is accredited by the Joint Commission. Saddle town community has not. Can both Christus Santa Rosa Hospital and Saddletown Community Hospital now care for Medicare patients after the merger?

   a. Yes, because the two organizations are one, they can share the Joint Commission accreditation.

   b. Yes, states have different Medicare conditions of participation, so they both have always cared for Medicare patients.

   c. No, Saddletown Community Hospital cannot care for Medicare patients until they meet the Medicare conditions of participation themselves.

   d. No, because Saddletown Community Hospital will be the legal entity, Christus Santa Rosa Hospital will lose their Medicare conditions of participation accreditation.

3. Which of the following is NOT considered an essential principle of Continuous Quality Improvement?

   a. Significance of accurate data collection and information analysis

   b. Inconsistency of variation

   c. Emphasis on improving the customer experience

   d. Value of teamwork

4. _____ is an example of an internal force of a healthcare facility.

   a. The closing of a local long-term care facility

   b. An elevated employee turnover rate

   c. The Joint Commission adding another data collection standard to maintain accreditation

   d. A local swine flu outbreak

5. Continuous data improvement focuses on meeting smaller goals to affect incremental change. All of the following are examples of smaller goals, EXCEPT:

   a. developing and publishing the steps for ROI for all healthcare facility staffers to review and implement.

   b. firing and replacing the entire team because the HIM department accuracy rate has risen significantly.

   c. direct messaging from the medical coder to the healthcare facility physician to reduce physician query time delay.

   d. uploading new patient paperwork on facility website to save intake time at the appointment.

6. San Antonio Community Hospital is analyzing the correlation between the number of staff and patient satisfaction. Which quality indicator would they use to measure the quantitative attributes of the healthcare facility?

   a. Process indicators

   b. Outcome indicators

   c. Process improvement indicators

   d. Structure indicators

7. Outcome indicators are quality indicators that:

   a. measure quantitative attributes.

   b. count the steps needed to complete the process.

   c. measure the satisfaction of the delivery of care to the patient.

   d. identify the performance level of care delivered.

8. All of the following are techniques used by teams to prioritize tasks, EXCEPT:

   a. nominal group technique (NGT).

   b. fishbone diagram.

   c. multivoting.

   d. affinity grouping.

9. The movement diagram is used to:

    a. provide a floorplan of the office space and indicate directions of work flow.

    b. determine the root cause of problems the healthcare facility is facing.

    c. display team task prioritization.

    d. present the frequency based on continuous collected data.

10. The technique used by teams in which the members determine the priority of various tasks by assigning a specific number of points to each team member is:

    a. affinity grouping.

    b. multivoting.

    c. brainstorming.

    d. nominal.

11. Review the plots on this scatter graph. What conclusions can be made?

    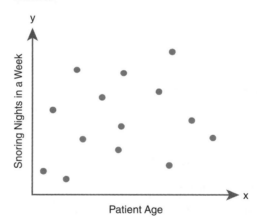

    a. The older the age, the more nights snoring.

    b. The younger the age, the fewer nights snoring.

    c. The older the age, the fewer nights snoring.

    d. Because the data does not correlate, we cannot confirm a relationship.

12. Review this Pareto chart. What does the Pareto Principle of the 80/20 rule mean?

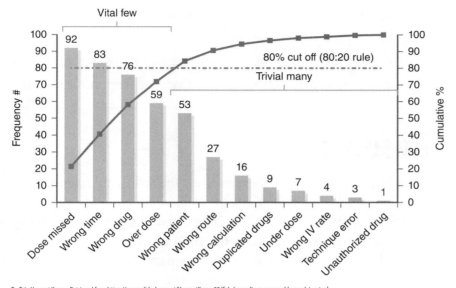

Dr. Brig Hemant Kumar, Retrieved from https://www.slideshare.net/HemantKumar98/fish-bone-diagram-a-problem-solving-tool

   a. 80% of actual problems caused by 20% of resources
   b. 80% of resources caused by 20% of the actual problem
   c. 80% of projected problems caused by 20% actual problems
   d. 80% of resources caused by 20% of limited resources

13. The three to four categories on the fish diagram represent:
   a. solutions.
   b. problems.
   c. causes.
   d. data.

14. Overordering and utilizing the last-in–last-out inventory method are examples of which type of misuse?
   a. Wasting time
   b. Transportation
   c. Inventory
   d. Defects and errors

15. Why does the Joint Commission require healthcare facilities to research the cause of sentinel events?

   a. To prevent data and information breaches

   b. To prevent disease outbreak

   c. To prevent misuse of healthcare facility resources

   d. To protect patients, staff, and visitors from future harm

Resources

For additional resources, please review the following references:

Abdelhak, M., & Hanken, M. A. (2016). *Health Information: Management of a Strategic Resource.* St. Louis, MO: Elsevier.
- Chapter 12: Performance Management and Patient Safety
- Chapter 17: Operational Management
  - Design and Management of Space in Health Information Services

Oachs, P. K., & Watters, A. (2016). *Health Information Management: Concepts, Principles, and Practice.* Chicago, IL: AHIMA, American Health Information Management Association.
- Chapter 25: Work Design and Performance Improvement

Sayles, N. B., & Gordon, L. L. (2016). *Health Information Management Technology: An Applied Approach.* Chicago, IL: AHIMA, American Health Information Management Association.
- Chapter 18: Performance Improvement

CHAPTER 23

HR Management, Training, and Development

In this chapter, we review the following subdomains:
- VI.D.1. Report staffing levels and productivity standards for health information functions
- VI.D.2. Interpret compliance with local, state, and federal labor regulations
- VI.D.3. Adhere to work plans, policies, procedures, and resource requisitions in relation to job functions
- VI.E.1. Explain the methodology of training and development
- VI.E.2. Explain return on investment for employee training/development

The following topics are covered in this subdomain:
- Staffing levels and productivity standards
- Labor/employment laws
- HR structure and operations
- Orientation and training
- Recruitment, retention, and sizing

MAIN TERMS

Conflict management

Disciplinary action

Fair Labor Standards Act

Family and Medical Leave Act (FMLA)

Flex time

Full-time equivalent

Genetic Nondiscrimination Act

Handling grievances

Orientation

OSHA

Part-time employee

Per diem

Performance management

Staff recruitment

Staff retention

Telecommuting

Practice Questions

1. The medical coder supervisor determines that out of the total 535 operative reports in the month of February, 23 were coded incorrectly. What is the coding accuracy rate?

    a. 2.7%
    b. 4.3%
    c. 43.0%
    d. 95.7%

2. San Antonio Community Hospital added 12 new hospital beds to the med-surg wing. Considering the Joint Commission standard of 8 patients per nurse per shift, and that each nurse can only work up to 40 hours per week, how many nurses are needed to meet the staffing needs of the hospital addition? (Hint: no overtime can be awarded.)

    a. 7
    b. 9
    c. 10
    d. 11

3. An hourly billing clerk has been working 30 minutes before clocking in for her daily shift because she feels that there is too much work. Which federal labor regulation is in violation in this case?

    a. Fair Labor Standards Act
    b. Civil Rights Act
    c. OSHA
    d. Family and Medical Leave Act

4. Emily is working 50 hours per week, but she does not earn overtime pay. This must mean she is:

    a. an exempt employee.
    b. a nonexempt employee.
    c. a part-time employee.
    d. a per-diem employee.

5. A well-qualified candidate for a surgical tech position comes to the interview with a head covering indicating a different religion. After reviewing her appearance, the HR representative sends her home because she thinks the head covering will get in the way of her performing her job adequately. According to Title VII, what is the employer responsible for?

    a. To protect the patient in case the head covering gets in the way of the surgical tech performing her job duties in the operating room

    b. To protect the healthcare facility's best interest so as to not discriminate against the candidate when she becomes part of the healthcare team

    c. To make reasonable accommodations to assist the employee to perform her duties effectively

    d. To hire the candidate because the healthcare facility needs a more diverse healthcare team

6. Molly works for a home healthcare agency. While preparing to bathe a patient, she noticed that the glove box was empty. The healthcare administrator stated that the facility was cutting back on unnecessary expenses, and that Molly should be re-using her gloves for multiple patients to prevent waste. The healthcare facility's new policy is a violation of which federal regulation?

    a. Fair Labor Standards Act

    b. Civil Rights Act

    c. OSHA

    d. Family and Medical Leave Act

7. Pamela has been a medical coder with Corona Regional Hospital for the past 6 years. She recently was diagnosed with breast cancer. Which federal regulation protects her job if she takes time off work to care for her health?

    a. Fair Labor Standards Act

    b. Civil Rights Act

    c. OSHA

    d. Family and Medical Leave Act

8. Greg has been diagnosed with the gene for early onset Alzheimer's disease. Currently he does not current show any signs of the disease, but his physicians assure him that the disease will manifest eventually. The employer-sponsored health plan wants to exclude Greg from the plan because they obtained his genetic test results. What federal regulation protects his rights?

   a. OSHA

   b. Family and Medical Leave Act

   c. Genetic Nondiscrimination Act (GINA)

   d. Fair Labor Standards Act

9. What are some of the benefits of maintaining detailed job descriptions for every position in the healthcare facility?

   a. To regularly audit all employee work

   b. To attract highly qualified candidates for open positions

   c. To benchmark workloads compared to other employees working at the same healthcare facility

   d. To report to the US Department of Labor

10. An essential tool utilized by the HR department in performance appraisal is:

    a. work sampling.

    b. production time study.

    c. time log.

    d. all of the above.

11. All of the following information should be included in a new employee orientation, EXCEPT:

    a. maintaining confidentiality through HIPAA training.

    b. how to determine which race of patients is more important.

    c. an employee handbook detailing corporate culture and standards.

    d. the organizational chart that provides the chain of command.

12. The HR department has received many complaints about the swing shift telemetry floor charge nurse and the Director of Health Information not getting along. The communication issues have resulted in potential patient injury. Which HR function should be employed?

    a. Staffing

    b. Handling grievance

   c. Conflict resolution

   d. Retention

---

13. Christa Santa Rosa Hospital, a Catholic institution, is hiring a nurse. If a religious non-Catholic applies, which federal legislation would protect them from being discriminated against?

   a. Fair Labor Standards Act

   b. Title VII

   c. Family and Medical Leave Act

   d. Genetic Nondiscrimination Act

---

14. Which of the following federal agencies compiles employment statistics on industries in the United States?

   a. US Bureau of Labor

   b. US Department of Labor

   c. Employment and Training Administration

   d. US Department of Commerce

---

15. Mary needs to take 6 weeks off for a surgery and recovery time. As per the employer policy, Mary informed HR of the surgery date and the time she needed off by submitting a note on her physician's letterhead. Mary is a lead coder for San Antonio Community Hospital, so the facility hired a temp coder to keep up with the workload. After 6 weeks, Mary returned to the hospital to work. However, the facility was so impressed by the temp's work that they want to keep her and place Mary in the billing department instead, which meant that her work hours would change to swing shift, she would lose quarterly commissions, and she would get paid less per hour. Should Mary accept the new position under these terms?

   a. Yes; San Antonio Community Hospital was generous in giving Mary the time off for her procedure and recovery, so the fact that they kept her job was a favor.

   b. Yes; although the employer cannot terminate Mary for taking the personal time off, they can choose the type of work they want her to move into after she returns.

   c. No; Mary can make more money as a coder, so she should find a job at a different hospital.

   d. No; the employer is required to allow Mary to return to her job or a similar job because she followed the employer's regulations of informing them that she was going to have the procedure.

Resources

For additional resources, please review the following references:

Abdelhak, M., & Hanken, M. A. (2016). *Health Information: Management of a Strategic Resource*. St. Louis, MO: Elsevier.
- Chapter 16: Human Resources Management Chapter
  - Human Resource Management

Oachs, P. K., & Watters, A. (2016). *Health Information Management: Concepts, Principles, and Practice*. Chicago, IL: AHIMA, American Health Information Management Association.
- Chapter 23: Human Resources Management

Sayles, N. B., & Gordon, L. L. (2016). *Health Information Management Technology: An Applied Approach*. Chicago, IL: AHIMA, American Health Information Management Association.
- Chapter 20: Human Resources Management and Professional Development

CHAPTER 24

Strategic, Organizational, and Financial Management

In this chapter, we review the following subdomains:

- VI.F.1. Summarize a collection methodology for data to guide strategic and organizational management
- VI.F.2. Understanding the importance of healthcare policy-making as it relates to the healthcare delivery system
- VI.F.3. Describe the differing types of organizations, services, and personnel and their interrelationships across the healthcare delivery system
- VI.F.4. Apply information and data strategies in support of information governance initiatives
- VI.F.5. Utilize enterprisewide information assets in support of organizational strategies and objectives

The following topics are covered in this subdomain:

- Internal and external workflow
  - Process monitors
  - Outcome measures and monitoring
  - Resource allocation
- Corporate compliance
  - Patient safety
  - Risk assessment
  - Customer satisfaction
- State, local, and federal policies
  - Healthy People 2020
  - Institute of Medicine (IOM) reports
- Centers for Disease Control and Prevention (CDC)
- Patient Centered Outcomes Research Institute (PCORI)
- Information and data strategy methods and techniques
- Government standards
  - Data information visualization, models, and presentation

MAIN TERMS

Accountable care organizations (ACOs)

Centers for Disease Control (CDC)

Compliance officer

Controlling

Corporate compliance

External customer

External forces

Functional definition

Leading

Opportunities

Organizing

Patient Centered Outcomes Research Institute (PCORI)

Planning

Risk assessment

Span of control

Specialization

Practice Questions

1. Which of the following is an example of a strategic goal?

    a. Adding a 35-bed maternity ward in 3 years

    b. Telemetry floor staffing schedule

    c. Planning inventory ordering for the fiscal year

    d. Updating the RIO process to meet Joint Commission standards

2. Zack regularly reviews coder accuracy reports and trains the coders who need to improve. Which management function would this activity fall into?

    a. Planning

    b. Controlling

    c. Leading

    d. Organizing

3. Bonnie is a new inpatient coder that the facility hired. She has 15 years of experience working with outpatient pain management and surgery center billing using CPT codes. However, the coding manager assigned her to code ICD-10-PCS for hospital cases. Which principle of organization has the coding manager failed to apply?

    a. Functional definition

    b. Hierarchical chain

    c. Unity of command

    d. Specialization

4. Donna, the new Director of Health Information, wants to be involved and hands-on with all of the functions in the department, so she calls a meeting with the managers of the various HIM departments, such as ROI, coding, billing, collections, and accounts receivable. At the meeting she tells all her line managers that employees should be communicating with her in addition to the line managers. Which principle of organization is Donna struggling with?

    a. Unity of command

    b. Functional definition

    c. Span of control

    d. Specialization

5. Which of the following is a characteristic of the operational plan?

    a. Long-term goals

    b. Developed by executive management

    c. List of daily functions

    d. Decision making based on mission statement

6. For 2019, Medicare is requesting medical records for all patients admitted with a gallstone diagnosis. This is an example of an _____ force.

    a. internal

    b. external

    c. operational

    d. executive

7. Mary has the certifications to be a nursing supervisor, but the nursing staff does not like working with her regularly. As a result, the skilled nursing facility has been facing a higher-than-normal turnover rate. This is an example of an _____ force.

    a. internal

    b. external

    c. operational

    d. executive

8. The healthcare facility's inability to collect reimbursements has been due to coding errors and poor medical billing practices. Which category on the SWOT does this issue fall?

    a. Strength

    b. Weakness

    c. Opportunity

    d. Threat

9. A generous donor gave the hospital an endowment to build a pediatric cancer wing. Which category on the SWOT does this issue fall?

    a. Strength

    b. Weakness

    c. Opportunity

    d. Threat

10. The goal of corporate compliance includes all of the following, EXCEPT:

    a. reporting staff to accrediting agencies.

    b. preventing injury to the staff and the patient.

    c. monitoring for fraudulent activity and conduct.

    d. resolution of regulation violations.

11. The program that collects health data to inform the public of potential health risks to prevent disease, injury, and disability is known as:

    a. Healthy People 2020.

    b. Institute of Medicine.

    c. Centers for Disease Control and Prevention.

    d. Patient Centered Outcomes Research Institute.

12. Which of the following insurance plans utilizes accountable care organizations (ACOs), which include a team of healthcare providers and supplies that work together to coordinate and improve care for patients?

    a. Medicare

    b. Blue Cross

    c. TRICARE

    d. Workers' compensation

13. Not all healthcare providers can bill health insurance for services rendered. Which of the following providers CAN bill health insurance for services rendered?

    a. Clinical lab scientist

    b. Nurse practitioner

    c. Endocrinologist

    d. Surgical technologist

14. Which of the following healthcare specialists is not considered to be an allied health professional?

    a. Pharmacist

    b. Nurses

    c. Nutritionist

    d. Health information technologist

15. According to governance standards, what is a healthcare organization's most strategic asset?

    a. Strategic plan

    b. Organizational plan

    c. Information

    d. Staff

Resources

For additional resources, please review the following references:

Abdelhak, M., & Hanken, M. A. (2016). *Health Information: Management of a Strategic Resource*. St. Louis, MO: Elsevier.
- Chapter 16: Human Resources Management
  - Human Resource Management

Oachs, P. K., & Watters, A. (2016). *Health Information Management: Concepts, Principles, and Practice*. Chicago, IL: AHIMA, American Health Information Management Association.
- Chapter 23: Human Resources Management

Sayles, N. B., & Gordon, L. L. (2016). *Health Information Management Technology: An Applied Approach*. Chicago, IL: AHIMA, American Health Information Management Association.
- Chapter 20: Human Resources Management and Professional Development

CHAPTER 25

Financial Management

In this chapter, we review the following subdomains:

- VI.G.1. Plan budgets
- VI.G.2. Explain accounting methodologies
- VI.G.3. Explain budget variances

The following topics are covered in this subdomain:

- Budgets
  - Staffing
  - Department
  - Capital
- Basic accounting methodology
  - Cost and cash accounting
- Budget variances

MAIN TERMS

Allocated cost

Assets

Balance sheet

Budget adjustment

Budget variance

Capital budget

Cash accounting

Corrective controls

Financial plan

Financial statements

Forecasted revenue and expense

Income statement

Liabilities

Operating budget

Preventative controls

Ratio analysis

Practice Questions

1. On a balance sheet, the financial analyst can find which of the following categories?

    a. Income

    b. Revenue

    c. Net loss

    d. Liabilities

2. The income statement includes all of the following categories, EXCEPT:

    a. income.

    b. revenue.

    c. net loss.

    d. assets.

3. Since the transition from a paper record to the EHR management system, the HIM department's sheet paper expense has dropped considerably. As such, the department set the 20XX fiscal budget to $500 for the year. At the end of the year, the sheet paper expense was $750. What is the budget variance?

    a. −$125

    b. −$250

    c. +$500

    d. +$750

4. Rhonda has been a nurse for San Antonio Community Hospital for the past 5 years and she would like a raise. Which budget should the line manager consult?

    a. Department budget

    b. Employment budget

    c. Capital budget

    d. Allocated cost budget

5. San Antonio Community Hospital decided to pay off the lease for the CT scans. What financial statement would reflect the large payoff of debt?

    a. Balance sheet

    b. Statement of retained earnings

c. Income statement

d. Statement of cash flows

6. Expenses that remain the same every period, such as equipment lease payments, are known as:

a. direct costs.

b. indirect costs.

c. fixed costs.

d. variable costs.

7. Which accounting method, cash or accrual, do many healthcare organizations choose and why?

a. Cash accounting because reimbursements are posted in the same period as the date of service, not the date received

b. Cash accounting because reimbursements are posted in the period as the date received, not the date of service

c. Accrual accounting because reimbursements are posted in the same period as the date of service, not the date received

d. Accrual accounting because reimbursements are posted in the same period as the date received, not the date of service

8. The pediatric office uses tongue depressors for just about every patient evaluation. Because these are used in patient care, the cost of the tongue depressors can be considered:

a. direct costs.

b. indirect costs.

c. fixed costs.

d. variable costs.

9. The balance sheet accounting equation is:

a. Assets = Revenue − Expenses.

b. Assets = Liabilities + Retained Equity.

c. Liabilities = Assets + Retained Equity.

d. Retained Equity = Assets + Liabilities.

10. Financial analysts use ratio analysis to:

    a. appraise the healthcare organization's assets.

    b. detail the healthcare organization's liabilities.

    c. examine the healthcare organization's variable costs.

    d. determine the financial health of the healthcare organization.

Resources

For additional resources, please review the following references:

Abdelhak, M., & Hanken, M. A. (2016). *Health Information: Management of a Strategic Resource*. St. Louis, MO: Elsevier.
- Chapter 18: Revenue Cycle and Financial Management
  - The Budget and the Business Plan
  - Financial Accounting
  - Capital Expense and Investment Decisions

Oachs, P. K., & Watters, A. (2016). *Health Information Management: Concepts, Principles, and Practice*. Chicago, IL: AHIMA, American Health Information Management Association.
- Chapter 26: Financial Management

Sayles, N. B., & Gordon, L. L. (2016). *Health Information Management Technology: An Applied Approach*. Chicago, IL: AHIMA, American Health Information Management Association.
- Chapter 19: Management
  - Financial Management

CHAPTER 26
Health Information Management Ethics

In this chapter, we review the following subdomains:

- VI.H.1. Comply with ethical standards of practice
- VI.H.2. Evaluate the consequences of a breach of healthcare ethics
- VI.H.3. Assess how cultural issues affect health, healthcare quality, cost, and HIM
- VI.H.4. Create programs and policies that support a culture of diversity

The following topics are covered in this subdomain:

- Professional and practice-related ethical issues
  - AHIMA Code of Ethics
- Breach of healthcare ethics
- Healthcare professionals and cultural diversity
  - Cultural competence and self-awareness
- Assumptions, biases, and stereotypes
- Americans with Disabilities Act (ADA)
- Equal Employment Opportunity Commission (EEOC)

MAIN TERMS

AHIMA Code of Ethics

American's with Disabilities Act (ADA)

Assumptions

Bias

Breach

Cultural competence

Cultural diversity

Diversity awareness

Equal Employment Opportunity Commission (EEOC)

Ethics committee

Healthcare ethics

Stereotypes

Practice Questions

1. What year was the health information profession established?

   a. 1919

   b. 1928

   c. 1998

   d. 2006

2. Which HIM professional value focuses on appreciating the contributions of other departments in the healthcare organization?

   a. quality

   b. integrity

   c. respect

   d. leadership

3. On the announcement board, the Director of Health Information lists five professional behaviors that all HIM department employees should maintain when speaking to a patient. Which of the seven AHIMA Code of Ethics purposes would this represent?

   a. summarize broad ethical principles that reflect the profession's core values

   b. establish a set of ethical principles to be used to guide decision-making and actions

   c. establish a framework for professional behavior and responsibilities when professional obligations conflict or ethical uncertainties arise

   d. provide ethical principles by which the general public can hold the HIM professional accountable

4. The medical bylaws for San Antonio Community Hospital state that health records are stored for 4 years. The AHIMA standard for health records retention is 7 years. The state of California's standard for health records retention is 10 years. If the HIM department applies ethical decision-making principles, how many years should the facility store health records for?

   a. 4 years

   b. 7 years

   c. 10 years

   d. forever

5. Which of the following ethical principles focuses on keeping patient's information safe and preventing unauthorized access?

   a. Privacy

   b. Security

   c. Confidentiality

   d. Compliance

6. When a healthcare facility realizes that there has been a breach of health information, who gets involved to review possible ethical violations to determine how to remedy the situation?

   a. The Joint Commission

   b. Agency for Healthcare Research and Quality

   c. American Hospital Association

   d. Ethics committee

7. Which of the following would be considered minimally acceptable wheelchair accommodations, according to ADA standards that employers should meet to assist those with disabilities perform their work?

   a. Lower the desk and bring some office machines within reach.

   b. Install elevators in the office building.

   c. Move department operations to the first floor.

   d. Create a separate office for the wheelchair user away from the rest of the department.

8. David Macias came in through the ER after an on-the-job accident. He fell from the roof of a construction site and broke his leg. Annie, the ER triage nurse, noticed that Mr. Macias was Hispanic, and so she started speaking English in a louder, condescending tone. When Annie closed the curtain, she spoke up to a coworker stating she was annoyed when patients don't speak English even though they live in America. What type of training is needed to address this incident?

   a. Equal Employment Opportunity

   b. Diversity awareness

   c. Breach of healthcare ethics

   d. Americans with Disabilities

9. Two injured individuals are transported to the hospital ER after a serious automobile accident. Neither patient was identified as the driver when they arrived; however, Dr. Harris, the ER attending physician, believes the Chinese male caused the accident. This behavior is known as:

   a. bias.

   b. stereotyping.

   c. prejudice.

   d. discrimination.

10. A new EHR user printed and left a copy of the labs of a patient who resides on the same floor; these were left at the nurses' station. This is an example of:

    a. information breach.

    b. privacy issue.

    c. security issue.

    d. intentional breach.

Resources

For additional resources, please review the following references:

Abdelhak, M., & Hanken, M. A. (2016). *Health Information: Management of a Strategic Resource*. St. Louis, MO: Elsevier.
- Chapter 16: Human Resource Management
  - Legal, Regulatory, and Accreditation

Oachs, P. K., & Watters, A. (2016). *Health Information Management: Concepts, Principles, and Practice*. Chicago, IL: AHIMA, American Health Information Management Association.
- Chapter 24: Employee Training and Development
  - Elements of Workforce Training
- Chapter 28: Ethical Issues in Health Information Management

Sayles, N. B., & Gordon, L. L. (2016). *Health Information Management Technology: An Applied Approach*. Chicago, IL: AHIMA, American Health Information Management Association.
- Chapter 20: Human Resources Management and Professional Development
  - Employment Law, Ethics, and Labor Relations
- Chapter 21: Ethical Issues in Health Information Management

CHAPTER 27

Project and Enterprise Information Management

In this chapter, we will review the following subdomains:
- VI.I.1. Summarize project management methodologies
- VI.J.1. Explain vendor/contract management
- VI.K.1. Apply knowledge of database architecture and design

The following topics are covered in this subdomain:
- Project management planning (PMP)
- Systems acquisition and evaluation
- Data dictionary and interoperability

MAIN TERMS

Data dictionary	Interoperable	Project management planning
Data fields	Object-orientated database	Project management professional
Database	Program evaluation and review technique (PERT)	Relational database
Gantt chart		

Practice Questions

1. In which phase of the database life cycle is the data dictionary established?

    a. Design

    b. Implementation

    c. Operation

    d. Evaluation

2. Two or more databases that contain at least one common data element and that are seamlessly interoperable are known as:

    a. databases.

    b. data architecture.

    c. a relational database.

    d. an object-oriented database.

3. Where can a user determine the data element formatting for the date of birth for a database?

    a. Data elements

    b. Data map

    c. Data set

    d. Data dictionary

4. The Gantt chart shows three activities for the project that are scheduled during the same time frame. What does this mean?

    a. The timeline should display a new activity starting when another activity ends.

    b. The Gantt chart must not be displaying the timeline and the project activities at the same time.

    c. The project team manager should consult the PERT chart to confirm the critical path to ensure the utilization of all available resources.

    d. The Gantt chart only displays the percent completion of the project, not the activities timeline.

5. The difference between the Gantt chart and the PERT chart is that the PERT chart graphically displays:

    a. the project timeline.

    b. all interdependent activities of the project.

    c. the project activities in detail.

    d. the percent of the project complete.

6. Which of the following activities is NOT included in the design phase of the project management life cycle?

    a. Tracking project progress

    b. Defining project objectives

    c. Estimating total project costs

    d. Determining the project timeline

7. The project to implement the upgraded EHR system is in place. However, the lab department feels that their module in the EHR does provide enough detail. They would prefer that each entry be time stamped; this project idea was not part of the original project plan. Which phase of the project management life cycle would this update be a part of?

    a. Design

    b. Tracking

    c. Revision

    d. Change control

8. The project team is working on assembling priorities for the project. In which phase of the project management life cycle would this activity be included?

    a. Design

    b. Tracking

    c. Revision

    d. Change control

9. Which of the following projects are common for the HIM department?

    a. Training physicians on accurate documentation standards and practices for all consultations

    b. Upgrading the bar-code medication software

    c. Implementing a nursing instant messaging feature

    d. Evaluating the quality of patient care delivery

10. The project manager is watching the costs of the project very closely. Which phase of the project management life cycle would this update be a part of?

    a. Design

    b. Tracking

    c. Revision

    d. Change control

Resources

For additional resources, please review the following references:

Abdelhak, M., & Hanken, M. A. (2016). *Health Information: Management of a Strategic Resource.* St. Louis, MO: Elsevier.
- Chapter 4: Health Data Concepts and Information Governance
  - Data Collection Standards
- Chapter 17: Operational Management
  - Project Management

Oachs, P. K., & Watters, A. (2016). *Health Information Management: Concepts, Principles, and Practice.* Chicago, IL: AHIMA, American Health Information Management Association.
- Chapter 3: Data Governance and Stewardship
  - Data Management Definitions
- Chapter 27: Project Management

Sayles, N. B., & Gordon, L. L. (2016). *Health Information Management Technology: An Applied Approach.* Chicago, IL: AHIMA, American Health Information Management Association.
- Chapter 6: Data Management
  - Databases
- Chapter 19: Management
  - Project Management

CHAPTER 28

Prepping for the RHIA Exam

In this module, we explore the following:
- Compare the RHIA exam content outline with the RHIT exam content outline
- Examine each domain in the RHIA exam content outline

Compare the RHIA Exam Content Outline with the RHIT Exam Content Outline

We have reviewed every subject and topic that you learned through your RHIT education. As you will see, most of what we covered so far also represents most of the required knowledge to successfully pass the RHIA exam. Just as a review, let's compare the two exams in **TABLE 28-1**.

TABLE 28-1 Comparing the RHIT and the RHIA Certification Exams

Exam	RHIT	RHIA
Number of questions	150 multiple-choice	180 multiple-choice
Exam time	3.5 hours	4 hours
Minimum education requirements	Associates degree	Baccalaureate degree
Career level	Technologist	Administrator

The most significant difference between these two certifications is the career level. Because RHIA candidates will be qualified for administrator positions, they are tested more on developing, creating, and managing. For example, RHIA candidates are tested on their knowledge of developing policies instead of just being familiar with policies, as RHIT candidates are tested on. There are more critical thinking and case study application type multiple-choice questions on the RHIA exam.

Examine Each Domain in the RHIA Content Outline

When comparing the exam content outlines for both the RHIT and RHIA exams, at initial glance it seems that there are significant differences. The RHIA exam content outline contains five domains whereas the RHIT contains seven. Let's review the maps of each of the RHIA exam domains.

Domain I: Data Content, Structure, and Standards (Information Governance)

The domain of data content, structure, and standards represents 18%–22% of the total questions for the RHIA exam. Reviewing **TABLE 28-2**, much of the content in this section is similar to the RHIT content outline. Just remember, all of the subjects are tested from the administrator perspective, so candidates should be familiar enough with the information to apply their knowledge for critical thinking and case study questions.

Domain II: Information Protection: Access, Disclosure, Archival, Privacy, and Security

The domain of information protection, including access, disclosure, archival, privacy, and security, represents 23%–27% of the RHIA exam. Much of this section focuses on establishing, developing, and maintaining training programs for healthcare facility staff on privacy, security, and confidentiality. Although the RHIT exam content outline addresses the principles of data and information privacy, security, and confidentiality, the RHIA candidate knowledge level should be on the administrative level. Reviewing Table 28-2 shows that there are some similarities

TABLE 28-2 Domain I Data Content Structure and Standards RHIA to RHIT Map				
Map to RHIT Exam Content Outline*				**Textbook Chapters**
DOMAIN I	Data content, structure, and standards (Information governance) (18%–22%)			
	A. Classification systems	A1. Code diagnosis and procedures according to established guidelines	2.1, 2.2	2
	B. Health record content and documentation	B1. Ensure accuracy and integrity of health data and health record documentation (paper or electronic)	1.4, 1.5, 1.7, 1.8	3
		B2. Manage the contents of the legal health record (structured and unstructured)	6.1	3, 7
		B3. Manage the retention and destruction of the legal health record	1.3, 1.6, 1.18	3
	C. Data governance	C1. Maintain data in accordance with regulatory requirements	1.9, 1.10, 1.16, 1.17	4
		C2. Develop and maintain organizational policies, procedures and guidelines for management of health information	1.15, 1.19	4
	D. Data management and secondary data sources	D1. Manage health data elements and/or data sets	1.16, 1.17, 1.18, 1.19	5
		D2. Assist in the maintenance of the data dictionary and data models for database design	1.22	5
		D3. Manage and maintain databases (e.g., data migration, updates)	1.21	6

* The numbers represent the domain and the competency according to the RHIT exam content guideline. For example, 6.1 represents domain 6, competency 1: Ensure confidentiality of the health records (paper and electronic). Review Appendix A for a complete RHIT exam content outline as the reference.

between the RHIA and the RHIT exam content outlines. However, there are a few competencies in this outline that are not thoroughly addressed in the RHIT exam content outline, including:

- B1. Design policies and implement privacy practices to safeguard protected health information
- B2. Design policies and implement security practices to safeguard protected health information
- C2. Develop policies and procedures for uses and disclosures/redisclosures of protected health information

Designing, Developing, and Implementing Policies

Designing, developing, and implementing policies is an administrative function. The administrator's level of knowledge should include standards from federal and state agencies, Joint Commission standards, hospital bylaws, and any other patient quality standards that govern the policy implementation process. The administrator also is able to identify situations in which a new policy is necessary based on collected and analyzed data. For additional practice, review Chapter 8, Data Privacy, Confidentiality, and Security (**TABLE 28-3**).

Domain III: Informatics, Analytics, and Data Use

The domain of informatics, analytics, and data use represents 22%–26% of the RHIA exam. There is an emphasis on data analytics, healthcare statistics, and decision support. Although the RHIT exam content outline covers knowledge about health information technologies and some healthcare statistics, for the most part, analytics represents an administrative function. This textbook reviews these additional administrative functions; please review the assigned chapters in **TABLE 28-4**.

Domain IV: Revenue Management

The revenue management domain represents 12%–16% of the RHIA exam. The RHIT exam content outline has a revenue management domain that focuses more on reimbursement collection. The RHIA exam revenue management domain represents an administrative perspective, which includes the management of clinical data used in the reimbursement process, processing and performing audit requests, and investigating medical identity theft. Review **TABLE 28-5** for the respective textbook chapters that cover this information.

TABLE 28-3 Domain II: Information Protection: Access, Disclosure, Archival, Privacy, and Security RHIA to RHIT Map

Map to RHIT Exam Content Outline				Textbook Chapters
Domain II	Information protection: access, disclosure, archival, privacy and security (23%–27%)			
	A. Health law	A1. Maintain healthcare privacy and security training programs	6.5, 6.11	7
		A2. Enforce and monitor organizational compliance with healthcare information laws	6.2, 6.4, 6.12	18
	B. Data privacy, confidentiality, and security	B1. Design policies and implement privacy practices to safeguard protected health information		8
		B2. Design policies and implement security practices to safeguard protected health information		8
		B3. Investigate and resolve healthcare privacy and security issues/breaches	6.9	8, 9
	C. Release of information	C1. Manage access, disclosure, and use of protected health information to ensure confidentiality	3.17, 6.3, 6.7, 6.10	9
		C2. Develop policies and procedures for uses and disclosures/re-disclosures of protected health information		9

Domain V Leadership

The leadership domain in the RHIA exam content outline goes above and beyond the RHIT exam content outline. This domain represents 12%–16% of the RHIA exam. Leadership is an administrative function,

TABLE 28-4 Domain III: Information Protection: Access, Disclosure, Archival, Privacy, and Security RHIA to RHIT map

Map to RHIT Exam Content Outline				Textbook Chapters
Domain III	Informatics, analytics, and data use			
	A. Health information technologies	A1. Implement and manage use of, and access to, technology applications	4.3, 4.5, 4.6, 4.8, 4.12	10
		A2. Evaluate and recommend clinical, administrative, and specialty service applications (e.g., financial systems, electronic record, clinical coding)	4.9, 4.10	11
	B. Information management strategic planning	B1. Present data for organizational use (e.g., summarize synthesize, and condense information)	1.12	11
	C. Analytics and decision support	C1. Filer and/or interpret information for the end customer	4.10	12
		C2. Analyze and present information to organizational stakeholders	4.4	14
		C3. Use data mining techniques to query and report from databases		14
	D. Healthcare statistics	D1. Calculate healthcare statistics for organizational stakeholders	1.20	13
		D2. Critically analyze and interpret healthcare statistics for organizational stakeholders (e.g., CMI)		13

E. Research methods	E1. Identify appropriate data sources for research		13
F. Consumer informatics	F1. Identify appropriate data sources for research		15
	F2. Provide support for end-user portals and personal health records		15
G. Health information exchange	G1. Apply data and functional standards to achieve interoperability of healthcare information systems		15
	G2. Manage the health information exchange process entitywide		15
H. Information integrity and data quality	H1. Apply data/record storage principles and techniques associated with the medium (e.g., paper, hybrid, electronic)	1.1, 1.2, 1.5, 1.8, 5.2	12
	H2. Manage master person index (e.g., patient record integration, customer/ client relationship management)	1.6	12
	H3. Manage merge process for duplicates and other errors entitywide	1.7	12

so the RHIT content outline does not address any of these competencies. There is a lot of information in all of these sections, and an RHIA candidate can easily be overwhelmed. However, keep a few tips in mind in terms of this domain (**TABLE 28-6**):

- The leadership domain represents one of the smallest sections of the RHIA exam, so spending too much time memorizing all of these competencies may not be beneficial.
- Review all of the textbook chapters listed.
- Apply the administrative perspective to the subject review.

TABLE 28-5 Doman IV: Revenue Management RHIA to RHIT Map

Map to RHIT Exam Content Outline				Textbook Chapters
Domain IV	Revenue management (12%–16%)			
	A. Revenue cycle and reimbursement	A1. Manage the use of clinical data required in reimbursement systems and prospective payment systems		16
		A2. Optimize reimbursement through management of the revenue cycle (e.g., charge master maintenance, DNFB, and AR days)	7.7, 7.8, 7.9	17
	B. Regulatory	B1. Prepare for accreditation and licensing processes (e.g. Joint Commission, Det Norske Veritas [DNV], Medicare, state regulators)	5.14, 7.11	18
		B2. Process audit requests (e.g., RACs or other payors, chart review)		18
		B3. Perform audits (e.g. chart review, POC)		18
	C. Coding	C1. Manage and/or validate coding accuracy	2.1, 2.2, 2.3, 2.4	19
	D. Fraud surveillance	D1. Participate in investigating incidences of medical identify theft		20
	E. Clinical documentation improvement	E1. Query physicians for appropriate documentation to support reimbursement	2.14	19
		E2. Educate and train clinical staff regarding documentation requirements	2.3, 2.7, 2.14, 2.16	19

TABLE 28-6 Domain V: Leadership RHIA to RHIT Map

Map to RHIT Exam Content Outline				Textbook Chapters
Domain V	Leadership (12%–16%)			
	A. Leadership roles	A1. Develop, motivate, and support work teams and/or individuals (e.g., coaching, mentoring)	21	
		A2. Organize and facilitate meetings	21	
		A3. Advocate for department organization and/or profession	21	
	B. Change management	B1. Participate in the implementation of new processes (e.g., systems, EHR, CAC)	22	
		B2. Support changes in the organization (e.g., culture changes, HIM collaborations, outsourcing)	22	
	C. Work design and process improvement	C1. Establish and monitor productivity levels	22	
		C2. Analyze and design workflow processes	22	
		C3. Participate in the development and monitoring of process improvement plans	22	
	D. Human resources management	D1. Perform human resource management activities (e.g., recruiting staff, creating job descriptions, resolving personal problems)	23	
	E. Training and development	E1. Conduct training and educational activities (e.g., HIM systems, coding, medical and institutional terminology, documentation and regulatory requirements)	23	

(continues)

TABLE 28-6 Domain V: Leadership RHIA to RHIT Map *(continued)*

F. Strategic and organizational management	F1. Monitory industry trends and organizational needs to anticipate changes	24	
	F2. Determine resource needs by performing analyses (e.g., cost benefit, business planning)	24	
	F3. Assist with preparation of capital budget	25	
G. Financial management	G1. Assist in preparation and management of operating and personnel budgets	25	
	G2. Assist in the analysis and reporting on budget variances	25	
H. Ethics	H1. Adhere to the AHIMA code of Ethics	26	
I. Project management	I1. Utilize appropriate project management methodologies	27	
J. Vendor/Contract management	J1. Evaluate and manage contracts (e.g., vendor, contract personnel, maintenance	27	
K. Enterprise information management	K1. Develop and support strategic and operational plans for entitywide health information management	27	

CHAPTER 29

Planning for a Career with an RHIT or RHIA Credential

In this module, we explore the following:

- Conduct a successful, planned, and organized job search
- Construct an industry-specific resume
- Build a job-specific cover letter
- Establish a career portfolio
- Develop skills to have a successful interview
- Prepare for your new position
- Assess the ethical implications of your new career
- Maintain and update industry knowledge through continuing education

Conduct a Successful, Organized, and Planned Job Search

Throughout your associate's or bachelor's degree program, you have learned about the variety of responsibilities that health information professionals possess. Closer to graduation you should have a clearer idea of the career that you would like to pursue. For example, many Registered Health Information Technician (RHIT) and Registered Health Information Administrator (RHIA) professionals choose a career in medical coding and billing. Others choose to work directly with establishing and maintaining health documentation standards. There are also career opportunities in striving to maintain HIPAA standards by working with privacy and security of patient information. The release of information department holds many rewarding positions as well. Whatever the career path you choose, with your education and an AHIMA certification under your belt, you will be better prepared for your future career.

If you are still not sure which career path in Health Information Management (HIM) is right for you, not to worry! AHIMA provides a career map at https://my.ahima.org/careermap. This map provides the path from an entry-level position to multiple career-advancement positions. Each position provides typical education, certification, and professional experience levels. You can use this tool to project your career trajectory over the future 5–10 years!

Advanced Education

Further advanced education than what you have just completed may be required for the position that you want. Not to worry! You've made it this far, so you've already accomplished so much. Enrolling in additional education programs will enhance your HIM knowledge, and will help you to qualify to reach your career goals faster.

Before enrolling in any HIM bachelor's, master's or doctorate programs, be sure that your degree is compatible with your career goals. CAHIIM, an educational program accrediting agency that is used to in conjunction with AHIMA to ensure HIM learning competencies are met, provides further professional AHIMA certification opportunities not open to graduates of non-CAHIIM approved educational programs.

RHIT to RHIA Proviso

AHIMA is allowing a special opportunity for RHIT professionals who have a bachelor's degree in a non-HIM–related field to meet the qualifications to take the RHIA exam.

RHITs who meet the following eligibility requirements will be eligible to sit for the RHIA examination during the time frame of July 1, 2017–June 30, 2021:

- Have at least a baccalaureate degree from a regionally accredited institution or nationally recognized accreditor; and
- Have received their RHIT credential on or before August 31, 2018; and
- Have complied with the standards for maintenance of the RHIT credential.

This opportunity is for a limited time; be sure you contact AHIMA if you have any additional questions about eligibility.

An Effective Job Search

Now that you have an HIM career path in mind, it's time to start planning a job search. HIM positions are difficult to find in a general job-search website for a number of reasons. Because these positions are so specialized that most candidates need to have an RHIT/RHIA credential to qualify, they are advertised through private facilities, industry accreditation websites, and professional networking.

But let's not underestimate the power of web job searches! Conducting a job search for health care in your local area provides a list of potential employers. Using this employer information, visit the healthcare facility's private website for any job listings. Popular websites used to search for healthcare jobs include the following:

- Careerbuilder.com
- Indeed.com
- USAjobs.gov
- Monster.com

There may be job opportunities listed on government job boards, especially if you have experience working in the government or were enlisted in the military before. Be sure to check job postings for the local county and cities, as they may sponsor healthcare initiatives that require HIM professionals on staff.

As we mentioned, these positions require highly skilled and credentialed professionals, so they may prefer to post their job openings through industry-specific accrediting agencies. Many times these positions posted are for positions requiring more experience; it wouldn't hurt to reach out to the employer to find out if any entry-level positions are available. Some of these HIM-related organizations include the following:

- AHIMA
- AHRQ
- HIMSS
- Healthcare IT News

Networking is essential for HIM career planning. We discuss the importance of networking later in the chapter.

Organize Your Job Search

The first step to organize your job search is to find 3–5 job descriptions that meet the following criteria:

- The position is in the sector of HIM that you have chosen.
- The job description describes activities you feel confident you can do and that you are interested in.
- You have met the education/credentialing qualifications.

Once you have identified these few jobs, compare and contrast them. Finally, prioritize them. If you feel you need to work on some of the required skills, open your HIM textbooks and start refamiliarizing yourself with these competencies. Work to prepare yourself as best as possible for your top choice!

Construct an Industry-Specific Resume

Creating a resume can seem like a daunting task, especially if you have limited experience in the HIM industry. Believe that your work experience is valuable, whether you have worked as an HIM professional or not. Your job longevity shows that you are responsible and dedicated to your work. Your computer skills indicate that you are not intimidated by information systems, and are strongly competent to learn new software programs. Listing your education, degree earned, and credentials designates the sacrifice you are making to prepare yourself for success in the HIM profession. So, no or limited HIM professional experience is no problem!

Credential Designation

Adding your credential to your name is essential. Although you may not have work experience in HIM, if you have earned your credential, use it proudly! Once you have your credential, AHIMA publishes your name on their website as an approved HIM professional at this link: https://my.ahima.org/pages/certification/newlycredentialed.aspx! Here are a few qualified formats you can use:

John Doe, RHIA, BA

Jane Doe, MBA, RHIT

Richard Brown, BA, RHIT, CPC, CCA

Payel Madero, MBA, RHIT

As you can see, these are all correct, so your name should be designated in the format that you like the most. Of course, if you have an HIM professional mentor, ask his or her advice on the format as well!

Professional Email Address

As you are now looking for a professional HIM position, it is wise to maintain a professional email address. Having an email like cuteycupid@gmail.com is great for personal use, but it doesn't sound very professional, so refrain from using these email types on your resume. Create a new email address, preferably one using your first and last name.

Also, as you are preparing for potential employers to call you, be sure to set up your voicemail with a professional outgoing message. Some candidates use a generic voicemail message; although this is professional, it doesn't provide the potential employer with an introduction to your professionalism. Review the following professional message example:

"Hello, you have reached the voicemail box for Payel Madero. I am not available to answer your call right now, but I look forward to returning your call soon. Please leave your name, reason for your call, a return phone number, and a good time to return your call, and I will return your call within 24 hours. Thanks and have a nice day."

Career Objective

Writing a career objective is sometimes challenging when you probably just want to say "Just please hire me! I will work really hard!" It's important to understand why the objective is so important. It shows that you know what kind of HIM job you want. It also reflects the time you have spent planning and organizing your job search, which reflects how serious you are about wanting the position.

The career objective should match some of the verbiage written in the job description posted, however formulated in your own words. Review the following example:

Job Description: Understands the industry standards on release of information for patients, physician's offices, subpoenas, and state and federal governing agencies, including maintaining confidentiality in accordance with hospital bylaws.

Sample Objective: A novice, credentialed HIM professional seeking a position in release of information to gain professional experience by maintaining confidentiality in accordance with hospital bylaws.

Education

If you have limited HIM professional experience, then I prefer to include education right below the objective. List the title of the program, the college, and your GPA if it is above 3.5. If you have received any special distinctions such as the Dean's List, a scholarship, a special position, or if you were chosen as team leader on a course project, list them here. Consider including your graduation date if you are still enrolled in the education program; you may also like to include the date of the certification exam if you haven't taken it and the exam has been scheduled.

Do not include your high school graduation information unless the following pertain to you:

- Your GPA was 4.0 or higher.
- You were valedictorian or salutatorian.
- Earned a scholarship based on academic excellence.
- Include high school graduation only if it was 5 or fewer years ago.

Skills and Qualifications

Skills and qualifications are essential to a successful resume. First of all, use the technical name of all software that you have used. Some inexperienced students include each and every program in the Microsoft Office Suite, including Word, Excel, Access, OneNote, Outlook, and so on—this is a waste of valuable space on the resume! HIM professionals should obviously know how to use most of these programs, but they should also be familiar with industry-specific software programs.

Many of you may have used AHIMA Virtual Lab in your HIT/HIA educational programs. AHIMA Virtual Lab uses some of the following common HIM software:

- EPIC
- Tableau
- 3M Encoder
- Medisoft
- Practice Fusion

If you have used any of these software programs, review your lab assignments to ensure that you are still familiar with how to use them. Once you are confident that you can maneuver through the software program if asked, then list it in your skills and qualifications.

Typing Speed

A proficient typing speed is an essential skill for HIM professionals. Visit www.typingtest.com to determine what your current typing speed is. If your results are less than 50WPM, then use this website to practice until you can consistently reach this speed. It is wise to include the typing speed only if it is higher than 40WPM.

Affiliations and Associations

As discussed in Chapter 1, becoming an AHIMA student member carries many benefits, including being able to list this membership on your resume. Being associated with AHIMA means that you are affiliated with one of the largest HIM professional organizations in the United States. However, there are other professional organizations that support specific sectors of the HIM industry. If you want to pursue career opportunities in one of these sectors, it will be wise to become a member of those organizations as well. **TABLE 29-1** provides a list of HIM professional organizations and the HIM industry sector that is supported.

Narrating Job Responsibilities

When describing job responsibilities, be sure to include details. Adding numbers to the descriptions helps the reader understand the depth of your responsibilities. Review the following example:

Manage the registers at store close

Manage the closing of up to eight registers at the end of business, which includes reconciling upwards of $5,500 each

Both descriptions describe the same job duties; however, the second statement reflects authority and responsibility.

TABLE 29-1 HIM Professional Organizations

Organization	HIM Industry Support
AHIMA	Takes the lead in the advancement and use of health data and information management for the delivery of quality health care worldwide.
HIMSS	A global, cause-based, not-for-profit organization focused on better health through information and technology.
AHRQ	Mission is to produce evidence to make health care safer, higher quality, more accessible, equitable, and affordable, and to work within the US Department of Health and Human Services and with other partners to make sure that the evidence is understood and used. AHRQ priorities are described.
ONC	The organization is at the forefront of the administration's health IT efforts and is a resource to the entire health system to support the adoption of health information technology and the promotion of nationwide health information exchange to improve health care.
CDC	A federal department that works 24/7 to protect America from health, safety, and security threats, both foreign and in the U.S.
TJC	An accrediting agency dedicated to continuously improving health care for the public, in collaboration with other stakeholders, by evaluating healthcare organizations and inspiring them to excel in providing safe and effective care of the highest quality and value.
NCRA	A credentialing organization whose data information specialists capture a complete history, diagnosis, treatment, and health status for every cancer patient in the U.S.

Regardless of the career path you choose, with your education and an AHIMA certification under your belt, you will be better prepared. Include any jobs related to the health field and use technical terms to show you do have relevant experience. When including specific jobs, include the most recent employment history, regardless of whether it was working in the HIM industry.

By this point, you might be running out of space on the first page. If you are new to the HIM profession, your resume should not be longer than one page. Sometimes you may need to alter text size, spacing, and the use of tables in order to fit everything in one page.

Build a Job-Specific Cover Letter

Remember when we discussed how we want our objective to say "hire me please!"? This ability is harnessed through the cover letter. Every resume we submit should have an accompanying cover letter that has been customized to the job it is for. The cover letter should follow the format of a business letter. The closer to the standard business letter format you keep, the more professional your presentation will be.

The letter should not be more than a page long and the healthcare facility should be mentioned. Excerpts from the job posting should be included, such as skills and qualifications the organization is looking for. This is an opportunity to tell them how you meet those skills and qualifications. If you are limited in your HIM professional experience, then focus more on skills such as time management, organization, customer-friendliness, effective communication, multitasking, and so on, and apply these to the position offered.

Establish a Career Portfolio

A career portfolio is a literal folder representing your career that you can present to the interviewer. Each career portfolio contains at least a resume, a list of references, a general cover letter, an RHIT or RHIA credential certificate, college transcripts, and a salary history. Just a tip: you should keep multiple copies of all of these items just in case your interviewer requests a copy. Your career portfolio should include a cover page, a title page, and a table of contents, these should include tabs that put your organizational skills on display. All pages should be included in sheet protectors as well.

For novice professionals entering the HIM industry, the following items can be added to the career portfolio:

- Certificates of attendance for AHIMA or local HIA meetings
- Certificate of training completion from employers or credentialing organizations
- Successful HIM projects that earned high grades or that you successfully implemented
- Letters of recommendation
- A narrative summary of a 5–10-year career plan

List of References

Employers use references to build trust in their interview candidate, so they are just as important as the resume. Appropriate references follow these guidelines:

- Each portfolio should have at least three references; one can be an HIM professor.
- Reference letters should be renewed every 2 years.
- At least one reference should have an RHIT or RHIA credential (not the professor).
- Try to avoid family members and/or fellow students.
- Include someone with whom you have worked for more than a year, even if he or she is not an HIM professional.

College Transcripts

You will need your college transcripts for a variety of reasons after your graduate, so it is wise to keep an unofficial copy in your career portfolio and order at least five certified transcripts via mail.

DO NOT OPEN THE CERTIFIED TRANSCRIPTS. Transcripts lose their certification when they are opened. Sometimes it can take a while to order a transcript from the college, so having some on hand may expedite some of these activities.

Five- to 10-Year Career Plan

The career plan is developed through the job planning process. Employers want to meet candidates that are career and goal oriented. Reviewing the AHIMA career map helps you to put into words where you see yourself and your career in the following 5–10 years.

Develop Skills to Have a Successful Interview

According to Glassdoor.com, each corporate job opening attracts, on average, 250 resumes.[1] So when you get a call for an interview, you should be so proud!! The interview process depends on the employer. Some employers conduct a telephone interview first. Other employers may ask you to come in to take a test before they schedule an interview.

The phone interview can be intimidating because they may start interviewing you right when you answer, so you might feel unprepared. In those cases, if you are very nervous, you may mention that you would like to schedule a time to talk so you are more prepared for the interview. The interviewer may be impressed with your effort to get ready for the interview, so you will earn their respect.

At times, the employer may send an email requesting an interview. These emails may provide some company information, a job description, and available interview times. Take some time to research the healthcare facility online. Review their mission and vision statement. Think about some questions that you might have for the interviewer about the company as well.

Employers that request you to come in to test are looking for a specific candidate. The test will most likely be related to the job posting that you applied for. For example, if you are applying for a coding auditor position, you may be tested in medical coding. As discussed earlier, prior to applying for the position, familiarize yourself with the activities listed in the job description so you feel confident that you will be successful.

---

[1] https://www.glassdoor.com/employers/topics/hiring-recruiting/

Depending on the position, you may be interviewed by only one individual or by a panel of interviewers. Interviewers recognize that candidates can be nervous, so take a few deep breaths. Take the time to answer the interview questions completely; don't rush through or say "I don't know." It's okay to take a few moments to collect your thoughts to answer effectively.

Preparing for the Interview

When going to the healthcare facility for the interview, prepare in advance. Get the correct address, including the suite number if applicable, and map out your route in advance. Plan to arrive at least 30 minutes early, which is enough time to gather your thoughts and review your career portfolio to refresh yourself before you enter the healthcare facility. Walk into the healthcare facility about 10 minutes prior to the interview time because you may need to complete some additional paperwork.

1. "Tell me about yourself." This is probably the hardest question that is asked, and it is the most important. Don't start talking about your pet or your baby sister. Prepare a 30-minute monologue on yourself. This should include the following:
   - Your full name; this is a great opportunity to share a nickname or a preferred name, if you have one.
   - Share your educational achievements. If you are still in school, feel free to share your anticipated graduation date, your GPA if its higher than 3.5, and/or any other commendations or certificates such as Dean's List or a scholarship.
   - In one sentence, share your passion for the HIM industry.
   - Focus in on two of your strengths, such as time management, attention to detail, strong communication strategies, and so on. Don't just mention them; provide at least two examples (albeit summarized) to back up your claim.
   - Explain why you are interested in the position you are interviewing for. This reflects that you took the time to review the job position prior to applying and shows that you have an interested in working there.
2. "What are your greatest professional/personal strengths?" Don't brag here, but mention ways your skills can be an asset to the company.
3. "What are some of your weaknesses?" A skilled interviewer will mention a weakness that is a benefit to the company. For example, I am so detail-oriented that I can be a perfectionist at times.
4. "What are some of your career goals?" Don't say nothing here. Share some highlights of your career plan.

5. "Tell me about a challenge or conflict that you faced at work and how you managed through it." This can be a challenging question; keep in mind that you don't want to come out looking like a difficult employee. If you went through a challenging time, mention how you grew professionally from the experience.

6. "Where do you see yourself in 5 years?" Another opportunity to share your 5–10 year plan.

7. "Why are you leaving your current job?" If you aren't currently working in the HIM industry, this is an easy question: you want to work in the industry you have been working towards. If you are already working in the HIM profession, mention that you are seeking professional growth.

8. "What is your management style?" You may not be applying for a management position, but if you show that you are prepared by sharing your 5-year plan, it is a next-step question. Be sure to review the chapters on leadership styles in your HIM textbooks to confirm the type of leader you hope to be and how.

9. Share a time that you disagreed with management about an important issue. How did you handle it? Again, a tricky question. The interviewer just wants to confirm that you can contribute to a respectful working environment.

10. How would your current boss and/or fellow employees describe you and your work ethic? Again, don't brag, but be honest.

Dressing for the Interview

The dress code for an interview is typically business attire. For men, wear a sports jacket; borrow one from someone if you don't have one. Men should wear business shoes, not sports shoes. It's been said that a lot can be said about someone's shoes; they don't need to be fancy, but they should be clean and polished. A collared button-down shirt should be accompanied with a tie as well.

For women, keep comfort in mind, especially when it comes to your shoes. Stiletto shoes are very cute, but they will be uncomfortable quickly if you wear them on an extended tour of the healthcare facility; heels should be shorter than 2 inches. Women can wear business slacks or a skirt; just be sure that the skirt is not more than 2 inches shorter than your knee. A blazer is appropriate, but not a requirement. Your appearance should be comfortable, yet professional.

We would be amiss if we didn't discuss tattoos. Many candidates have them and would like to display them. To maintain a level of professionalism, some healthcare facilities require employees to cover up their tattoos and/or other body ornaments. Although candidates have the right to display these, it may not bode well for your interview depending on the natural preferences of the interviewer. You want the interviewer to address you for your job qualifications, not your tattoos! See if you are able to cover up what you can through your professional outfit, but be sure to ask about the healthcare facility policy during the interview.

An essential accessory to your outfit is a smile. It is normal to be nervous, but feel free to be yourself as well. Shake hands with everyone you meet and take down names of those you meet during the interview.

How to Talk about Money during the Interview

In your career portfolio, you should keep a salary history. Although you may have a longer work history, starting in the HIM industry fresh means your starting salary would be lower than your current position.

Discussion about salary and benefits should occur towards the end of the interview. By this time, you and the interviewer should have already discussed your skills, the needs of the position, and the responsibilities required. Typically, more job responsibilities equate to a higher salary. A non-intimidating way to bring up the subject is to ask, "What is the budget allocated for this position?"

Following Up after the Interview

The first thing you should ask for after the interview is the interviewer's business card. Later that evening, make some to time to reflect on the interview, and think about how it went. Put some of the highlights down on paper. If you didn't think the interview went well, jot down a few areas you think there might be room for improvement so you will be more prepared for the next interview.

Very importantly, write out a thank you card for your interviewer. Include some of the highlights from the interview and thank them for considering you as a candidate for the position. Follow up a few days afterwards to see whether the interviewer has additional questions for you by sending an email or leaving a voicemail.

Prepare for Your New Position

You passed your interview and the healthcare facility wants you to join their team! You are well on your way at this point! But there are still a number of steps to take prior to starting your position.

Analyzing Job Offers

Think about an offer before you say yes! Weigh the benefits with the potential challenges. Being new to the HIM industry, your goal should be to stay at your first job for at least a year. The following are a list of questions to ask about the job offer:

- How long will it take to get to work every day?
- What are the hours?
- How is the traffic that time of day?
- Is the facility transit-friendly?
- What are the benefits? Is there a probationary period?
- Do they support further education? Regular training?

It is a great feeling getting a job offer after you've worked so hard to complete your education and complete your AHIMA certification. But before jumping into the first job you find, be sure that the position supports your 5–10-year career plan.

Background Check and Health Mandates

All job offers are made under the stipulation that the candidate will pass the background check and additional health mandates; these are known as conditions for employment. The background check will review some of the following topics:

- Criminal records (state, county, and city)
- Credit history
- Employment history
- Work authorization
- Education history (high school, university, and so on)
- Social media profiles
- Driving record

Be sure that you are prepared for them to check some or all of these things. If you have a criminal history, it may hinder your ability to get hired. It's best to be honest with the interviewer about your situation; they may make an exception for you. And just a friendly reminder, you do need a copy of your Social Security number for employment. In case you don't have your actual card, apply for one through the Social Security Administration to have it when you get to this point.

Working in the healthcare environment also requires additional precautions. Most healthcare facilities require all workers, including HIM professionals to have their TB test every 2–3 years and a yearly flu shot. Most healthcare facilities maintain the right to have employees complete random drug testing at any given time as well. Depending on the type of facility, there may be other medical interventions that may be necessary, but the facility will let you know.

Just as a side point, some medications and substances are legal to possess and use, but are prohibited by healthcare facilities. Just because a substance is legal does not mean that a healthcare facility has to accept candidates who use it. The most compelling reason is that, in health care, it is inappropriate for healthcare professionals to work under the influence. One such example is marijuana. Some healthcare facilities conduct random drug tests, and if marijuana is found, it could cost your job.

Assess the Ethical Implications of Your New Career

Applying for an AHIMA credentialing exam comes with the stipulation that you will uphold and adhere to all of the AHIMA Code of Ethics.

The AHIMA Code of Ethics serves seven purposes:

1. Promotes high standards of HIM practice
2. Identifies core values on which the HIM mission is based
3. Summarizes broad ethical principles that reflect the profession's core values
4. Establishes a set of ethical principles to be used to guide decision making and actions
5. Establishes a framework for professional behavior and responsibilities when professional obligations conflict or ethical uncertainties arise
6. Provides ethical principles by which the general public can hold the HIM professional accountable
7. Mentors practitioners new to the field to HIM's mission, values, and ethical principles

According to AHIMA Code of Ethics,

Violation of principles in this code does not automatically imply legal liability or violation of the law. Such determination can only be made in the context of legal and judicial proceedings. Alleged violations of the code would be subject to a peer review process. Such processes are generally separate from legal or administrative procedures and insulated from legal review or proceedings to allow the profession to counsel and discipline its own members, although in some situations, violations of the code would constitute unlawful conduct subject to legal process.

Guidelines for ethical and unethical behavior are provided in this code. The terms "shall and shall not" are used as a basis for setting high standards for behavior. This does not imply that everyone "shall or shall not" do everything that is listed. This concept is true for the entire code. If someone does the stated activities, ethical behavior is the standard. The guidelines are not a comprehensive list. For example, the statement "safeguard all confidential patient information to include, but not limited to, personal, health, financial, genetic and outcome information" can also be interpreted as "shall not fail to safeguard all confidential patient information to include personal, health, financial, genetic, and outcome information."

A code of ethics cannot guarantee ethical behavior. Moreover, a code of ethics cannot resolve all ethical issues or disputes or capture the richness and complexity involved in striving to make responsible choices within a moral community. Rather, a code of ethics sets forth values and ethical principles, and offers ethical guidelines to which a HIM professional can aspire and by which actions can be judged. Ethical behaviors result from a personal commitment to engage in ethical practice.

Professional responsibilities often require an individual to move beyond personal values. For example, an individual might demonstrate behaviors that are based on the values of honesty, providing service to others, or demonstrating loyalty. In addition to these, professional values might require promoting confidentiality, facilitating interdisciplinary collaboration, and refusing to participate or conceal unethical practices. Professional values could require a more comprehensive set of values than what an individual needs to be an ethical agent in one's own personal life.

The AHIMA Code of Ethics is to be used by AHIMA members and certificants, consumers, agencies, organizations, and bodies (such as licensing and regulatory boards, insurance providers, courts of law, government agencies, and other professional groups) that choose to adopt it or use it as a frame of reference. The AHIMA Code of Ethics reflects the commitment of all to uphold the profession's values and to act ethically. Individuals of good character who discern moral questions and, in good faith, seek to make reliable ethical judgments, must apply ethical principles.

The code does not provide a set of rules that prescribe how to act in all situations. Specific applications of the code must take into account the context in which it is being considered and the possibility of conflicts among the code's values, principles, and guidelines. Ethical responsibilities flow from all human relationships, from the personal and familial to the social and professional. Further, the AHIMA Code of Ethics does not specify which values, principles, and guidelines are the most important and ought to outweigh others in instances when they conflict.[2]

---

[2] AHIMA Code of Ethics. http://bok.ahima.org/doc?oid=105098#.XMfsVi2ZN0s

Maintain and Update Industry Knowledge through Continuing Education

Once you get hired, don't put your 5-year career goal plan aside! No one should want to stay at an entry-level job forever. Start on learning as much as you can at your new position. Use your HIM textbooks to help you apply what you learned in class to your new job, and keep learning. Get to know members of the HIM department and their roles. Express an interest in a position and ask to be trained on specialized HIM activities.

AHIMA offers the following additional credentials beyond the RHIT and RHIA credentials:

- Certified Coding Associate (CCA)
- Certified Coding Specialist (CCS)
- Certified Coding Specialist—Physician-based (CCS-P)
- Certified Health Data Analyst (CHDA)
- Certified in Healthcare Privacy and Security (CHPS)
- Certified Documentation Improvement Practitioner (CDIP)
- Certified Healthcare Technology Specialist (CHTS) Certified Professional in Health Informatics (CPHI)

Please confirm the education and/or professional experience requirements for each of these credentials through AHIMA.org.

Continuing Education Units

Continuing education units, or CEUs, are required every 2 years to maintain the AHIMA credential. The most credentials you have, the more CEUs are required (refer to **TABLES 29-2** and **29-3**). There are several opportunities to earn CEUs, including the following:

- Attending the yearly AHIMA convention
- Attending the yearly state-sponsored HIM conventions
- Participation in educational programs on topics relevant to HIM
- Participation in formal education programs of study that address HIM-relevant subject areas
- Publication and presentation of material relevant to HIM
- Independent study activities relevant to the HIM profession
- Writing a scholarly article contributing to the HIM profession
- Other activities, including the oversight and involvement of directed clinical practice on behalf of CAHIIM-accredited programs, visiting AHIMA exhibits at a national or state meeting, facilitating for an AHIMA Engage community, and activities

defined by the guidelines for approval of CE programs for state, local, and regional HIM associations and exceptional events recognized by CCHIIM

TABLE 29-2 CEU Requirements for a Single Credential	
If You Have A(n)...	**You Must Earn...**
RHIA, CHPS, CHDA, CDIP, CPHI	30 CEUs
RHIT, CHTS-CP, CHTS-PW, CHTS-IM, CHTS-IS, CHTS-TS, CHTS-TR	20 CEUs
CCA, CCS, CCS-P	20 CEUs, including two mandatory annual coding self-reviews**
Physician Coding Specialist (PCS)*	20 CEUs, including two mandatory annual coding self-reviews**
Certified in Healthcare Privacy (CHP)*	30 CEUs
Certified in Healthcare Security (CHS)*	30 CEUS

If you have more than one AHIMA credential, you must earn 10 additional CEUs per credential during your 2-year recertification cycle up to a maximum of 50 CEUs. These CEUs may not be duplicated or used for more than one credential.

TABLE 29-3 CEU Requirements for Multiple Credentials	
Credential	**Required Number of CEUs**
CCS and CCS-P	30
CHPS with RHIT	40
RHIA with CHDA	40
RHIA with CDIP	40
RHIA with CCS and CCS-P	50
CHDA with CCS, CHPS, and CDIP	50
RHIA with CCS, CCS-P, CHDA, and CDIP	50

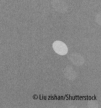

Answer Key

Chapter 2

1. Correct option: c
   ICD-10-PCS Guideline A9 emphasizes that the code-building process has to take place by selecting values from a given row. It will not be accurate to choose values for a given character in one row and then select a value from a different row for the next character.

2. Correct option: c
   When a reduction of a fracture occurs and a cast is placed, the application of the cast is included in the reduction of the fracture and would not be coded separately.

3. Correct option: b
   ICD-10-PCS guideline B3.11a states "Inspection of a body part(s) performed in order to achieve the objective of a procedure is not coded separately."

4. Correct option: d
   The abdominal pain would be the principal diagnosis. In those rare instances where two or more contrasting or comparative diagnoses are documented as either/or (or similar terminology), they are coded as confirmed and sequenced according to the circumstances of the admission.

5. Correct option: d
   Probable diagnoses are coded as if confirmed, whereas symptoms, which in this case is abdominal pain, are not coded when they are integral to the underlying condition.

6. Correct option: c
   The size of a lesion that is removed can be found on the pathology report. The pathologist documents the size of the lesion being analyzed.

7. Correct option: b
   Blood test levels are reported on the laboratory report.

8. Correct option: b
    As a result of the disparity in documentation practices by providers, querying has become a common communication and educational method to advocate proper documentation practices. No coding can be performed without proper physician documentation.

9. Correct option: a
    Hypocalcemia is the presence of an abnormally small concentration of calcium ions in the circulating blood.

10. Correct option: d
    A complication is a secondary condition that arises during hospitalization.

11. Correct option: a
    A patient can only be assigned to one MS-DRG for any given hospitalization.

12. Correct option: d
    The principal diagnosis determines the MDC assignment. The principal diagnosis is the condition established after study to have resulted in the inpatient admission.

13. Correct option: c
    Data quality review is an examination of health records to determine the level of coding accuracy and to identify areas of coding problems.

14. Correct option: c
    One of the elements of the auditing process is identification of risk areas. Examples of various case selection possibilities include medical and surgical MS-DRGs by high dollar and volume.

15. Correct option: a
    The National Practitioner Data Bank (NPDB) was mandated under the Health Care Quality Improvement Act of 1986 to provide a database of medical malpractice payments, adverse licensure actions, and certain professional review actions (such as denial of medical staff privileges) taken by healthcare entities such as hospitals against physicians, dentists, and other health-care providers, as well as private accrediting organizations and peer review organizations.

16. Correct option: d
    Members of the medical staff are generally referred to as independent practitioners. They include individuals permitted by law and the organization to provide patient care services without direction or supervision, within the scope of their license and individually granted clinical privileges.

17. Correct option: a
    One coding convention in the CPT code set uses *and* for *and/or*.

18. Correct option: c

    In the ICD-10-CM code set, Z codes represent Factors Influencing Health Status and Contact with Health Services.

19. Correct option: c

    Modifier −22 is used for unusual procedural services. Modifier −52 is used for reduced services, and Modifier −57 is used for decision for surgery. The correct answer is Modifier −53, which is used for procedures that are discontinued.

20. Correct option: b

    External causes of morbidity codes are used to report external causes of injury and poisoning.

21. Correct option: c

    The resection root operation is cutting out or off, without replacement, all of a body part.

22. Correct option: a

    The Healthcare Effectiveness Data and Information Set is used to regulate Medicare cost control.

23. Correct option: d

    The coder should not query the physician prior to reviewing the entire medical record for accurate documentation.

24. Correct option: d

    The seventh character in an injury, poisoning, or certain other consequences of external causes is used to determine the encounter. A is used for the initial encounter, D is used for subsequent encounters, and S is used for sequela encounters.

25. Correct option: b

    The pacemaker leads are placed on the heart, and the approach is percutaneous. The device is an intracardiac pacemaker.

26. Correct option: c

    The DSM V is used for behavioral diagnosis; while it includes the same codes as ICD-10-CM, this specific code set is used exclusively for behavior diagnosis.

27. Correct option: b

    The patient Social Security number is not collected through the UHDDS.

28. Correct option: d

    Unbundling is a fraudulent practice in which the goal is to obtain more reimbursements by coding for line items separately.

29. Correct option: c

    The UACDS is used to collect outpatient clinical data.

30. Correct option: d

    The detachment root operation is defined as cutting off all or part of the upper or lower extremities.

31. Correct option: b
Crohn's disease and gastritis are conditions coded in the Chapter 11 Diseases of the digestive system.

32. Correct option: b
The correct option includes eight for the approach (via natural opening, endoscopic), and the X diagnostic qualifier for character seven.

33. Correct option: c
Because the laceration is as deep as subcutaneous tissue, it is considered complex.

34. Correct option: b
SNOMED CT is designated as a standard for electronic exchange of clinical health information.

35. Correct option: c
Signs, symptoms, abnormal test results, or other reasons for the outpatient visit are used when a physician qualifies a diagnostic statement as "possible," "probable," "suspected," "questionable," "rule out," "working diagnosis," or other similar terms indicating uncertainty. So the symptoms should be coded.

36. Correct option: a
The case meets the three specific key components, so the correct answer is 99201.

Chapter 3

1. Correct option: d
The records delinquency rate is calculated by $12/20 \times 100\% = 60\%$.

2. Correct option: b
When the patient leaves against medical advice, a discharge order is not recorded in the medical record.

3. Correct option: d
The MPI for a healthcare facility should be maintained indefinitely.

4. Correct option: c
Errors in the paper medical record are corrected by drawing a single line through the error and by signing and dating the correction.

5. Correct option: b
The consent for treatment is used to ensure the patient has agreed to accept and undergo the treatments and procedures suggested by the physician.

6. Correct option: c
The operative report should be dictated and filed in the EHR within 48 hours.

7. Correct option: d
    The American Health Information Management Association (AHIMA) establishes the standardization of records and data collection in a variety of healthcare facilities.

8. Correct option: a
    PHI belongs to the patient to review their health information to make healthcare decisions.

9. Correct option: b
    The principal diagnosis is used to explain to the health insurance company the purpose of the hospital stay.

10. Correct option: d
    The discharge summary includes information related to the discharge of patient, so it will include instructions for continual care.

11. Correct option: d
    Secondary data resources can be collected for research and legal purposes.

12. Correct option: b
    The master patient index (MPI) collects demographic data on every patient's admission to the healthcare facility.

13. Correct option: b
    Hospice care delivers palliative care for terminally ill patients.

14. Correct option: b
    The mission of the National Institutes of Health is to research communicable diseases, environmental health, and foreign quarantine activities.

15. Correct option: c
    Some government-sponsored hospitals, specifically VA hospitals, provide care to military personnel and their immediate families.

16. Correct option: c
    Ambulatory surgery centers are facilities where surgeries can take place and patients are sent home the same day.

17. Correct option: b
    Because Mr. Branson has already spent 30 days in the acute care facility, the insurance will not cover another acute care facility for the same episode. Because he needs continuous nursing care, the skilled nursing facility would be the best choice.

18. Correct option: a
    All options listed are characteristics of quality data. Data consistency means that the data are reliable.

19. Correct option: c
    The second surgeon would complete a consultation to record their findings, provide their impressions, and report their recommendations.

20. Correct option: c
    The Joint Commission uses ORYX initiatives to collect intra-hospital mortality data.

21. Correct option: a
    The terminal digit filing system is the most efficient use of space because medical records are spaced by numbers evenly.

22. Correct option: b
    Vital signs are recorded in the objective section of the SOAP progress notes.

23. Correct option: b
    Data timeliness is a data characteristic that ensures patient information is collected within established time guidelines.

24. Correct option: b
    Health insurance information is considered administrative data.

25. Correct option: c
    Data accessibility is the characteristic of quality data that allows easy and multi-user access to pertinent patient care data.

26. Correct option: a
    The primary purpose of the health record is to use patient health information to deliver quality health care.

27. Correct option: d
    The OASIS data set is used by home health agencies.

28. Correct option: b
    Delinquent records are incomplete within the timeframe defined by the medical staff rules and regulations.

29. Correct option: c
    The Joint Commission uses health record information to ensure the documentation supports the standard of quality care.

30. Correct option: d
    The Joint Commission accreditation is needed for healthcare facilities to participate in Medicare and Medicaid government insurance programs.

31. Correct option: d
    Obtaining accreditation is considered voluntary compared to these other options; however, accreditation is needed for healthcare providers to participate in government health insurance programs.

32. Correct option: b
    Medical bylaws determine the rules and regulations of the healthcare facility, including documentation standards.

33. Correct option: a
    Each healthcare facility should maintain a clinical forms committee to ensure that documentation capture meets the guidelines established by the medical bylaws.

34. Correct option: d
    Nurses document and reconcile the medication record.

35. Correct option: c
    Data relevancy ensures that data collected are relevant to patient health.

Chapter 4

1. Correct option: a
   The data dictionary standardizes medical terminology to organize data in a database.

2. Correct option: b
   HL7, or Health Level 7, is an organization that is dedicated to providing a comprehensive framework and related standards for the exchange, integration, sharing, and retrieval of electronic health information that supports clinical practice and the management, delivery, and evaluation of health services.

3. Correct option: d
   Medical bylaws are developed by the healthcare facility and are managed within the facility.

4. Correct option: c
   Audit trails are used to monitor authorized access for healthcare professionals; this ensures that only users that "need to know" are accessing patient information.

5. Correct option: c
   X12 establishes data interchange standards between health insurance payers and the healthcare facility.

6. Correct option: b
   Management information systems are used by health information department managers to monitor daily hospital admissions and discharges.

7. Correct option: d
   Metadata are descriptive data that characterize other data to create a clearer understanding of their meaning and to achieve greater reliability and quality of information.

8. Correct option: a
   Data aggregation is any process in which information is gathered and expressed in a summary form that can be used to evaluate performance measures.

9. Correct option: d
   Data integrity ensures that data and data elements do not change as they are transmitted.

10. Correct option: c
    Structure and content standards are used in managing electronic information that includes data elements with defined data descriptors.

11. Correct option: a
    The governing board bylaws are established by the board of directors of the healthcare facility, which defines the use of PHI in their facilities.

12. Correct option: b
    All health records, including psychotherapy medical records, can be released to the patient's health insurance company for reimbursement.

13. Correct option: d
    The Certification Commission for Healthcare Information Technology (CCHIT) is an independent, not-for-profit group that certifies electronic health records (EHR) and networks for health information exchange (HIE) in the United States.

14. Correct option: c
    Validation checks imbedded in the practice management software would alert the coding data analyst of the possible data entry errors.

15. Correct option: c
    The goal of data exchange standards is to connect and communicate with other healthcare organizations; to separate facility health data would go against that objective.

16. Correct option: c
    Data stewardship is the responsibility of all health information management professionals to ensure the knowledge and appropriate use of data from patient personal health information.

17. Correct option: c
    Licensure requirements are maintained by county and state authorities; a healthcare facility must have and maintain a license to practice medicine as long as care is provided to patients.

18. Correct option: b
    The Joint Commission promotes the delivery of quality patient care by encouraging healthcare facilities to implement performance improvement measures.

19. Correct option: a
    The clinical practice guidelines established by the board of directors determine the outcomes from the delivery of patient care.

20. Correct option: a
    Automated data entry is the most common collection method used for secondary databases.

Chapter 5

1. Correct option: b
    The data dictionary defines the type and value of each field in the database.

2. Correct option: a
    The electronic health record collects CPOE transactions and stores them in the database.

3. Correct option: a
    The search feature is able to find any patient record in the database.

4. Correct option: c
    SQL is the language used for all databases, so the query will use SQL.

5. Correct option: d
    AHIMA requires that all MPI records are retained permanently for all healthcare facilities.

6. Correct option: d
    The pie chart is the best graphical tool used to present percentages.

7. Correct option: c
    The bar graph can provide the frequency per coder, so all coders with their coding completion rates can be compared.

8. Correct option: c
    The flow chart provides the list of sequential processes needed to complete the project.

9. Correct option: c
    The primary key is a unique value for each database and is independent of any other value in the database.

10. Correct option: b
    The software interface is used to collect data fields defined by the EHR for the patient medical record.

11. Correct option: d
    Structured data have predetermined choices in which the user cannot choose or add information that is not provided, so the drop-down menu option is correct.

12. Correct option: a
    Data is the simplest form; it does not have a determining value.

13. Correct option: d
    Data fields define the data collected for the database.

14. Correct option: b
    The bar chart is the most effective graphic presentation tool used to compare the frequency of information breaches when comparing different months.

15. Correct option: c
    The line chart is useful in displaying aggregate data over a period of time.

16. Correct option: d
    The Social Security number is a unique number issued to each US citizen.

17. Correct option: c
    Because the scanned documents represent an object maintained in the database, it should be object-oriented. It is relational as well because of the different patient records which is compromised of data from different database.

18. Correct option: a
    All data elements are defined so all users understand the purpose of the data collected.

19. Correct option: c
    Granularity is the characteristic that the data that are collected for patient care meet the appropriate level of detail required. In order to provide appropriate patient care, the ER must know which medications the patient is currently using.

20. Correct option: c
    The line chart can display the expenses over a specified amount of time.

21. Correct option: b
    The bar chart is used to compare the frequency among multiple groups.

Chapter 6

1. Correct option: b
   In order to query secondary data, there should be multiple records with the same data.

2. Correct option: b
   The physician index includes information credentialing for the healthcare facility.

3. Correct option: c
   The purpose of collecting patient data for the disease registry is to analyze data to determine trends in disease management.

4. Correct option: b
   A cancer registry reference date should be set on January 1 of a given year.

5. Correct option: d
   Delivery of care directly to the patient, health insurance reimbursement, and development of a patient care plan are related to primary purposes of health information.

6. Correct option: a
   Data collected through the patient delivery process is primary data.

7. Correct option: b
   The National Cancer Registrars Association established educational and professional standards to credential Certified Tumor Registrars.

8. Correct option: d
   The National Center for Health Statistics collects data on birth, marriage, divorce, fetal death, and death.

9. Correct option: c
   Primary data includes any data that can identify the patient.

10. Correct option: a
    The objective of the NPDB (National Provider Data Bank) is to report adverse physician actions in a national wide database; it is unrelated to clinical research or patient care.

11. Correct option: b
    The physician index is a facility-based index that can be queried to determine if there is a connection between the physician and the patients becoming ill.

12. Correct option: d
    Primary data collection tools collect data used to directly provide care to the patient; the computerized order entry collects data for patient care delivery.

13. Correct option: d
    When patient data are used to analyze birth defects in a specific geographical area, they can be used to develop community policies and procedures for prevention.

14. Correct option: b
    According to the Commission on Cancer, an 80% follow-up rate is maintained for all eligible patients from the cancer registry reference data.

15. Correct option: c
    The facility-based trauma index uses the abbreviated injury scale data.

16. Correct option: d
    The immunization registry is a nationwide database that would report on the health objectives established by Healthy People 2020.

17. Correct option: c
    The facility index indicates that care should be delivered in the facility. While the patient is receiving education from the facility, they are not receiving medical care and thus clinical data cannot be collected, so this example is excluded.

18. Correct option: a
    March of Dimes specializes in reporting, supporting, and researching birth defects in the United States.

19. Correct option: d
    Population-based registry includes facility, community, and state level clinical data.

20. Correct option: a
    Clinical investigators are secondary users of clinical data.

Chapter 7

1. Correct option: d
   The facility bylaws determine the required elements to complete the patient's legal record as defined by accrediting agencies such as the Joint Commission.

2. Correct option: c
   The Director of the Health Information department of an accredited facility is known as the custodian of records.

3. Correct option: a
   The plaintiff is the party that files a claim against another party in the court of law.

4. Correct option: b
   The objective of a subpoena from the court is to collect patient health record data related to the dates of services requested.

5. Correct option: d
   The nonmaleficence ethical principle is first do no harm, so the physician who prevents harm to the patient is exercising this principle.

6. Correct option: a
   Autonomy is the ethical principle that allows patients to choose and/or refuse health care based on their personal choices.

7. Correct option: b
   The advance directive is the legal document used to communicate patient healthcare preferences when they cannot communicate them verbally.

8. Correct option: c
   The informed consent form informs the patient on the benefits and risks of the medical procedure.

9. Correct option: d
   Legislative bodies enact statutes.

10. Correct option: b
    The power of attorney gives Mary the right to make healthcare decisions for her father when he is unconscious.

11. Correct option: b
     If the facility failed to obtain a signed informed consent form, then the facility assaulted and battered the patient.

12. Correct option: d
     All three standards are required in order for a legal health record to be admitted in a court of law.

13. Correct option: d
     The AHIMA minimum record storage time is trumped by the state minimum requirements if it is longer than 7 years.

14. Correct option: a

15. Correct option: d
     The defendant is the legal party that the legal charge is made against.

16. Correct option: b
     The Constitution provides details on the powers issued to the three branches of government in the United States.

17. Correct option: c
     If the subpoena is not responded to in time, the Director of Health Information is in contempt of court.

18. Correct option: a
     Statutes of limitations refers to the limited amount of time issued.

19. Correct option: b
     Slander is when an individual speaks negatively against a party in which embellishments are included.

20. Correct option: b
     The physician–patient relationship is established when they meet the first time.

21. Correct option: b
     The purpose of the notice of privacy practice is to be given to every patient at the first encounter.

22. Correct option: a
     While administrative government agencies can pose the need for laws, they cannot enact laws on their own; they must rely on the branches of government that have the power to do so.

23. Correct option: c
     The healthcare facility accepts patient health information under contract that they will keep it private, secure, and confidential. Unauthorized release is a breach of contract.

24. Correct option: d
     The court order is issued by the judge, and the subpoena is a request from the court.

25. Correct option: d
     While the healthcare organization owns the medical records, disclosure of patient health information without patient

authorization is not permitted under the HIPAA Privacy Rule. However, there are exceptions in which health information can be disclosed, specifically when reporting and releasing vital statistics such as births, deaths, and autopsies if the patient is not able to provide a release.

26. Correct option: c
    Justice is the ethical principle that requires all people to be treated equally.

Chapter 8

1. Correct option: a
   Covered entities include healthcare facility, health insurance plans, and healthcare clearing houses.

2. Correct option: c
   PHI elements include identifying data elements such as the Social Security number, geographic elements, and contact information.

3. Correct option: d
   Workforce members include employees of covered entities as well as volunteers, student interns, trainees, and employees of out-sourced vendors that work onsite at the covered entity's facility.

4. Correct option: b
   The objective of administrative simplification is to standardize the management of protected health information. This allows health information to be stored, transmitted, and managed while maintaining specific standards to ensure privacy, security, and confidentiality.

5. Correct option: b
   The ARRA expands the definition of business associates to include patient safety organizations, health information organizations, e-prescribing gateways, and personal health record vendors.

6. Correct option: a
   The objective of administrative simplification is to standardize the management of protected health information.

7. Correct option: c
   Confidentiality is the expectation that personal health information shared between the patient and the provider will be used only for its intended purpose.

8. Correct option: d
   Information that is deidentified information does not identify individual patients because personal characteristics have been removed from the record. Blackening the eye area is the process of deidentifying the patient in full-face photos.

9. Correct option: b

   The Security Rule is flexible in that HIPAA allows the covered entity to adopt security protection measures that are reasonable and appropriate for the size of their organization.

10. Correct option: d

    The contingency plan outlines the emergency procedures when a covered entity's normal operating processes and procedures are interrupted.

11. Correct option: a

    Workstation security is an example of a physical safeguard in which employees lock their workstation when they step away from it.

12. Correct option: b

    The ARRA expands the definition of business associates to include patient safety organizations, health information organizations, e-prescribing gateways, and personal health record vendors.

13. Correct option: d

    The Security Rule is flexible in that HIPAA allows the covered entity to adopt security protection measures that are reasonable and appropriate for the size of their organization.

14. Correct option: c

    The principle in determining record retention rules is that the longest retention time is applied.

15. Correct option: c

    The American Hospital Association recommends retaining records for a minimum of 10 years; however, if the patient was older than the age of majority when treated (10 years), then the minimum retention schedule applies. He is 12 years old at his procedure; adding 7 years would make him 19.

16. Correct option: d

    The MPI of a facility is permanent and should never be destroyed.

17. Correct option: d

    The objective of destroying the medical record is to remove all traces of the dates of service. Any evidence of the record should be destroyed as well as the medical record from the file room.

18. Correct option: a

    It is common for the number of patients to increase and decrease with time; the other situations represent interruptions in daily activities that can affect the quality of patient care delivered, so these can use the contingency plan.

19. Correct option: c

    All healthcare facilities, as part of the bylaws, should keep paper medical records to continue documentation if and when access to the EHR is disrupted.

20. Correct option: b
    External data threats happen outside the healthcare facility. Because the tree is located inside the facility campus, this can be considered an internal threat.

21. Correct option: a
    While a facility is access controls, transmission security, and access controls are part of a successful security program, network safeguards are used to monitor the security program.

22. Correct option: a
    Protecting the privacy of data, ensuring the integrity of data, and ensuring the availability of data are essential tools to control unauthorized access to PHI.

23. Correct option: b
    Every health record that an employee accesses, whether he or she is authorized or not, is recorded in the patient record. That way, if and when a breach of information occurs, the audit log can be reviewed to determine who had access to the patient information. Audit logs should be monitored regularly by the chief privacy officer.

24. Correct option: c
    The facility medical bylaws should contain every medical form used at the healthcare facility. Facilities should hold drills to prepare their employees for contingency situations.

25. Correct option: a
    Privacy is the right of individuals to control access to their personal health information. The clinic does not have the right to report the condition to the employer, but they can state that the patient did not pass the physical exam.

Chapter 9

1. Correct option: d
   Health records that contain highly sensitive information must require additional consent.

2. Correct option: c
   Bryan Henderson should call the clinic in Idaho to request the information.

3. Correct option: b
   The health information department has the right to charge the patient a reasonable copy fee.

4. Correct option: c
   Hospitals have 45 days to respond to the date on the request letter.

5. Correct option: d
   The Privacy Officer is responsible to provide training for the healthcare facility staff on privacy issues.

6.	Correct option: b
The 72-year-old is older, but they are still considered legally competent, whereas the other individuals do not qualify for legal competency according to the HIPAA Privacy Rule.

7.	Correct option: d
A physical driver's license needs to be presented to complete the release of information authorization form.

8.	Correct option: b
The Privacy Officer would be responsible for investigating alleged privacy violations.

9.	Correct option: a
In order for the authorization for release of information to be valid, it needs to have an authorized signature.

10.	Correct option: c
HIPAA Privacy Rule administrative requirements include implementing policies and procedures to ensure compliance.

11.	Correct option: a
PHI standards for protected health information, which the HIPAA Privacy Rule administrative requirements protect.

12.	Correct option: b
The release of information authorization can be approved if a legally competent caregiver can accept the record.

13.	Correct option: d
The penalty for willful neglect that was not corrected is $50K per violation.

14.	Correct option: b
The contingency plan, which details decisions that the facility will make when an emergency takes place; PHI breach is considered an emergency situation.

15.	Correct option: c
Prevention is the number one defense against a health information breach.

16.	Correct option: d
The authorization is specific to the facility named, even though the expiration is still valid.

17.	Correct option: a
The HIPAA Privacy Rule requires the privacy officer to communicate with the OCR, protects the rights of the patients above the healthcare facility, and investigates privacy violations.

18.	Correct option: c
The healthcare facility should deliver the record to the patient in the medium that it is stored in, so if the record is in paper and electronic form, both formats can be delivered.

19. Correct option: d
All healthcare records from any healthcare facility that are kept in paper or electronic format are covered by the HIPAA Privacy Rule.

20. Correct option: c
The healthcare facility is obligated to follow a court order, regardless of having a signed patient authorization for information release on file.

Chapter 10

1. Correct option: c
The certified EHR will hold scanned images of X-rays.

2. Correct option: b
The alert warns the healthcare team of the patient's allergies, thus it promotes patient safety.

3. Correct option: b
Patient financial system applications include applications that verify eligibility, perform prior authorization, generate health insurance claims, and include coding encoders.

4. Correct option: d
Clinical decision support systems assist healthcare providers to make decisions about patient care.

5. Correct option: d
The patient health record (PHR) is always maintained by the patient and/or caregiver.

6. Correct option: c
The expert system asks "what if" questions to assist with problem analysis by comparing data.

7. Correct option: b
The chart locator search tool is used in the EHR to find the patient medical record.

8. Correct option: b
The Digital Imaging and Communications in Medicine (DICOM) standards are used to standardize PACS.

9. Correct option: d
The health information exchange can be accessed by any authorized healthcare provider to retrieve patient records in different healthcare facilities.

10. Correct option: b
Information is a collection of data that is defined and analyzed.

11. Correct option: d
Telemedicine includes the process videoconferencing an encounter when the healthcare provider is not able physically present.

12. Correct option: d
    The Internet is made up of local area networks (LANs) and wide area networks (WANs).

13. Correct option: a
    Wi-fi Protected Access (WPA) is the strongest security protocol system.

14. Correct option: a
    The IP address is a unique address assigned to each computer on the Internet.

15. Correct option: b
    Healthcare providers enter orders in the EHR through the Computerized Provider Order Entry (CPOE).

16. Correct option: a
    PACS represents picture archiving and communication system.

Chapter 11

1. Correct option: a
   The planning stage asks the needs of the healthcare facility.

2. Correct option: d
   A strategic plan is long term, including a period of at least 3 years.

3. Correct option: c
   The implementation step includes installation of the software and hardware of the health information system.

4. Correct option: b
   For the systems development life cycle, the planning stage asks what is needed, and the development stage asks how to meet the healthcare facility needs.

5. Correct option: b
   The request for proposal is essential to the design or acquire stage.

6. Correct option: b
   SMART goal statement categories used in the planning stage are Specific, Measurable, Attainable, Relevant, and Time-based.

7. Correct option: c
   The implementation stage should include staff training. Part of the training process is to ensure that staff recognizes the importance of using the health information system according to facility guidelines.

8. Correct option: b
   The contingency plan will provide the continuity of business and operations plan in case of a natural disaster.

9. Correct option: d
   Nancy is scanning records because the lab information system and the facility EHR are not interoperable.

10. Correct option: d
    In order to ensure the delivery of quality patient care, the patient's medication allergy should be documented in all health information systems within the enterprise system.

Chapter 12

1. Correct option: b
   Diagnostic analytics explains why something happened.

2. Correct option: c
   Predictive analytics explains what will happen in the future based on the analysis of past data.

3. Correct option: c
   The three types of data collected for data analytics are clinical, financial, and operational.

4. Correct option: d
   Health data analysts start by investigating the process of how the data were captured to ensure that it is accurate.

5. Correct option: a
   The dashboard is the clinical summary that includes allergies, patient name, date of birth, medical record number, account number, and recent labs and test results.

6. Correct option: c
   Executive information systems are a decision support system used for performance data analytics.

7. Correct option: d
   Skilled nursing facilities should use the SNFPPS payment system.

8. Correct option: c
   Using patients to complete the medical record is not appropriate because the record is populated with physician signed records. Increasing the hospital medical records delinquency rates to 6 months is again Joint Commission standards for medical records.

9. Correct option: a
   The healthcare facility defines a complete record, not the Joint Commission.

10. Correct option: a
    Medicare pays according to the fee schedule, not according to the physician or facility charges for the procedure or service. The Joint Commission does not maintain a fee schedule.

11. Correct option: b
    The assembly process can only occur with paper records because it is the process of organizing the paper record into the format established by the healthcare facility.

12. Correct option: c
     The concurrent review method allows deficiencies to be resolved before patients are discharged.

13. Correct option: b
     Physician signatures are not required on notes, only on orders.

14. Correct option: a
     Quantitative analysis determines the presence of required elements of the health record.

15. Correct option: d
     Qualitative analysis determines the quality of care provided through documentation.

16. Correct option: d
     The legal record requirement states that a line should be drawn through the additional space on the page to prevent tampering. Throwing away medical documentation is illegal.

17. Correct option: c
     Legal documents require documentation in black ink.

18. Correct option: c
     The attending physician must authenticate the report, in addition to the resident physican.

19. Correct option: c
     Quantitative analysis determines the authentications needed in the medical record.

20. Correct option: a
     Establishing a 1-week turnaround time for all dictated reports will drastically improve the delinquency rate.

Chapter 13

1. Correct option: c
    The correct option is 10 days. Although the actual average is 9.2 days, it is rounded to the next higher complete day.

2. Correct option: b
    Because the standard deviation is 18, 2 standard deviations would be 2 times the standard deviation, or 36. Because the question asks for 2 standard deviations *below* the mean, this would equal −36. So, 186 mean length of stay days − 36 standard deviation (x2) = 150 days.

3. Correct option: c
    Mode is the sample that occurs most frequently in a data set, so the answer is 16.

4. Correct option: b
    First, sort the data from the smallest sample to the greatest

sample. Then, apply the quartile formula (n + 1) ÷ 4. In this case, there are 15 samples, so the first quartile is sample4. This corresponds with 5.

5. Correct option: a
A larger standard deviation indicates that the data samples are further from the mean.

6. Correct option: b
The variance formula does not require data samples to be organized from least to greatest.

7. Correct option: a
There is not enough information to determine the quartiles or the mode, so these responses are incorrect. The wider the range, the larger the standard deviation. The variance is directly related to the standard deviation.

8. Correct option: c
Death is considered a discharge, so it is subtracted from the inpatient census.

9. Correct option: b
To calculate the census, we start with the census on December 1, which is 144. Five patients were admitted, 3 from the ER and 2 from surgery; adding these patients brings the census to 149. One patient died, which is subtracted, so the census would be 148. Patients admitted and discharged on the same day do not affect the census.

10. Correct option: d
The length of stay is calculated from the admission date to the discharge date. July has 31 days and she was admitted on July 5. 31 − 5 = 26 days. She was discharged on August 15, so add 15 days to the 26 days from July. Total discharge days = 41 days.

11. Correct option: c
The gross death rate is the total number of inpatient deaths, including newborns, for a period divided by the total number of discharges, including adults, children, and newborns, in the same period. Dividing 8 total deaths (including adults, children, and newborns) by 223 total discharges and then multiplying by 100 equals 3.59%.

12. Correct option: a
The fetal death rate is the total number of intermediate and late fetal deaths for a given period divided by the total number of live births plus the total number of intermediate and late fetal deaths for the same period.

13. Correct option: a
The formula for the bed turnover rate is the total number of discharges for a given period divided by the average bed count for the same period. The total number of discharges for adults and children is 873 and the average bed count is 300, so the correct answer is 2.91%.

14.   Correct option: b

The gross hospital death rate formula is the total deaths in a given period divided by the total number of discharges for the same period. So 31 deaths divided by 2,989 discharges x 100 is 0.95%.

15.   Correct option: c

The net autopsy rate formula is the total inpatient autopsies in a given period divided by the total number of inpatient deaths minus the number of unautopsied medical examiner's cases for the same period. So 15 autopsies divided by 31 deaths minus 3 medical examiner's cases x 100 is 54%.

16.   Correct option: a

The bed turnover rate is the total number of discharges for a given period divided by the average bed count for the same period. So 2,989 discharges divided by 283 bed count is 10.56.

17.   Correct option: d

The inpatient bed occupancy rate formula is the total number of inpatient service days for a given period divided by the total number of inpatient bed count days for the same period. To calculate the total number of inpatient bed count days, we take the number of days in June 20XX and multiply this by the number of beds; 30 days in the month of June multiplied by 283 equals 8,490. The total inpatient service days, 7,848, is then divided by 8,490 and multiplied by 100, which is 92.44%.

18.   Correct option: c

The average daily census is the total number of service days for a given period by the total number of days in the same period. There are 30 days in June. So, 7,848 divided by 30 days is 261.6 days, or 262 days.

19.   Correct option: b

The inpatient occupancy rate formula is the total number of inpatient service days for a given period divided by the total number of inpatient bed count days for the same period. The first step is to determine the inpatient bed count days for each time period, as seen in this table:

Inpatient Days for Period			
1-Apr	15-Apr	325	4,875
16-Apr	30-Apr	300	4,500
1-May	15-May	290	4,350
16-May	31-May	325	5,200
			18,925

The total inpatient bed count days is 18,925. We divide 17,324 inpatient service days by 18,925 inpatient bed count days, and then multiply by 100 to get 91.5%.

Use the following data to answer questions 17 and 18.

Fetal Death Rate for San Antonio Community Hospital

20. Correct option: a

The fetal death rate is the total number of intermediate and late fetal deaths for a given period divided by the total number of live births plus the total number of intermediate and late fetal deaths for the same period. From this data, the total number of intermediate and late fetal deaths is 2, and the total number of live births plus intermediate and late fetal deaths is 52, so the rate is 3.84%.

21. Correct option: a

The newborn death rate is the total number of newborn deaths for a given period divided by the total number of newborn discharges, including deaths, for the same period. The total number of deaths is 2, and the total number of discharges is 50, so the rate is 4%.

22. Correct option: c

Adults, children, and newborns are included in the hospital mortality rate.

23. Correct option: d

Because the patient was admitted and discharged on the same day, the census does not change.

24. Correct option: b

To calculate the average length of stay, all data EW summed and divided by the number of patients. The total of all lengths of stay is 65, and the number of patients is 18, which gives you an average of 3.6 days.

25. Correct option: d

Because the standard deviation is 6, every additional 6 births represents one standard deviation. March had 63 births, 17 higher than average. Because 3 standard deviations represents 18 births, the increase is within the 3 standard deviations over the mean.

26. Correct option: b

The C-section occurrence rate is the number of C-section deliveries over the total number of deliveries. The denominator is the total number of deliveries, which is 159.

27. Correct option: c

The average daily census is the total number of inpatient service days over the total number of days in the same period. This would be 3,000 IPSD/30 days in June = 100 patients.

28. Correct option: c
    Vital statistics include data on births, deaths, fetal deaths, marriages, and divorces.

29. Correct option: d
    The prevalence rate is the proportion of persons in a population who have a particular disease at a specific point in time or over a specific period of time.

30. Correct option: c
    The incidence rate is the probability or risk of illness in a population over a period of time.

Chapter 14

1. Correct option: d
   Data analysis is the method used to measure the quality and effectiveness of the health care delivered.

2. Correct option: a
   The Joint Commission maintains the conditions of participation for accreditation.

3. Correct option: c
   Aggregate data is used to develop information and make conclusions.

4. Correct option: b
   Individual data is used to deliver direct patient care.

5. Correct option: d
   A retrospective study reviews the medical records of all patients undergoing the colonoscopy for the past 3 months to determine the cause of infection.

6. Correct option: a
   Because the correlation coefficient is close to +1, there is a strong positive correlation, so these populations are most likely going to develop gastrointestinal infections.

7. Correct option: d
   To calculate the odds ratio, use AD/BC. This results in 6,800 divided by 300, which is 22.667.

8. Correct option: c
   The odds ratio result means that the patient is more likely to develop the condition.

9. Correct option: b
   Participants in the prospective study have the risk for the disease, but the disease has not manifested.

10. Correct option: d
    The first step in conducting any research study using human participants should be to contact and apply for IRB approval.

11. Correct option: b
     The HEDIS performance measures are sponsored by the NCQA.

12. Correct option: d
     Aggregate data is when all levels of data, including individual and comparative data, are used to draw conclusions about specific healthcare topics.

13. Correct option: a
     Because the increase in patient satisfaction is directly correlated to the healing hands program, the increase in patient satisfaction is the dependent variable of the healing hands program.

14. Correct option: c
     The main difference between descriptive studies and correlation studies is that correlation studies have more than one variable.

15. Correct option: b
     Prospective studies are used for patients who exhibit risk factors for disease but are free from the disease.

Chapter 15

1. Correct option: b
    Health informatics is the management of all health data and information through computer applications and technology.

2. Correct option: c
    The patient manages the personal health record (PHR).

3. Correct option: d
    The patient uses the patient portal to share some of their personal health information with the physician.

4. Correct option: a
    A smart glucose monitor is a wireless device that sends patient data to the physician wirelessly.

5. Correct option: a
    Patient-generated health data are collected through a mobile technology or application.

6. Correct option: c
    Connected personal health records are populated through the healthcare facility EHR.

7. Correct option: d
    The detached personal health record is maintained by the patient, so they determine how the record is maintained.

8. Correct option: c
   Health information exchange use is a requirement for Meaningful use Stage II.

9. Correct option: c
   Interoperability occurs seamlessly between health information systems. The case of accessing the health information system in the same physician network is an example of interoperability.

10. Correct option: b
    Interoperability is not a standard to meet meaningful use standards. Most Certified EHR systems maintain different data dictionaries.

11. Correct option: d
    Fewer medical errors, increased patient safety, and enhanced health data and information reporting are all benefits from health information exchange.

12. Correct option: c
    The second data element used to search the health information exchange is the date of birth.

13. Correct option: c
    The problem list includes symptoms that the patient experiences that are reported to the physician.

14. Correct option: a
    The Office of the National Coordinator develops and maintains standards for secure correspondence between the physician and the patient.

15. Correct option: b
    The different types of health information exchange include the direct exchange, query-based exchange, and consumer-mediated exchange.

Chapter 16

1. Correct option: b
   The Joint Commission establishes the conditions of participation, which must be met to become a Medicare participating provider.

2. Correct option: d
   Lucy would be ineligible for Medicare because of age. CHIP would require the parents to have a higher income. Lucy cannot qualify for Blue Shield, but she can apply for healthcare coverage. Medicaid plans are state funded for lower income patients.

3. Correct option: a
   The copayment is assigned by the health insurance plan, can be identified on the patient's health insurance ID card, and is paid at the time of service.

4. Correct option: d
    Medicare was established in 1965 as an amendment of the Social Security Act.

5. Correct option: b
    Medicare will allow a maximum amount based on the PPS rate.

6. Correct option: a
    The prospective payment system is based on diagnosis codes, procedure codes, and a historical average of charges made in the past, not physician charges.

7. Correct option: d
    While both the PPO and the HMO are considered managed care plans, the major difference is that HMO plans require the patient access care through the gatekeeper.

8. Correct option: c
    Patients assigned the same DRG have the same diagnosis, health-care protocol, and resource utilization management. Length of stay will depend on patient health status, which differs from patient to patient.

9. Correct option: b
    To calculate the hospital case mix, all values should be added together and divided by the total number of cases in the given period.

10. Correct option: c
    When the physician's office is has a capitation agreement with the managed care plan, they cannot bill the plan for office visits.

11. Correct option: d
    In the fee-for-service payment arrangement, the physician's office first assigns the respective procedure and diagnosis, and then they assign a fee to each procedure code.

12. Correct option: c
    The indemnity plan reimburses patients for medical expenses up to a specified amount.

13. Correct option: a
    Medicare Part A plans cover hospital coverage only.

14. Correct option: d
    The OPPS, the outpatient prospective payment system, is used for Medicare reimbursements for outpatient services.

15. Correct option: c
    Sally has Medicare Part C because her HMO plan covers inpatient, outpatient, and prescription services in one health plan.

16. Correct option: b
    The provider's office charges are taken from the provider's fee schedule.

17.   Correct option: a
      As a participating Medicare provider, the provider agrees to adjust their reimbursements based on the Medicare allowed amount.

18.   Correct option: b
      Medicare secondary insurances cover the 20% deductible based on the Medicare allowable fee, which is $120. So the amount Secure Horizons should pay for is $24.

19.   Correct option: a
      The case indicates that Herman pays for his own insurance, and does not qualify for state assistance. COBRA is used for those who have let go of their job and want to continue the same health plan as before.

20.   Correct option: d
      Medicaid is known as the payer of last resort. Because the amount reimbursed by Medicare is higher than the Medicaid-allowed amount for the same procedure, they will not pay any more.

21.   Correct option: a
      Being that the Riverside Medical Clinic has a capitation agreement with Blue Shield HMO, they cannot charge additional amounts for office visits, but can only accept the copay from the patient.

22.   Correct option: b
      Workers' compensation plans are typically used for on-the-job–related injuries.

23.   Correct option: c
      Because David can choose his own provider access, including specialists, and has a high deductible, he most likely has a PPO.

24.   Correct option: d
      Under the current Affordable Care Act, children can still be considered dependents until age 26.

25.   Correct option: A
      The Agency for Healthcare Research and Quality does not maintain physician databases to report medical experience.

26.   Correct option: c
      While funded through the federal government, the administration, which includes program eligibility, is handled through the state program.

27.   Correct option: d
      Because the physician's office did not obtain a surgical authorization prior to the procedure, they are at risk of not getting paid. Some insurance companies have an appeals process, but there is no guarantee of payment.

28. Correct option: a
    Birthing centers do not use MS-DRGs for reimbursement.

29. Correct option: b
    The DRG payment system is organized my diagnosis codes, which is currently based on the ICD-10-CM.

30. Correct option: c
    The MS-DRG weight is directly related to healthcare resources, so the higher the weight, the more healthcare resources are required.

31. Correct option: a
    Although the MS-DRG is based on the diagnosis or ICD-10-CM code, it is not included in the MS-DRG description.

32. Correct option: d
    The RBRVS is based on the CPT code set because it is used by Medicare Part B.

33. Correct option: b
    While all of these circumstances are true for in-network participating providers, the essential benefit is patient referrals.

34. Correct option: c
    The Office of the Inspector General monitors fraud and abuse in government-sponsored health insurance plans.

35. Correct option: c
    Because Diane has an HMO, the gatekeeper, or primary care physician, must be consulted with the patient concern first. Then they only can offer a referral to a specialist in network.

36. Correct option: b
    Because gastroenterology and oncology are both considered specialists, she would pay $50 per office visit. Because she has one gastroenterologist appointment and two oncologist appointments in 1 month, her copayment would add up to $150 in September.

37. Correct option: b
    The deductible includes all the surgical and therapy costs for the year. Because she had the knee arthroscopy and the colonoscopy earlier in the year, she already met $1,950 prior to starting the chemotherapy. She would need to spend another $1,550 to reach the deductible, and based on the cost of chemotherapy, she would reach the deductible in July.

38. Correct option: b
    Because Edna has a coinsurance up to $5,000 and she gets $1,250 chemotherapy every month, she would reach the coinsurance max in September.

39. Correct option: c
    Copayments are not reflected in the deductible and coinsurance minimums.

40. Correct option: b
    January 1 of the following year restarts the coinsurance and deductibles. So she would pay the standard copayment for chemotherapy.

Chapter 17

1. Correct option: a
   The revenue code is a three-digit code that is listed only on the UB-04 form, not the CMS-1500 form.

2. Correct option: d
   The capitation covers all routine office visits, so the physician will not bill the insurance plan for these services.

3. Correct option: c
   The reason code is a code with an accompanying legend that explains the reason the claim was denied.

4. Correct option: c
   The insurance company will never correct a health insurance claim; it needs to be corrected and rebilled. Because the error was from the physician's office, the patient cannot be held responsible. Because the diagnosis states the right arm but the CPT modifier states the left arm, the insurance company will deny based on medical necessity.

5. Correct option: d
   The Social Security number and the procedure and diagnosis code descriptions are not present on any health insurance claim form.

6. Correct option: a
   The difference between the charged amount and the allowed amount listed on the explanation of benefits is written off the patient account.

7. Correct option: b
   The Advanced Beneficiary Notice, or ABN, is a required document for Medicare patients that want care from a healthcare provider that is not covered under their health insurance plan.

8. Correct option: b
   The Uniform Ambulatory Care Data set (UACDS) is used to complete the CMS-1500 form.

9. Correct option: a
   The primary diagnosis in the CMS-1500 is the reason for encounter and the UB-04 form is known as the admitting diagnosis.

10. Correct option: d
    Both the ICD-10-CM and the HCPCS codes can be used for both the CMS-1500 and the UB-04 forms.

11. Correct option: b

   The place of service codes can be found in the cover of the CPT coding manual.

12. Correct option: c

   The healthcare facility manages the chargemaster, which lists all the charges posted in the patient accounts, organized by the date of service.

13. Correct option: d

   The health insurance company and the physician are not financially responsible because the lapse of coverage was due to the patient nonpayment.

14. Correct option: b

   The NCCI edit table indicates which codes and modifiers cannot be matched together to ensure accuracy.

15. Correct option: d

   The physician should send an appeal letter requesting additional funds based on the contractual fee schedule.

16. Correct option: b

   If the secondary insurance is listed on the remittance advice, Medicare will electronically file the claim with the secondary insurance.

17. Correct option: c

   When a provider is not in-network with the health insurance plan, the reimbursement check is sent directly to the patient.

18. Correct option: a

   Successful reimbursement begins in admitting because the health insurance ID is verified, compared with the patient ID, and the health insurance plan is contacted to verify coverage, review eligibility, and obtain preauthorization.

19. Correct option: b

   The aging in a patient account begins on the date of service.

20. Correct option: d

   The process of coding each single activity in the operative report is an example of unbundling.

21. Correct option: a

   The chargemaster lists all patients and the procedures performed by the date of service.

22. Correct option: a

   Patient verification is completed in the front end cycle.

23. Correct option: c

   By providing patient resources after the patient has been diagnosed with a life-changing disease, the case manager coordinates care for the patient.

24. Correct option: c
    The admitting clerk is responsible for coordinating benefits to confirm the primary insurance plan. If the patient is still working and has coverage through work, then their Medicare coverage is secondary.

25. Correct option: b
    Anesthesia is billed on the CMS-1500 form. However, because this is submitted electronically, the correct submission would be through the HIPAA X12 837p.

26. Correct option: c
    A utilization management (UM) plan is a requirement for condition of participation for Medicare and Medicaid plans.

27. Correct option: c
    The advanced beneficiary notice is used to confirm patient financial responsibility for services not covered by Medicare.

28. Correct option: b
    Because Aetna denied the claim even though Medicare already paid, the appeal letter should be written to them.

29. Correct option: b
    Utilization management evaluation is based on the actual length of stay.

30. Correct option: c
    The most common reason why claims are denied is because inaccurate information is collected through the patient intake process.

31. Correct option: a
    Because the home healthcare facility does not have an operative room, these charges will not be found in the chargemaster of a home healthcare facility.

32. Correct option: c
    National Committee of Quality Assurance (NCQA) requires a utilization management plan for all managed care plans.

33. Correct option: b
    The goal of utilization review is to evaluate appropriateness of care. If there is little demand for this machine, then it may be wiser to sell the machine and convert the room into a treatment room to increase revenue.

34. Correct option: c
    Appeal letter should include a reference number, which is typically the number assigned by the insurance company.

35. Correct option: d
    The advanced beneficiary notice is used to inform the patient that the procedure and/or service is not covered by Medicare, so the patient is financially responsible.

Chapter 18

1. Correct option: d
    The Joint Commission accreditation lasts for 36 months.

2. Correct option: d
    Accreditation is voluntary, whereas certification is required.

3. Correct option: d
    The utilization management plan, the quality improvement organization review, and the Joint Commission accreditation are all required to meet conditions of participation standards.

4. Correct option: b
    The executive committee is a management group that permits healthcare professionals to have clinical privileges.

5. Correct option: b
    Risk management includes all activities involved in reducing potential and prospective liability.

6. Correct option: c
    According to the Joint Commission standard, the history and physical exam report should be documented into the patient record within 24 hours of admission.

7. Correct option: b
    The Joint Commission reviews the patient record to ensure that standards of patient safety and quality are delivered.

8. Correct option: a
    Medical clinics and offices are not bound by the condition of participation standards.

9. Correct option: c
    Handwritten orders are eliminated with the EHR system.

10. Correct option: b
    A sentinel event is a patient safety event that results in death or permanent harm to the patient.

11. Correct option: c
    Meaningful Use Stage III represents the evaluation of the impact of EHR on the delivery of quality patient care.

12. Correct option: d
    Quality Improvement Organizations are sponsored by Medicare and Medicaid and review patient records to determine the level of quality care delivered.

13. Correct option: a
    The American Association for Accreditation of Ambulatory Surgery Facilities (AAAASF) is an association that meets standards of a deeming authority who meets the Medicare's conditions of participation requirement.

14. Correct option: b
    The Joint Commission is a deeming authority for outpatient surgery centers.

15. Correct option: b
    This plan calls for an increase in the review of evaluation and management health insurance claims.

16. Correct option: c
    According to the compliance program basics, the individual assigned as compliance officer is the individual to report all violations.

17. Correct option: c
    The Joint Commission does not review or evaluate health insurance claims.

18. Correct option: d
    The overpayment amount is $450 × 50 patients = $22,500. The penalty is three times the overpayment amount, which is 3 × $22,500 which is $67,500. There is an additional $10,000 to the penalty, so the total due is $77,500.

19. Correct option: b
    XXX

20. Correct option: b
    According to HITECH, Dr. Chu can remain a Medicare participating provider and not upgrade his information systems as long as he is willing to accept a lower Medicare fee schedule.

Chapter 19

1. Correct option: b
   ICD-10-PCS and ICD-10-CM are both coding systems are used through the inpatient coding process.

2. Correct option: c
   The goal of a coding compliance program is to prevent fraudulent coding practices.

3. Correct option: b
   Because the patient was admitted with the tracheostomy, this is considered present on admission, so a POA code should be used.

4. Correct option: a
   Because the patient acquired the infection 48 hours after admission, this is considered a hospital-acquired condition, so a HAC indicator should be used.

5. Correct option: a
   The incision is part of the presurgical activities so it should not be coded either for the surgeon or the hospital.

6. Correct option: c
    The APR-DRG level 3 indicates that there is a major risk of mortality.

7. Correct option: d
    By regularly utilizing the copy-and-paste documentation method, specific symptoms can be overlooked when comparing patients, so this can lead to reduced reimbursements; it can force medical coders to assign a more generalized code; and this practice does not reflect the goals of the facility's coding compliance plan.

8. Correct option: b
    DSM V is a diagnosis coding system used to diagnosis mental health patients.

9. Correct option: b
    A facility coding compliance plan should emphasize coding accuracy and timeliness, not either/or.

10. Correct option: c
    The indicator HAC, or hospital-acquired condition, should be reported to Medicare.

11. Correct option: b
    In order to benchmark, the comparing facility should have similar resources. The military hospital and the privately owned facility have different resources than the 275-bed community hospital. If we were to compare "apples to apples," we would choose the 275-bed community hospital.

12. Correct option: c
    The clinical documentation improvement process begins the day after patient admission.

13. Correct option: a
    The standards and criteria for a clinical documentation improvement program do not come from the Centers for Medicare and Medicaid Services. The American Medical Association publishes the CPT every year, so even they contribute documentation standards.

14. Correct option: b
    Health information management professionals are responsible for training the staff on appropriate and required documentation standards.

15. Correct option: d
    The coder should query the physician to have the documentation clarified and updated, which would include a review of the lab results, to include the comorbidity.

Chapter 20

1. Correct option: a
   The first step to the Medicare appeal is redetermination.

2. Correct option: b
   The local coverage determinations are published by Medicare Administrative Contractors to determine medical necessity under specific clinical circumstances.

3. Correct option: a
   According to the Office of the Inspector General, the most common error found on health insurance claims is missing documentation.

4. Correct option: b
   Performing internal audits for medical coding and billing can identify potential issues to prevent higher ADRs in the following quarters.

5. Correct option: d
   According to the Balanced Budget Act, on his second offense Dr. Johnson can no longer be a participating provider with Medicare again.

6. Correct option: b
   This example is fraudulent because the physician intentionally upcoded even though he knew he did not perform the service for every office visit.

7. Correct option: c
   Waste occurs when unnecessary costs have been created to the healthcare facility and/or the health insurance plan.

8. Correct option: a
   The first step to determine the source of the upcoding is to review Dr. Trees's documentation in patient records through an internal audit.

9. Correct option: d
   Access controls, contingency plans, and a security plan are all requirements of HIPAA legislation for healthcare facilities.

10. Correct option: c
    When Dr. Walter provides a financial incentive for client referrals, this is considered a kickback.

11. Correct option: b
    Qui tam is the whistleblower provision.

12. Correct option: b
    This case is an example of abuse. Dr. Jackson did not intentionally code for ambulatory services in his medical office instead of shorter visits to the dialysis center, but the error cost the insurance plan money.

13. Correct option: d
    The False Claims Act issues penalties to healthcare facilities that knowingly submitted fraudulent claims.

14. Correct option: c
    The Stark Law states that the physician is prohibited from recommending a business to the patient in which they have a self-interest.

15. Correct option: c
    The Whistleblower Protection Act legislation is used to strengthen and improve protection for the rights of federal employees, to prevent reprisals, and to help eliminate wrongdoing within the government.

16. Correct option: b
    Federal employees can report to the Office of the Special Counsel when reporting misconduct and offenses in the government.

17. Correct option: a
    The Office of the Inspector General represents the largest team of auditors and leading healthcare law enforcement agencies in the United States.

18. Correct option: c
    RACs increase the requests of information to review more Medicare patient medical records.

19. Correct option: a
    The higher the Medicare denial rate, the higher the ADR rate will be; to reduce the ADR, it would be essential to reduce the Medicare denial rate.

20. Correct option: b
    Upcoding is the practice of assigning diagnostic and/or procedure codes that represent higher healthcare services than those actually delivered.

Chapter 21

1. Correct option: a
   The facility bylaws policies and procedures are based on federal, state, and local documentation standards and the facility mission and vision statements.

2. Correct option: c
   The Director of Health Information is considered part of middle-level management.

3. Correct option: d
   The Chief Executive Officer has the role as the head of the board of directors.

4. Correct option: c
   The contingency theory states that leaders in one circumstance may not necessary lead in another circumstance.

5. Correct option: a
   Trait theory explains that leadership skills are inherited, and such leaders have a natural ability.

6. Correct option: b
   The four essential management functions are leadership, planning, controlling, and organizing.

7. Correct option: c
   The authoritarian leadership style is domineering and this style includes making all decisions by the leader.

8. Correct option: b
   Because the president does not participate in strategic decision-making, he is a laissez-faire leader.

9. Correct option: a
   The Chief Information Officer is responsible for planning, budgeting, and training for information technology.

10. Correct option: b
    Authoritarianism is not an essential characteristic of effective team leaders.

11. Correct option: b
    The team charter includes a list of all team members and their respective responsibilities.

12. Correct option: b
    During team meetings, silence is an indicator of consensus, so for the sake of time, not every team member needs to vocally agree.

13. Correct option: c
    Brainstorming is a critical-thinking process that is essential in team building and communication.

14. Correct option: a
    The root-cause analysis is a critical-thinking tool that can be used to determine the cause of a sentinel event.

15. Correct option: b
    The designated team leader is responsible to release the meeting agenda for each meeting.

Chapter 22

1. Correct option: a
   The nominal group technique (NGT) encourages team members to review a number of different ideas and rank them by impor-

tance to the team member. Once all ideas are ranked, the ranks are summed and calculated to determine the ideas that have more priority.

2. Correct option: c
    Through the merger process, Saddletown Community Hospital must meet their own Medicare conditions of participation accredited through the Joint Commission in order to care for Medicare patients.

3. Correct option: b
    The six essential principles of continuous quality improvement (CQI) are constancy of variation, importance of data, vision and support of executive leadership, focus on customers, investment in people, and importance of teams.

4. Correct option: b
    An internal force occurs within the organization. An elevated employee turnover could pose problems with the operations of the facility in that more training is needed to replace the employee that leaves the position.

5. Correct option: b
    Incremental changes are small changes; firing and replacing the entire department will have too big of an impact to improve healthcare processes.

6. Correct option: d
    Structure indicators measure the quantitative attributes of the healthcare setting, including the number of qualified staff on duty, the number of fully operational medical equipment machines, and the amount of medical supply inventory needed to provide care to the patient.

7. Correct option: c
    Outcome indicators measure the outcomes of patient care; these indicators can also include patient satisfaction with the care they received.

8. Correct option: b
    The fishbone diagram, also known as the root-cause analysis, is a data visualization tool that assists the team to determine the possible causes of a problem the facility is facing.

9. Correct option: a
    A movement diagram is a graphical presentation of the workspace. This includes the entire floorplan, including all furniture such as desks, chairs, office equipment, cabinets, and anything that is on the office floor.

10. Correct option: b
    Multivoting technique also is used to prioritize ideas, but each team member is assigned the same number of points, which they to the ideas they believe should be prioritized.

11. Correct option: d

     The plots on the scatter graph are not presented in a clear direction, so a relationship cannot be confirmed.

12. Correct option: a

     The Pareto chart is a reflection of the Pareto Principle, which states that 20% of the sources are responsible for 80% of the actual problem.

13. Correct option: b

     The team defines a few problems, which become categories in the diagram.

14. Correct option: c

     Overordering of inventory can lead to throwing out expired medical supplies. Also, following the last-in–last-out practice leaves older medical supply inventory in the back and unused.

15. Correct option: d

     The Joint Commission requires that the hospital investigate the root cause of sentinel events so as to prevent injury in the future.

Chapter 23

1. Correct option: d

    The coding accuracy rate is (535 operative reports − 23 incorrectly coded reports)/(535 operative reports) = 95.7%.

2. Correct option: d

    The 12 new hospital beds need 24-hour nurse care, which equals 288 total work hours. If each nurse works only 40 hours, 288 total hours/40 hours possible per week, we need 7.2 nurses. However, each nurse can only care for 8 patients, so technically we need 1.5 nurses per hour to meet the Joint Commission standard. So 1.5 nurses × 7.2 nurses needed for the total work hours equals 10.8 nurses. Because no overtime is allowed, we need to round up to 11 nurses.

3. Correct option: a

    According to the Fair Labor Standards Act, the hourly employee must be paid for every hour that they are working, especially if they work overtime.

4. Correct option: a

    Exempt employees are full-time employees who are not covered by the Fair Labor Standards Act.

5. Correct option: c

    If the candidate is qualified for the position, the employer has the obligation to make reasonable accommodations to assist the employee to perform her duties effectively.

6. Correct option: c
The Occupational Safety and Health Act is regulated by the US Department of Labor to ensure a healthy and safe work environment. Sharing gloves is a violation because the sharing of gloves can contaminate Molly and multiple patients.

7. Correct option: c
Because Pamela has been working as a medical coder for the past 6 years, which is beyond the minimum 1 year of employment required by the Family and Medical Leave Act, she is able to take up to 12 weeks of personal time to address her health issues.

8. Correct option: c
According to the Genetic Nondiscrimination Act, Title I states health plans may not use genetic information to make eligibility, coverage, underwriting, or premium setting decisions or impose pre-existing condition exclusions.

9. Correct option: b
A major benefit to maintaining strong job descriptions for every position in the healthcare facility is to benchmark workloads compared to other employees working at the same healthcare facility.

10. Correct option: d
Work sampling, production time study, and time logs can all be used by the HR department for performance appraisals.

11. Correct option: b
Never should HR indicate to employees that some patients are more important than others based on a discriminatory bias.

12. Correct option: c
Conflict resolution is a tool used by the HR department to improve communication in the healthcare facility departments.

13. Correct option: b
Title VII of the Civil Rights Act of 1964 protects applicants against discriminatory hiring practices based on religion.

14. Correct option: a
The US Bureau of Labor collects and analyzes data on employment statistics on industries in the United States.

15. Correct option: d
Mary should demand her original position because she followed the employer's regulations on medical leave based on the Family and Medical Leave Act.

Chapter 24

1. Correct option: a
Strategic goals represent long-term, 3- to 5- year goals.

2. Correct option: b
    Controlling is the process of monitoring the application of healthcare facility policies and procedures.

3. Correct option: d
    Because each employee is qualified in a specific set of skills, management assigns duties to employees based on their skill set. Some employees have an extensive skill set but do not have the work ethic to handle too many cases or a larger workload. An efficient manager knows how to use all of their assets, including employees, to achieve the organization's goals with the knowledge of employee specialization.

4. Correct option: a
    Employees should be made aware of the manager that they report to; they should not have to report to more than one manager.

5. Correct option: c
    Operational plans focuses on daily functions, not long-term goals.

6. Correct option: b
    Because Medicare is an external agency to the healthcare facility and is adding pressure by requesting medical records, this is an external force.

7. Correct option: a
    The pressure on the healthcare organization in this case is coming from management, so this is an internal force.

8. Correct option: b
    The healthcare facility's inability to collect reimbursements is an internal force, and therefore it represents a weakness.

9. Correct option: c
    The donor's endowment opens a future opportunity for the hospital; because the donor is not affiliated with the hospital, this is an external force.

10. Correct option: a
    Corporate compliance is the process of leading the organization to ensure that all employees work to meet patient safety standards including injury prevention, detection of fraudulent conduct, and resolution of regulation violations.

11. Correct option: c
    The Centers for Disease Control and Prevention's mission is to collaborate with the public to provide the public the tools they need to prevent disease, injury, and disability.

12. Correct option: a
    Accountable care organizations include a team of healthcare providers and supplies that work together to coordinate and improve care for Medicare patients.

13.   Correct option: c
Out of these healthcare professionals, only the endocrinologist can bill the health insurance company for services rendered.

14.   Correct option: b
Nurses are not considered allied health professionals.

15.   Correct option: c
Information is the healthcare organization's most strategic asset.

Chapter 25

1.   Correct option: d
Liabilities can be found on the balance sheet.

2.   Correct option: d
Income, revenue, and net loss are all found on the income statement.

3.   Correct option: b
The budget variance is the difference between the budgeted amount and the actual amount expensed.

4.   Correct option: a
The line manager would review her department budget to determine if there is room to fit a raise.

5.   Correct option: b
Retained earnings can be affected by net income, distribution of stock dividends, and payment of long-term debt.

6.   Correct option: c
Fixed costs are the same costs for each fiscal period.

7.   Correct option: c
Healthcare organizations many times choose accrual accounting, so the date of service charges can be balanced out in the same fiscal period.

8.   Correct option: a
The tongue depressors can be considered a direct cost because they are directly used in the delivery of patient care.

9.   Correct options: b
The balance sheet accounting equation is Assets = Liabilities + Retained Equity.

10.   Correct options: d
Financial analysts use ratio analysis to determine the financial health of the healthcare organization.

Chapter 26

1. Correct option: b
   The health information profession was started in 1928.

2. Correct option: c
   Respect is the HIM professional value that shows an appreciation of contribution and collaboration to successfully protect and secure patient information.

3. Correct option: c
   The AHIMA Code of ethics principle that applies is Establish a framework for professional behavior and responsibilities when professional obligations conflict or ethical uncertainties arise.

4. Correct option: c
   Ethical decision making takes into context state laws, so the facility to retain records 10 years to meet the state standard.

5. Correct option: c
   Confidentiality is the principle of keeping patient information safe and preventing unauthorized access.

6. Correct option: d
   The ethics committee is responsible for determining the scope of the health information breach, reviewing ethical violations, and determining how to remedy the situation.

7. Correct option: A
   The most feasible option for the wheelchair user would be to lower the desk and bring some office machines within reach. Installing an elevator and moving the department operations to the first floor are expensive and not reasonable. Isolating the wheelchair user away from the department may be construed as discrimination.

8. Correct option: b
   In order to build trust, HIM professionals should undergo diversity awareness training to prevent prejudice, stereotyping, and bias.

9. Correct option: b
   Stereotyping makes assumptions that everyone in specific cultural categories have the same thoughts, behaviors, and habits.

10. Correct option: a
    A breach is a violation or patient information, either intentional or accidental.

Chapter 27

1. Correct option: a
   The data dictionary is established in the design phase of the database life cycle.

2. Correct option: c
   Relational databases are two or more databases that contain at least one common data element and that are seamlessly interoperable.

3. Correct option: d
   The data dictionary will include the format descriptions for all data elements in a database.

4. Correct option: c
   The Gantt chart includes the project activities and the timeline of the activities. Although many activities can have the exact same timeline, it is important to consult the PERT chart to confirm the project timeline.

5. Correct option: b
   The PERT chart graphically displays the interdependency of the activities of the project, whereas the Gantt chart displays the percent of the project completion.

6. Correct option: a
   Tracking project progress is not included in the design phase of the project management life cycle.

7. Correct option: d
   As the project plan is implemented, the project team may identify areas where significant change in the project objectives and activities may be needed.

8. Correct option: a
   Defining project objectives is part of the design phase of the project management life cycle.

9. Correct option: a
   The HIM department is very involved in training the medical staff to ensure accurate documentation standards and practices for all consultations.

10. Correct option: b
    Project costs are monitored in the tracking phase of the project management life cycle.

APPENDIX A

Formulas for Commonly Computed Healthcare Rates and Percentages

$$\text{Average Daily Census} = \frac{\text{Total service days for the unit for the period}}{\text{Total number of days in the period}}$$

$$\text{Average Length of Stay} = \frac{\text{Total length of stay (discharge days)}}{\text{Total discharges (including deaths)}}$$

$$\text{Percentage of Occupancy} = \frac{\text{Total service days for a period}}{\text{Total bed count days in the period}} \times 100$$

$$\text{Hospital Death Rate (Gross)} = \frac{\text{Number of deaths of inpatients in the period}}{\text{Number of discharges (including deaths)}} \times 100$$

$$\text{Hospital Death Rate (Net)} = \frac{\text{Inpatient deaths} < 48 \text{ hours}}{\text{Number of discharges (including deaths)} - \text{inpatient deaths} < 48 \text{ hours}} \times 100$$

$$\text{Gross Autopsy Rate} = \frac{\text{Total inpatient autopsies for a given period}}{\text{Total inpatient deaths for the period}} \times 100$$

$$\text{Net Autopsy Rate} = \frac{\text{Total inpatients for a given period}}{\text{Total inpatient deaths} - \text{Total unautopsied coroners'}} \times 100$$
$$\text{or medical examiners' cases}$$

$$\text{Hospital Autopsy Rate (Adjusted)} = \frac{\text{Total hospital autopsies}}{\text{Number of deaths of hospital patients whose}} \times 100$$
$$\text{bodies are available for hospital autopsy}$$

$$\text{Postoperative Death Rate} = \frac{\text{Postoperative deaths}}{\text{Number of people who die within 10 days of surgery}} \times 100$$

$$\text{Total number of intermediate and/or Fetal Death Rate} = \frac{\text{Total number of intermediate and/or late}}{\text{Total number of live births} + \text{intermediate and}} \times 1$$
$$\text{late fetal deaths for the period}$$

$$\text{Neonatal Mortality Rate (Death Rate)} = \frac{\text{Total number of newborn deaths for a period}}{\text{Total number of newborn infant discharges}} \times 100$$
$$\text{(including deaths) for the period}$$

$$\text{Maternal Mortality Rate (Death Rate)} = \frac{\text{Total number of obstetric maternal}}{\text{Total number of obstetric discharges}} \times 100$$
$$\text{(including deaths) for the period}$$

$$\text{Cesarean Section Rate} = \frac{\text{Total number of caesarean sections}}{\text{Total number of deliveries in the period}} \times 100$$
$$\text{(including caesarean sections)}$$

$$\text{Postoperative Infection Rate} = \frac{\text{Number of infections in clean}}{\text{Number of surgical operations}} \times 100$$
$$\text{in the period}$$

$$\text{Infection Rate} = \frac{\text{Number of infection occurences in a period}}{\text{Number of discharges in the period}}$$

APPENDIX B

Common Pharmaceuticals

Common Pharmaceuticals		
Generic Name	**Brand Name**	**Indications**
Albuterol	ProAir	Asthma, COPD
Alprazolam	Xanax	Anxiety, panic attacks
Amlodipine	Norvasc	Hypertension, coronary artery disease, angina
Amoxicillin	Amoxil	Bacterial infection
Atorvastatin	Lipitor	Hyperlipidemia, high cholesterol
Azithromycin	Zithromax	Bacterial infection
Budesonide	Pulmicort	Asthma
Cephalexin	Keflex	Bacterial infection
Cyclobenzaprine	Flexeril	Muscle spasm
Digoxin	Lanoxin	Atrial fibrillation, heart failure
Esomeprazole	Nexium	GERD
Fluoxetine	Prozac	Depressive disorders
Gabapentin	Neurontin	Epilepsy
Hydrochlorothiazide/ triamterene	Maxzide	Hypertension, edema

(continues)

Common Pharmaceuticals		*(continued)*
Generic Name	**Brand Name**	**Indications**
Hydrocodone	Vicodin	Severe pain
Levothyroxine	Synthroid	Hypothyroidism
Liraglutide	Victoza	Type 2 diabetes
Lisinopril	Zestril	Hypertension, heart failure, diabetic neuropathy
Memantine	Namenda	Alzheimer's disease
Methylphenidate	Concerta	Attention deficit-hyperactivity disorder
Metoprolol	Lopressor	Hypertension, angina pectoris, myocardial infarction
Prednisone	Deltasone	Severe allergic conditions
Rivaroxaban	Xarelto	Nonvalvular atrial fibrillation, deep vein thrombosis, pulmonary embolism
Sertraline	Zoloft	Major depressive disorder
Sitagliptin	Januvia	Type 2 diabetes
Tramadol	Ultram	Severe pain
Warfarin	Coumadin	Venous thrombosis, pulmonary edema, post-myocardial infarction, stroke
Zolpidem	Ambien	Insomnia

APPENDIX C

AHIMA Code of Ethics

The Code of Ethics and How to Interpret the Code of Ethics

Principles and Guidelines

The following ethical principles are based on the core values of the American Health Information Management Association and apply to all AHIMA members and certificants. Guidelines included for each ethical principle are a non-inclusive list of behaviors and situations that can help to clarify the principle. They are not meant to be a comprehensive list of all situations that can occur.

I. Advocate, uphold, and defend the individual's right to privacy and the doctrine of confidentiality in the use and disclosure of information.

A health information management professional **shall**:

1.1. Safeguard all confidential patient information to include, but not limited to, personal, health, financial, genetic, and outcome information.

1.2. Engage in social and political action that supports the protection of privacy and confidentiality, and be aware of the impact of the political arena on the health information issues for the healthcare industry.

1.3. Advocate for changes in policy and legislation to ensure protection of privacy and confidentiality, compliance, and other issues that surface as advocacy issues and facilitate informed participation by the public on these issues.

1.4. Protect the confidentiality of all information obtained in the course of professional service. Disclose only information that is directly relevant or necessary to achieve the purpose of disclosure. Release information only with valid authorization from a patient or a person legally authorized to consent on behalf of a patient or as authorized by federal or state regulations. The minimum necessary standard is essential when releasing health information for disclosure activities.

1.5. Promote the obligation to respect privacy by respecting confidential information shared among colleagues, while responding to requests from the legal profession, the media, or other non-healthcare related individuals, during presentations or teaching and in situations that could cause harm to persons.

1.6. Respond promptly and appropriately to patient requests to exercise their privacy rights (e.g., access, amendments, restriction, confidential communication, etc.). Answer truthfully all patients' questions concerning their rights to review and annotate their personal biomedical data and seek to facilitate patients' legitimate right to exercise those rights.

II. Put service and the health and welfare of persons before self-interest and conduct oneself in the practice of the profession so as to bring honor to oneself, peers, and to the health information management profession.

A health information management professional **shall**:

2.1. Act with integrity, behave in a trustworthy manner, elevate service to others above self-interest, and promote high standards of practice in every setting.

2.2. Be aware of the profession's mission, values, and ethical principles, and practice in a manner consistent with them by acting honestly and responsibly.

2.3. Anticipate, clarify, and avoid any conflict of interest, to all parties concerned, when dealing with consumers, consulting with competitors, in providing services requiring potentially conflicting roles (for example, finding out information about one facility that would help a competitor), or serving the Association in a volunteer capacity. The conflicting roles or responsibilities must be clarified and appropriate action taken to minimize any conflict of interest.

2.4. Ensure that the working environment is consistent and encourages compliance with the AHIMA Code of Ethics, taking reasonable steps to eliminate any conditions in their organizations that violate, interfere with, or discourage compliance with the code.

2.5.   Take responsibility and credit, including authorship credit, only for work they actually perform or to which they contribute. Honestly acknowledge the work of and the contributions made by others verbally or written, such as in publication.

A health information management professional **shall not**:

2.6.   Permit one's private conduct to interfere with the ability to fulfill one's professional responsibilities.

2.7.   Take unfair advantage of any professional relationship or exploit others to further one's own personal, religious, political, or business interests.

III.   Preserve, protect, and secure personal health information in any form or medium and hold in the highest regards health information and other information of a confidential nature obtained in an official capacity, taking into account the applicable statutes and regulations.

A health information management professional **shall**:

3.1.   Safeguard the privacy and security of written and electronic health information and other sensitive information. Take reasonable steps to ensure that health information is stored securely and that patients' data is not available to others who are not authorized to have access. Prevent inappropriate disclosure of individually identifiable information.

3.2.   Take precautions to ensure and maintain the confidentiality of information transmitted, transferred, or disposed of in the event of termination, incapacitation, or death of a healthcare provider to other parties through the use of any media.

3.3.   Inform recipients of the limitations and risks associated with providing services via electronic or social media (e.g., computer, telephone, fax, radio, and television).

IV.   Refuse to participate in or conceal unethical practices or procedures and report such practices.

A health information management professional **shall**:

4.1.   Act in a professional and ethical manner at all times.

4.2.   Take adequate measures to discourage, prevent, expose, and correct the unethical conduct of colleagues. If needed, utilize the Professional Ethics Committee Policies and Procedures for potential ethics complaints.

4.3.   Be knowledgeable about established policies and procedures for handling concerns about colleagues' unethical behavior. These include policies and procedures created by AHIMA, licensing and regulatory bodies, employers, supervisors, agencies, and other professional organizations.

4.4.   Seek resolution if there is a belief that a colleague has acted unethically or if there is a belief of incompetence or impairment by discussing one's concerns with the colleague when feasible and when such discussion is likely to be productive.

4.5.   Consult with a colleague when feasible and assist the colleague in taking remedial action when there is direct knowledge of a health information management colleague's incompetence or impairment.

4.6.   Take action through appropriate formal channels, such as contacting an accreditation or regulatory body and/or the AHIMA Professional Ethics Committee if needed.

4.7.   Cooperate with lawful authorities as appropriate.

A health information management professional **shall not**:

4.8.   Participate in, condone, or be associated with dishonesty, fraud and abuse, or deception. A non-inclusive list of examples includes:

- Allowing patterns of optimizing or minimizing documentation and/or coding to impact payment
- Assigning codes without physician documentation
- Coding when documentation does not justify the diagnoses or procedures that have been billed
- Coding an inappropriate level of service
- Miscoding to avoid conflict with others
- Engaging in negligent coding practices
- Hiding or ignoring review outcomes, such as performance data
- Failing to report licensure status for a physician through the appropriate channels
- Recording inaccurate data for accreditation purposes
- Allowing inappropriate access to genetic, adoption, health, or behavioral health information
- Misusing sensitive information about a competitor
- Violating the privacy of individuals

Refer to the <u>AHIMA Standards of Ethical Coding</u> for additional guidance.

4.9.   Engage in any relationships with a patient where there is a risk of exploitation or potential harm to the patient.

V. Advance health information management knowledge and practice through continuing education, research, publications, and presentations.

A health information management professional **shall**:

5.1. Develop and enhance continually professional expertise, knowledge, and skills (including appropriate education, research, training, consultation, and supervision). Contribute to the knowledge base of health information management and share one's knowledge related to practice, research, and ethics.

5.2. Base practice decisions on recognized knowledge, including empirically based knowledge relevant to health information management and health information management ethics.

5.3. Contribute time and professional expertise to activities that promote respect for the value, integrity, and competence of the health information management profession. These activities may include teaching, research, consultation, service, legislative testimony, advocacy, presentations in the community, and participation in professional organizations.

5.4. Engage in evaluation and research that ensures the confidentiality of participants and of the data obtained from them by following guidelines developed for the participants in consultation with appropriate institutional review boards.

5.5. Report evaluation and research findings accurately and take steps to correct any errors later found in published data using standard publication methods.

5.6. Design or conduct evaluation or research that is in conformance with applicable federal or state laws.

5.7. Take reasonable steps to provide or arrange for continuing education and staff development, addressing current knowledge and emerging developments related to health information management practice and ethics.

VI. Recruit and mentor students, staff, peers, and colleagues to develop and strengthen professional workforce.

A health information management professional **shall**:

6.1. Provide directed practice opportunities for students.

6.2. Be a mentor for students, peers, and new health information management professionals to develop and strengthen skills.

6.3. Be responsible for setting clear, appropriate, and culturally sensitive boundaries for students, staff, peers, colleagues, and members within professional organizations.

6.4. Evaluate students' performance in a manner that is fair and respectful when functioning as educators or clinical internship supervisors.

6.5. Evaluate staff's performance in a manner that is fair and respectful when functioning in a supervisory capacity.

6.6. Serve an active role in developing HIM faculty or actively recruiting HIM professionals.

A health information management professional **shall not**:

6.7. Engage in any relationships with a person (e.g. students, staff, peers, or colleagues) where there is a risk of exploitation or potential harm to that other person.

VII. Represent the profession to the public in a positive manner.
A health information management professional **shall**:

7.1. Be an advocate for the profession in all settings and participate in activities that promote and explain the mission, values, and principles of the profession to the public.

VIII. Perform honorably health information management association responsibilities, either appointed or elected, and preserve the confidentiality of any privileged information made known in any official capacity.
A health information management professional **shall**:

8.1. Perform responsibly all duties as assigned by the professional association operating within the bylaws and policies and procedures of the association and any pertinent laws.

8.2. Uphold the decisions made by the association.

8.3. Speak on behalf of the health information management profession and association, only while serving in the role, accurately representing the official and authorized positions of the association.

8.4. Disclose any real or perceived conflicts of interest.

8.5. Relinquish association information upon ending appointed or elected responsibilities.

8.6. Resign from an association position if unable to perform the assigned responsibilities with competence.

8.7. Avoid lending the prestige of the association to advance or appear to advance the private interests of others by endorsing any product or service in return for remuneration. Avoid endorsing products or services of a third party, for-profit entity that competes with AHIMA products and services. Care should **also** be exercised in endorsing any other products and services.

IX. State truthfully and accurately one's credentials, professional education, and experiences.

A health information management professional **shall**:

9.1. Make clear distinctions between statements made and actions engaged in as a private individual and as a representative of the health information management profession, a professional health information association, or one's employer.

9.2. Claim and ensure that representation to patients, agencies, and the public of professional qualifications, credentials, education, competence, affiliations, services provided, training, certification, consultation received, supervised experience, and other relevant professional experience are accurate.

9.3. Claim only those relevant professional credentials actually possessed and correct any inaccuracies occurring regarding credentials.

9.4. Report only those continuing education units actually earned for the recertification cycle and correct any inaccuracies occurring regarding CEUs.

X. Facilitate interdisciplinary collaboration in situations supporting health information practice.

A health information management professional **shall**:

10.1. Participate in and contribute to decisions that affect the well-being of patients by drawing on the perspectives, values, and experiences of those involved in decisions related to patients.

10.2. Facilitate interdisciplinary collaboration in situations supporting health information practice.

10.3. Establish clearly professional and ethical obligations of the interdisciplinary team as a whole and of its individual members.

10.4. Foster trust among group members and adjust behavior in order to establish relationships with teams.

XI. Respect the inherent dignity and worth of every person.

A health information management professional **shall**:

11.1 Treat each person in a respectful fashion, being mindful of individual differences and cultural and ethnic diversity.

11.2 Promote the value of self-determination for each individual.

11.3 Value all kinds and classes of people equitably, deal effectively with all races, cultures, disabilities, ages and genders.

11.4 Ensure all voices are listened to and respected.

http://bok.ahima.org/doc?oid=105098#.XMfsVi2ZN0s.

RHIT Examination Content Outline

Number of Questions on Exam:

> 150 multiple-choice questions (130 scored/20 pretest)
> Exam Time: 3.5 hours—Any breaks taken will count against your exam time

Domain 1

Data Analysis and Management (18%–22%)

Tasks:

1. Abstract information found in health records (i.e., coding, research, physician deficiencies, etc.).
2. Analyze data (i.e., productivity reports, quality measures, health record documentation, case mix index).
3. Maintain filing and retrieval systems for health records.
4. Identify anomalies in data.
5. Resolve risks and/or anomalies of data findings.
6. Maintain the master patient index (i.e., enterprise systems, merge/unmerge medical record numbers, etc.).
7. Eliminate duplicate documentation.
8. Organize data into a useable format.
9. Review trends in data.
10. Gather/compile data from multiple sources.
11. Generate reports or spreadsheets (i.e., customize, create, etc.).

12. Present data findings (i.e., study results, delinquencies, conclusion/summaries, gap analysis, graphical data).
13. Implement workload distribution.
14. Design workload distribution.
15. Participate in the data management plan (i.e., determine data elements, assemble components, set time-frame).
16. Input and/or submit data to registries.
17. Summarize findings from data research/analysis.
18. Follow data archive and backup policies.
19. Develop data management plan.
20. Calculate healthcare statistics (i.e., occupancy rates, length of stay, delinquency rates, etc.).
21. Determine validation process for data mapping.
22. Maintain data dictionaries.

Domain 2

Coding (16%–20%)

Tasks:

1. Apply all official current coding guidelines.
2. Assign diagnostic and procedure codes based on health record documentation.
3. Ensure physician documentation supports coding.
4. Validate code assignment.
5. Abstract data from health record.
6. Sequence codes.
7. Query physician when additional clinical documentation is needed.
8. Review and resolve coding edits (i.e., correct coding initiative, outpatient code editor, NCD, LCD, etc.).
9. Review the accuracy of abstracted data.
10. Assign POA (present on admission) indicators.
11. Provide educational updates to coders.
12. Validate grouper assignment (i.e., MS-DRG, APC, etc.).
13. Identify HAC (hospital-acquired condition).
14. Develop and manage a query process.
15. Create standards for coding productivity and quality.
16. Develop educational guidelines for provider documentation.
17. Perform concurrent audits.

Domain 3

Compliance (14%–18%)

Tasks:

1. Ensure patient record documentation meets state and federal regulations.
2. Ensure compliance with privacy and security guidelines (HIPAA, state, hospital, etc.).
3. Control access to health information.
4. Monitor documentation for completeness.
5. Develop a coding compliance plan (i.e., current coding guidelines).
6. Manage release of information.
7. Perform continual updates to policies and procedures.
8. Implement internal and external audit guidelines.
9. Evaluate medical necessity (CDMP—clinical documentation management program).
10. Collaborate with staff to prepare the organization for accreditation, licensing, and/or certification surveys.
11. Evaluate medical necessity (outpatient services).
12. Evaluate medical necessity (data management).
13. Respond to fraud and abuse.
14. Evaluate medical necessity (ISSI [utilization review]).
15. Develop forms (i.e., chart review, documentation, EMR, etc.).
16. Evaluate medical necessity (case management).
17. Analyze access audit trails.
18. Ensure valid healthcare provider credentials.

Domain 4

Information Technology (10%–14%)

Tasks:

1. Train users on software.
2. Maintain database.
3. Set up secure access.
4. Evaluate the functionality of applications.
5. Create user accounts.
6. Trouble-shoot HIM software or support systems.
7. Create database.
8. Perform end-user audits.
9. Participate in vendor selection.
10. Perform end-user needs analysis.
11. Design data archive and backup policies.

12.   Perform system maintenance of software and systems.
13.   Create data dictionaries.

Domain 5

Quality (10%–14%)

Tasks:

1.   Audit health records for content, completeness, accuracy, and timeliness.
2.   Apply standards, guidelines, and/or regulations to health records.
3.   Implement corrective actions as determined by audit findings (internal and external).
4.   Design efficient workflow processes.
5.   Comply with national patient safety goals.
6.   Analyze standards, guidelines, and/or regulations to build criteria for audits.
7.   Apply process improvement techniques.
8.   Provide consultation to internal and external users of health information on HIM subject matter.
9.   Develop reports on audit findings.
10. Perform data collection for quality reporting (core measures, PQRI, medical necessity, etc.).
11. Use trended data to participate in performance improvement plans/initiatives.
12. Develop a tool for collecting statistically valid data.
13. Conduct clinical pertinence reviews.
14. Monitor physician credentials to practice in the facility.

Domain 6

Legal (9%–13%)

Tasks:

1.   Ensure confidentiality of health records (paper and electronic).
2.   Adhere to disclosure standards and regulations (HIPAA privacy, HITECH Act, breach notifications, etc.) at both state and federal levels.
3.   Demonstrate and promote legal and ethical standards of practice.
4.   Maintain integrity of legal health record according to organizational bylaws, rules, and regulations.
5.   Follow state mandated and/or organizational record retention and destruction policies.
6.   Serve as the custodian of the health records (paper or electronic).

7. Respond to release of information (ROI) requests from internal and external requestors.
8. Work with risk management department to provide requested documentation.
9. Identify potential health record–related risk management issues through auditing.
10. Respond to and process patient amendment requests to the health record.
11. Facilitate basic education regarding the use of consents, healthcare power of attorney, advanced directives, DNRs, etc.
12. Represent the facility in court-related matters as they apply to the health record (subpoenas, depositions, court orders, warrants).

Domain 7

Revenue Cycle (9%–13%)

Tasks:

1. Communicate with providers to discuss documentation deficiencies (i.e., queries).
2. Participate in clinical documentation improvement programs to ensure proper documentation of health records.
3. Collaborate with other departments on monitoring accounts receivable (i.e., unbilled, uncoded).
4. Provide ongoing education to healthcare providers (i.e., regulatory changes, new guidelines, payment standards, best practices, etc.).
5. Identify fraud and abuse.
6. Assist with appeal letters in response to claim denials.
7. Monitor claim denials/over-payments to identify potential revenue impact.
8. Prioritize the work according to accounts receivable, patient type, etc.
9. Distribute the work according to accounts receivable, patient type, etc.
10. Maintain the chargemaster.
11. Ensure physicians are credentialed with different payers for reimbursement.

APPENDIX E

RHIA Exam Content Outline

Registered Health Information Administrator (RHIA) Examination Content Outline

Number of Questions on Exam:

180 multiple choice (160 scored/20 pretest)

Exam Time: 4 hours—Any breaks taken will count against your exam time

Domain 1

Data Content, Structure, and Standards (Information Governance) (18%–22%)

Tasks:

A. Classification Systems

   A1. Code diagnosis and procedures according to established guidelines.

B. Health Record Content and Documentation

   B1. Ensure accuracy and integrity of health data and health record documentation (paper or electronic).

   B2. Manage the contents of the legal health record (structured and unstructured).

   B3. Manage the retention and destruction of the legal health record.

C.   Data Governance

   C1.   Maintain data in accordance with regulatory requirements.

   C2.   Develop and maintain organizational policies, procedures, and guidelines for management of health information.

D.   Data Management and Secondary Data Sources

   D1.   Manage health data elements and/or data sets.

   D2.   Assist in the maintenance of the data dictionary and data models for database design.

   D3.   Manage and maintain databases (e.g., data migration, updates).

Domain 2

Information Protection: Access, Disclosure, Archival, Privacy, and Security (23%–27%)

Tasks:

A.   Health Law

   A1.   Maintain healthcare privacy and security training programs.

   A2.   Enforce and monitor organizational compliance with healthcare information laws, regulations, and standards (e.g., audit, report, and/or inform).

B.   Data Privacy, Confidentiality, and Security

   B1.   Design policies and implement privacy practices to safeguard protected health information.

   B2.   Design policies and implement security practices to safeguard protected health information.

   B3.   Investigate and resolve healthcare privacy and security issues/breaches.

C.   Release of Information

   C1.   Manage access, disclosure, and use of protected health information to ensure confidentiality.

   C2.   Develop policies and procedures for uses and disclosures/redisclosures of protected health information.

Domain 3

Informatics, Analytics, and Data Use (22%–26%)

Tasks:

A. Health Information Technologies

    A1. Implement and manage use of, and access to, technology applications.

    A2. Evaluate and recommend clinical, administrative, and specialty service applications (e.g., financial systems, electronic record, clinical coding).

B. Information Management Strategic Planning

    B1. Present data for organizational use (e.g., summarize, synthesize, and condense information).

C. Analytics and Decision Support

    C1. Filter and/or interpret information for the end customer.

    C2. Analyze and present information to organizational stakeholders.

    C3. Use data mining techniques to query and report from databases.

D. Healthcare Statistics

    D1. Calculate healthcare statistics for organizational stakeholders.

    D2. Critically analyze and interpret healthcare statistics for organizational stakeholders (e.g., CMI).

E. Research Methods

    E1. Identify appropriate data sources for research.

F. Consumer Informatics

    F1. Identify and/or respond to the information needs of internal and external healthcare customers.

    F2. Provide support for end-user portals and personal health records.

G. Health Information Exchange

    G1. Apply data and functional standards to achieve interoperability of healthcare information systems.

    G2. Manage the health information exchange process entity-wide.

H.   Information Integrity and Data Quality

  H1.   Apply data/record storage principles and techniques associated with the medium (e.g., paper-based, hybrid, electronic).

  H2.   Manage master person index (e.g., patient record integration, customer–client relationship management).

  H3.   Manage merge process for duplicates and other errors entity-wide (e.g., validate data sources).

Domain 4

Revenue Management (12%–16%)

Tasks:

A.   Revenue Cycle and Reimbursement

  A1.   Manage the use of clinical data required in reimbursement systems and prospective payment systems (PPS).

  A2.   Optimize reimbursement through management of the revenue cycle (e.g., chargemaster maintenance, DNFB, and AR days).

B.   Regulatory

  B1.   Prepare for accreditation and licensing processes (e.g., Joint Commission, Det Norske Veritas [DNV], Medicare, state regulators).

  B2.   Process audit requests (e.g., RACs or other payors, chart review).

  B3.   Perform audits (e.g., chart review, POC).

C.   Coding

  C1.   Manage and/or validate coding accuracy.

D.   Fraud Surveillance

  D1.   Participate in investigating incidences of medical identity theft.

E.   Clinical Documentation Improvement

  E1.   Query physicians for appropriate documentation to support reimbursement.

  E2.   Educate and train clinical staff regarding supporting documentation requirements.

Domain 5

Leadership (12%–16%)

Tasks:

A. Leadership Roles

    A1. Develop, motivate, and support work teams and/or individuals (e.g., coaching, mentoring).

    A2. Organize and facilitate meetings.

    A3. Advocate for department, organization, and/or profession.

B. Change Management

    B1. Participate in the implementation of new processes (e.g., systems, EHR, CAC).

    B2. Support changes in the organization (e.g., culture changes, HIM consolidations, outsourcing).

C. Work Design and Process Improvement

    C1. Establish and monitor productivity standards.

    C2. Analyze and design workflow processes.

    C3. Participate in the development and monitoring of process improvement plans.

D. Human Resources Management

    D1. Perform human resource management activities (e.g., recruiting staff, creating job descriptions, resolving personnel issues).

E. Training and Development

    E1. Conduct training and educational activities (e.g. HIM systems, coding, medical and institutional terminology, documentation, and regulatory requirements).

F. Strategic and Organizational Management

    F1. Monitor industry trends and organizational needs to anticipate changes.

    F2. Determine resource needs by performing analyses (e.g., cost benefit, business planning).

    F3. Assist with preparation of capital budget.

G. Financial Management

    G1. Assist in preparation and management of operating and personnel budgets.

    G2. Assist in the analysis and reporting on budget variances.

H.   Ethics

H1. Adhere to the AHIMA code of ethics.

I.   Project Management

I1.   Utilize appropriate project management methodologies.

J.   Vendor/Contract Management

J1.   Evaluate and manage contracts (e.g., vendor, contract personnel, maintenance).

K.   Enterprise Information Management

K1. Develop and support strategic and operational plans for entity-wide health information management.

Glossary

Abstracting The information management process of extracting information from the health record to create a brief summary of the patient's illness, treatment, and outcome.

Abuse Healthcare practices that either directly or indirectly undermine efforts to provide cost-effective, medically necessary, and high-quality healthcare services.

Access control Policies and procedures implemented to ensure that only authorized healthcare stakeholders have access to protected health information on a need-to-know basis.

Accountable care organizations (ACOs) A group of providers, healthcare facilities, and other members of the healthcare team who work together voluntarily to deliver coordinated high-quality care to Medicare patients; the goal is to ensure that patients receive the care needed at the right time while avoiding duplicate services and preventing medical errors.

Accreditation A determination given to a healthcare facility based on its voluntarily reaching healthcare delivery and medical record documentation standards by an accrediting organization.

Accrual accounting A recording process by which transactions are recorded in the appropriate time period before cash payments are expected or due.

Additional document request (ADR) An official request for additional documents for a specific patient's medical record from the recovery audit contractor (RAC), supported by the Centers for Medicare and Medicaid Services (CMS).

Adjustments The difference between the amount charged and the contracted health insurance payment that is written off; this amount is not billed to the patient directly.

Administrative safeguards Administrative actions, policies, and procedures to develop a security program to protect electronic health information and to manage the conduct of all covered entities and business associates handling access to private health information.

Administrative simplification Amended by HITECH, authorizes Health and Human Services (HHS) to (1) adopt standards for transactions and code sets that are used to exchange health data; (2) adopt standard identifiers for health plans, healthcare providers, employers, and individuals for use on standard transactions; and (3) adopt standards to protect the security and privacy of personally identifiable health information.

ADT system admission-transfer-discharge systems (ADT) that is used to manage patient census for a healthcare facility.

Advanced beneficiary notice (ABN) A Medicare waiver of liability form issued used to inform Medicare beneficiaries of services that are not covered by their insurance plan.

Affinity grouping An information analytics technique used for organizing ideas into relatable groups.

Affordable Care Act (ACA) Federal legislation passed in 2009 that changed health insurance eligibility for all Americans by eliminating preexisting conditions for all and by extending the age for dependent coverage to 26.

Agency for Healthcare Research and Quality (AHRQ) A branch of the U.S. Public Health Services that endorses general health research with the goal of improving the quality, appropriateness, and effectiveness of health care.

Agenda An outline of discussion topics, decisions, and progress updates that is distributed prior to a team or project meeting.

Aggregate data Data extracted and deidentified from the patient health record that is used for comparison and analysis.

AHIMA CDI toolkit A list of activities designed by AHIMA to support clinical documentation improvement (CDI) for the healthcare facility.

AHIMA Code of Ethics   A code of ethics that focuses on the ethical implications of medical coding, medical billing, documentation standards, and the management of protected health information.

All-Patient-defined Diagnosis-related Groups (APR-DRGs) System   The extension of the DRG inpatient classification system that includes four distinct classifications (minor, moderate, major, and extreme) based on the severity of a patient's health condition; classifications are assigned with severity of illness (SOI) and risk of mortality (ROM) indicators.

Allocated cost   An expense that is directly related to the delivery of patient care.

Alphabetic filing system   A filing and storage system used for paper medical records that uses the patient's last name alphabetically, with the first name providing additional filing guidance.

Ambulatory care   Health care delivered in an outpatient facility.

Ambulatory Payment Classification (APC)   The prospective payment system classification, which is a resource-based reimbursement system; the payment unit is the ambulatory payment classification group (APC group).

American Association for Accreditation of Ambulatory Surgery Facilities (AAAASF)   The organization that provides accreditation for ambulatory surgery centers.

American College of Surgeons (ASC)   A scientific and educational association formed to improve the quality of surgical care by setting high standards for surgical education and practice.

American Correctional Association (ACA)   An association that supports documentation standards for correctional facilities in the United States.

American Health Information Management Association (AHIMA)   A professional membership organization for managers of health record services, healthcare information systems, and medical coding services; the interest group also provides accreditation, advocacy, certification, and educational services.

American Osteopathic Association (AOA)   The medical association that certifies healthcare professionals for doctors of osteopathy.

American Recovery and Reinvestment Act of 2009 (ARRA)   The federal mandates related to health information technology are spread throughout the law; however, the bulk of these items are in Title XIII-Health Information Technology.

Americans with Disabilities Act (ADA)   Federal legislation that endorses equal opportunity for and elimination of discrimination against individuals with disabilities.

Analysis   Querying the electronic medical record to ensure adherence to documentation and accreditation standards.

ANSI X12   The standards used to electronically transfer health information through electronic data interchange (EDI).

Anti-kickback statute   A federal statute that supports penalties for any individual and/or business that knowingly and willfully offers, pays, solicits, or receives an incentive in order to increase business.

Appeal   An official request in writing for the health insurance claim payment to be re-considered.

Assembly   The process of organizing a paper medical record into a facility-established format in order to determine any deficiencies.

Asset   Something with economic value that an individual, corporation, or country owns or controls with the expectation that it will provide a future benefit; often reported on the balance sheet.

Audit controls   An electronic mechanism that records all of the different patient records and pages visited in the electronic health record.

Audit trails   A list of all patient health record pages visited by a user, which is used to determine security violations.

Authentication   An electronic proof of authorship attached to each physician's order that ensures the source of the health record entry.

Authoritarian leadership   A leadership style in which the leader dictates and controls all decisions in the group or team.

Authorization   The granting of permission to disclose confidential information; as defined in terms of the HIPAA Privacy Rule, an individual's formal, written permission to use or disclose his or her personally identifiable health information for purposes other than treatment, payment, or healthcare operation.

Authorized users   Users of healthcare information in a facility who have been approved to access the patient health record.

Autonomy An ethical principle that recognizes the patient's right to determine what health care is delivered to them.

Average daily census The arithmetic mean of the number of hospital inpatients admitted to the hospital each day or for a given period.

Average length of stay (ALOS) The arithmetic mean length of stay for hospital inpatients discharged during a given period of time.

Balance sheet A financial statement that represents the accounting formula: assets = liabilities + owner's equity.

Bar chart A chart that uses bars of varying length to represent data graphically.

Barcode medication administration record (BC-MAR) Health information system that uses barcoding technology to identify the correct patient in order to deliver medications accurately in the inpatient setting.

BASIC A computer programming language that performs according to a list of commands.

Bed count The number of inpatient beds set up and staffed for use on a given day.

Bed count day A unit of measure that denotes the presence of one inpatient bed (either occupied or vacant) set up and staffed for use in one 24-hour period.

Bed turnover rate The average number of times a bed swaps occupants during a given period of time.

Behavior theory A leadership theory whose advocates believe that successful leadership traits are learnable behaviors.

Benchmark The methodical comparison of the quality of healthcare delivery between similar and comparable organizations.

Benchmarking The process of methodically comparing the quality of healthcare delivery between similar and comparable organizations.

Bias A behavior trait that advocates partiality and/or prejudice.

Birth defects registry A registry of patients born with a major genetic defect that causes structural changes in one or more body parts.

Board of directors A group of elected or appointed officials who bear the ultimate responsibility for the success of the healthcare facility.

Brainstorming A team problem-solving technique that involves all members spontaneously sharing ideas.

Breach Under the HITECH Act, the acquisition, access, use, or disclosure of protected health information in a manner not permitted, which compromises the security or privacy of protected health information.

Breach notifications HITECH Act rule that requires both HIPAA-covered entities and business associates to identify unsecured PHI breaches and notify the involved parties of the breach.

Budget adjustment Approval from the finance department to move funds from one department budget to another.

Budget variance The difference between the amount budgeted for revenue and the actual expensed amount for a period.

Business associates (BA) A person or organization other than a member of a covered entity that performs functions or activities on behalf of or affecting a covered entity that involves the use or disclosure of protected health information. Involved activities can include claims processing (including medical coding, billing, and collection), administration, data analysis, utilization review, quality assurance, patient safety activities, and practice management.

Business continuity plan A plan established by the health information department of a facility that provides instructions on how to continue daily business operations in case of loss of EHR access.

Bylaws Operating documents that outline the rules and regulations of the healthcare facility.

C-suite executives Members of the board of directors that include the COO, CFO, CIO, and the CEO.

Cancer registry A database designed for the collection, management, and data analysis for patients who were diagnosed with a malignant or neoplastic disease.

Capital budget A financial planning process that plans and strategies long-term investment strategies.

Capitation A method of healthcare reimbursement in which an insurance carrier prepays a physician, hospital, or other healthcare provider a fixed amount per patient for a given population without regard to the actual number or nature of healthcare services provided to the population.

Case management An open-ended concurrent review of the necessity and effectiveness of healthcare services delivered to the patient.

Case mix index (CMI) The average relative weight of all cases treated in a given facility or provider; the index indicates the intensity of resource used or the clinical severity of a specific group in relation to other groups in the classification systems.

Cash-basis accounting Transactions are recorded when they occur to reflect that money has been received for services provided directly.

Cause-specific death rate The total number of deaths due to a specific illness during a given time period divided by the estimated population for the same time period.

Census The number of inpatients present in a healthcare facility on a single day at the same time daily.

Centers for Disease Control (CDC) A federal agency dedicated to protecting health and promoting quality of life through the prevention and control of disease, injury, and disability.

Centers for Medicare and Medicaid Services (CMS) A federal agency sponsored by the Department of Health and Human Services that provides health insurance coverage for American citizens 65 or older, permanently disabled individuals, and patients with end-stage renal disease.

Certificate of destruction A document that gives proof that a health record was destroyed and that includes the method of destruction, the signature of the person responsible for destruction, and inclusive dates for destruction.

Certification The process of receiving approval from an authorized organization that evaluates and recognizes the institution for meeting specific established standards.

Certification Commission on Health Information Technology (CCHIT) A commission whose effort was initiated by the private sector to evaluate and potentially test EHR products against specific criteria, drawn from the HL7 standard EHR system functionality.

Certified tumor registrar (CTR) An earned credential from the National Board for Certification of Registrars (NBCR); candidates must meet the eligibility requirements, which include a combination of experience and education.

CHAMPVA The federal health insurance benefit program for dependents or veterans having a total and permanent disability, or survivors of veterans who died in military service.

Chargemaster A financial management report that contains information about the healthcare organization's charges for the services it provides to patients.

Chief Executive Officer (CEO) The senior manager appointed by the board of directors, who directs the healthcare facility's long-term strategic planning.

Chief Financial Officer (CFO) The c-suite manager responsible for the overall financial management of the healthcare organization.

Chief Information Officer (CIO) The c-suite manager responsible for the overall health information management of the healthcare organization.

Chief Operation Officer (COO) The c-suite manager responsible for the overall operations of the healthcare organization.

Children's Health Insurance Program (CHIP) A state-sponsored program that provides health coverage to lower-income children whose parents make too much money to qualify for Medicaid.

Claim denials Insurance claim denial by the health insurance for reasons listed and explained on the explanation of benefits (EOB).

Classification systems A clinical vocabulary, terminology, or nomenclature that provides a list of words or phrases with their code descriptions; used to standardize terms.

Clearinghouse An entity positioned in the middle between the healthcare facility submitting the insurance claim and the health insurance company that is accepting the claim.

Clinical coding The process of assigning numeric or alphanumeric classifications to diagnostic and procedural statements.

Clinical data analytics A method of capturing data, reviewed and evaluated for effectiveness and necessity.

Clinical decision support (CDS) The activity that occurs when individual data elements are symbolized by a special code that is then used to make comparisons, identify trends, and create clinical reminders and alerts.

Clinical decision support system (CDSS) The information system that supports clinical decision activity by providing feedback to alert the appropriate information systems.

Clinical documentation improvement (CDI) A documentation evaluation program that is used in healthcare facilities to regularly monitor whether documentation meets AHIMA standards, and whether the policies and procedures adhere to the facility's bylaws.

Clinical documentation improvement (CDI) metrics Metrics, or ratios, that reflect clinical documentation improvement successes; these ratios include the case mix index (CMI), review rate, query rate, response rate, and the response time.

Clinical privileges The permission given by the healthcare facility's board of governors that enables a physician to provide patient care within the organization within specific practice limits.

Clinical protocols Specific instructions for performing clinical procedures, which are established by authoritative bodies of the healthcare facility.

Clinical trials An experimental study in which there are two groups, a control group and an experimental group. The goal is to determine whether the treatment delivered to the experimental group affects the health condition of that group's members positively.

Clinical vocabularies A structured list of terms designed to standardize the care and treatment of patients.

CMS 1450 form (UB-04) A paper health insurance claim form that is used by inpatient and outpatient hospitals to report services for procedures; uses ICD-10-PCS and HCPCS codes.

CMS 1500 form The universal paper insurance claim form developed and approved by the American Medical Association and the Centers for Medicare and Medicaid Services; physicians use it to bill Medicare, Medicaid, and private insurers for services provided.

COBOL A computer programming language used for data processing.

Coding Clinic A quarterly newsletter published by the American Hospital Association's central office, which is used to code complex medical cases.

Coding compliance plan The goals of the coding compliance plan should be to have improved documentation in the medical record, maintain high coding standards in accuracy and timeliness, and reduce health insurance claim denials based on coding errors.

Coinsurance The patient financial responsibility assigned by the health insurance contract, which is a percentage up to a cap amount that is paid after the insurance plan has paid.

Commission for the Accreditation of Birth Centers An accreditation association that establishes documentation standards for birthing centers in the United States.

Commission on Accreditation of Rehabilitation Facilities (CARF) An accreditation association that establishes documentation and care standards for rehabilitation centers in the United States.

Commission on Cancer (CoC) A program of the American College of Surgeons (ACS); it recognizes cancer care programs for their commitment to providing comprehensive, high-quality, and multidisciplinary patient-centered care.

Comparative data Data that is organized numerically and collated to make comparisons and benchmarks.

Complaint A written legal statement from a plaintiff that initiates a lawsuit.

Compliance A corporate culture that promotes the prevention, detection, and resolution of irregular practices.

Compliance officer A corporate official in charge of overseeing and managing compliance issues within an organization, ensuring, for example, that a company is complying with regulatory requirements and that the company and its employees are complying with internal policies and procedures.

Computer-assisted coding (CAC) Utilizes natural language processing (NLP) and algorithmic software to electronically analyze entire medical charts to pre-code with both CPT procedures and ICD-9 diagnostic nomenclatures.

Concurrent review The process of continually monitoring a patient's medical record during their hospital stay for medical necessity and the appropriateness of care delivered.

Conditions of participation (CoP) The administrative and operational rules and regulations governing the eligibility of an entity to become a participating provider with Medicare and Medicaid.

Confidentiality The principle that the healthcare professionals are ethically obligated to protect and secure private patient information.

Conflict management A problem-solving technique that endorses working with different individuals to find mutually acceptable compromises.

Consent A means for patients to convey to healthcare providers their implied or expressed permission to administer care or treatment or to perform surgery or other medical procedures.

Consultation rate The total number of hospital inpatients receiving consultations for a given period divided by the total number of discharges and deaths in the same period.

Consumer informatics An industry dedicated to technologies that provide consumers access to their personal health records.

Consumer-mediated exchange Consumer-mediated exchange allows patients to manage their healthcare information online just as they would manage their finances with online banking.

Contingency and disaster planning An essential planning process that incorporates policies and procedures for continuing business operations during a computer system shutdown; sometimes called business continuity plan.

Continuous Quality Improvement (CQI) A program used to improve the quality of care delivered by identifying problems, implementing and monitoring corrective actions, and studying their effectiveness.

Controlling A management function in which team performance is monitored according to facility policies and procedures.

Coordination of benefits A procedure used to determine the financial responsibilities when a patient has more than one health plan.

Copayment The patient's financial responsibility assigned by the health insurance contract, which is a set amount and is paid prior to consultation.

Core clinical EHR systems The Institute of Medicine identifies eight core EHR functions: health information and data, result management, order management, decision support, electronic communication and connectivity, patient support, administrative processes and reporting, and reporting and population health.

Corporate compliance The effort made to ensure a healthcare facility meets regulations and standards established by accreditation and/or certification organizations.

Corrective controls Controls that are designed to correct errors or risks and prevent future errors.

Correlation coefficient A statistical measure that calculates the strength of the relationship between two separate variables.

Correlational studies A study tool used in data analysis for research and to make conclusions.

Cost accounting An accounting method that includes all costs incurred during the delivery of healthcare services to determine accurate pricing.

Covered entities According to the HIPAA Privacy Rule, any health plan, healthcare clearinghouse, or healthcare provider that transmits specific healthcare transactions in electronic form that must adhere to the standard of health information transmission established by HIPAA.

Crude birth rate The number of live births divided by the total population at risk over a given period of time.

Crude death/mortality rate The total number of deaths in a given population for a given period of time divided by the estimated population for the same period of time.

Cultural competence A trait that enhances the ability to understand, communicate with, and effectively interact with people from different cultural backgrounds.

Cultural diversity A corporate culture that encourages tolerance of all cultural backgrounds in the workplace.

Current Procedural Terminology (CPT) A medical code set that is used to report professional and technical procedures for entities such as physicians, health insurance companies, and accreditation organizations.

Daily inpatient census The number of inpatients present at census-taking time each day, plus any inpatients who were both admitted and discharged after census-taking time the previous day.

Data analysis The process of evaluating aggregate data to make concluding information for decision making.

Data capture The process of collecting data through the definition of elements in the data dictionary.

Data dashboard A health information tool that is used as a visual aid in the EHR, which displays key indicators such as recent vital recordings or patient allergies.

Data dictionary A list of key terms that define the data in the database.

Data Elements for Emergency Department Systems (DEEDS) The uniform data elements collected through the delivery of care of the emergency room.

Data fields The smallest area in which data can be stored; the location is defined by the column and row of the database.

Data integrity A security principle that ensures the extent to which healthcare data is complete, accurate, consistent, and timely.

Data provisioning The process of making data available in an orderly and secure way to EHR users and applications.

Data sets A collection of related sets of data composed of separate data elements, which can be manipulated as a unit through query.

Data visualization A graphical representation of data and/or information.

Database A structured set of data that can be manipulated and then analyzed to make informational conclusions.

Decision support system A set of related databases required to assist with analysis and decision making within an organization.

Decision tree query A tool that uses a series of questions to deduce accurate and specific codes.

Deductible The amount set annually for which the patient is financially responsible before the health insurance pays the claim for medical services rendered.

Deemed status An official designation offered to healthcare organizations that meet minimum standards of participation, which is used to become a participating provider with Medicare.

Deeming authorities Organizations that establish standards for conditions of participation and that issue deeming status for well-qualified healthcare organizations.

Defendant The party against whom a case is brought. In a civil case, the civil complaint is made against the defendant; in a criminal case, the defendant is the party accused of a crime.

Deficiencies Missing elements from the healthcare record that need to be resolved before becoming a legal record (e.g., missing signatures).

Deidentified information Healthcare information from which personal identifying data elements have been removed; information that is commonly used for secondary data purposes such as research or education.

Democratic leadership A leadership style in which the leader is in support of decision-making processes and choices from the team.

Department of Health and Human Services (DHHS) A cabinet-level federal agency with the responsibility to protect and enhance the health of all Americans.

Dependent variable A statistical term in which the result is directly dependent on the independent variable.

Deposition A method of information discovery and collection used in the litigation process of a court case.

Descriptive analytics A set of statistical techniques used to describe data, such as the mean, mode, frequency distributions, and standard deviations.

Destruction The process of demolishing a health record so it is no longer legible, such as by shredding or magnetic degaussing.

Diagnosis-related group (DRG) A unit of case-mix classification developed by Medicare as a prospective payment system for inpatient patients.

Diagnostic analytics A set of statistical techniques used to study the patient through the collection of patient history, physical, laboratory, X-rays, and other medical tests.

Diagnostic and Statistical Manual of Mental Disorders (DSM-V) The code set used for mental health disorders.

Digital Image and Communications in Medicine (DICOM) An ISO standard that uses a digital image communications format and the picture archive and communications system for use with digital images.

Disciplinary action An administrative action used to improve the substandard employee work performance.

Discrete data Data that represents separate, distinct, specific, finite values.

Disease index An index that organizes admitting diagnoses from patient admissions during a particular time period.

Disease management process A healthcare system of coordinated healthcare interventions and communications for defined patient populations with conditions where self-care efforts can be implemented.

Disease registry A centralized data collection system used to improve the quality of care and measure the effectiveness of a therapeutic care.

Distal attributes Division of leadership traits that include personality, cognitive abilities, and values that define the leader as a person.

Diversity awareness Training delivered by the human resources department that encourages the acceptance of a variety of different cultures, races, ages, sexes, and disabilities.

Duplicate medical record number Occurs when a patient is assigned an additional medical record number when one has already been assigned; each patient should have only one medical record number per healthcare facility.

Effectiveness of health care Assessment of health care delivered to the patient to ensure the improvement of quality of life.

Electronic data interchange (EDI) A standard of data transmission that uses strings of data and links to communicate with various healthcare entities.

Electronic Health Record (EHR) An electronic record of patient health that conforms to nationally recognized interoperability standards and that can be created, managed, and consulted by authorized clinicians and staff within the healthcare organization.

Encoder Specialty software used for medical coding assignment based on coding guidelines.

Encryption The process of transforming data electronically into an unintelligible string of characters that can be transmitted via communications media with a high degree of security and then decrypted when it reaches a secure destination.

Epidemiologist Public health research professional who investigates the causes of disease and injury in humans.

Equal Employment Opportunity Commission (EEOC) A federal agency that administers and enforces civil rights laws against workplace discrimination.

Equity An accounting term that refers to the financial ownership of the healthcare facility.

Ethics committee A committee assigned to review clinical ethical violations to verify the courses of action required to alleviate those violations.

Ethnography A research method that investigates ethnicity in relation to race-specific diseases.

Evaluation The last stage in the information system implementation process that examines the successes and failure of the implementation.

Exclusive Provider Organization (EPO) A hybrid managed care organization that has a mix of the features of a health maintenance organization (HMO) and a preferred provider organization (PPO) that provides benefits to subscribers by an in-network provider.

Executive information systems (EIS) Information systems geared to meet the needs of executives of the healthcare facility.

Executive management Senior management employees of the healthcare organization who make strategic decisions for the facility.

Expense An accounting term that refers to the amounts charged as operational costs.

Experimental studies A study tool to establish the cause and effect of healthcare cases.

Expert system Software system that uses a database of expert knowledge to assist healthcare professionals in making decisions about patient care.

Explanation of Benefits (EOBs) A statement issued by the patient's health insurance that explains the insurance payment, the amount adjusted, and the patient's financial obligation.

External analysis An evaluation of the external environment to determine opportunities and threats to a healthcare organization.

External customer Individuals and businesses from outside a healthcare organization who receive services and products from within the organization.

Fair Labor Standards Act (FLSA) Federal legislation that establishes the minimum wage and overtime payment standards and practices for all employers in the United States.

False Claims Act Federal legislation that prohibits the filing of false health insurance claims to a government program; used to prevent healthcare fraud and abuse.

Family and Medical Leave Act (FMLA) Federal legislation that allows full-time employees up to 12 weeks' time off to care for themselves or family members without losing their position at work.

Fetal autopsy rate The number of autopsies performed on intermediate and late fetal deaths over a given time period divided by the total number of intermediate and late fetal deaths for the same time period.

Financial data Data collected that is related to the revenue and expenses of the healthcare facility.

Financial plan The development of a financial strategy to meet the constraints of a department's healthcare facility budget.

Financial statements A collection of accounting reports, including the balance sheet, income statement, and statement of cash flow, used to determine the financial status of a healthcare facility.

Firewall A computer defense system (including hardware and software) that provides a security barrier and/or supports an access control policy between two networks.

Fishbone diagram A performance improvement tool used to categorize the root causes of areas that need improvement.

Flex time A work schedule that allows employees to choose a pattern of work time differing from 8 am to 5 pm, Monday through Friday.

Food and Drug Administration (FDA) A federal agency that works under the U.S. Department of Health and Human Services (DHHS) that monitors the use of drugs and food for safe and appropriate consumption.

Forecasting An accounting technique that uses historical financial data to make future financial decisions.

Fraud The unethical and criminal practice of filing health insurance claims for services that were not rendered to the patient.

Fraud surveillance The process involved with monitoring activity in order to prevent fraud.

Full-time equivalent employee (FTE) A statistic representing the number of full-time employees as calculated by the reported number of hours worked by all employees, excluding part-time employees.

Gantt chart A project management tool used to display the time duration of activities involved in bringing project tasks to completion.

Gatekeeper The primary care physician responsible to care for the patient and refer to specialist care if a need presents; used to control costs of healthcare delivery.

Genetic Information Nondiscrimination Act (GINA) Federal legislation that prohibits health insurance companies and employers from discriminating on the basis of the results of genetic tests.

Gross autopsy rate The number of inpatient autopsies conducted during a given time period divided by the number of inpatient deaths for the same time period.

Gross death rate The number of inpatient deaths that occurred during a given time period divided by the total number of inpatient discharges, including deaths, for the same time period.

Grounded theory A management theory that focuses on current happenings instead of what should be happening.

Grouper A software application that assigns prospective payment groups based on the diagnosis codes assigned.

Health Care Finance Administration (HCFA) A federal agency sponsored by the Department of Health and Human Services that administers Medicare and Medicaid government insurance programs.

Health Care Fraud Prevention and Enforcement Action Team (HEAT) A joint initiative between HHS, OIG, and DOJ to prevent fraud and abuse in medical reimbursement.

Health informatics A computer science that uses information technology to analyze health records to improve patient healthcare outcomes.

Health information exchange (HIE) The electronic exchange of health information between providers within a collective group that maintains the same level of interoperability.

Health Information Portability and Accountability Act of 1996 (HIPAA) The federal legislation enacted to provide continuity of health coverage, control fraud and abuse in health care, reduce health costs, and guarantee the security and privacy of health information.

Health Information Technology for Economic and Clinical Health (HITECH) The federal legislation that updated the HIPAA federal law to improve the use of electronic health data in the healthcare delivery process.

Health Level 7 (HL7) A set of international standards used to transfer health information data and information between approved software applications used by a variety of healthcare providers.

Health maintenance organization (HMO) A managed care model that organizes the delivery of health care from a primary care physician, who is also known as the gatekeeper.

Healthcare Common Procedure Coding System (HCPCS)   Standardized code sets that are necessary for Medicare and other health insurance providers to report medical supplies, transport, drugs, and a variety of other healthcare services.

Healthcare Effectiveness Data and Information Set (HEDIS) A performance measurement tool used by health insurance companies to measure the effectiveness of care delivered to the patient.

Healthy People 2020 A community program that establishes health goals for the public every 10 years, which are used to attain high-quality, longer lives free of preventable disease, disability, injury, and premature death.

HIPAA X12 837i An electronic health insurance claim standard for reporting the data set collected by the CMB-1450 form (UB-04) used by healthcare institutions such as inpatient hospitals and ambulatory surgery centers.

HIPAA X12 837p An electronic health insurance claim standard for reporting the data set collected by the CMB-1500 form used by healthcare professionals.

Histogram A statistical presentation tool used to display the frequency distribution of continuous data.

Home Health Prospective Payment System (HHPPS) The prospective payment system classification used specifically for home healthcare facilities.

Hospital (nosocomial) infection rate The number of infections that occur in a hospital's various patient care units on a continuous basis.

Hospital-acquired condition (HAC) A health ailment that a patient acquired while hospitalized that could have been preventable.

Hospital autopsy rate The total number of autopsies performed by a hospital pathologist for a given time period divided by the number of deaths of hospital patients (inpatients and outpatients) whose bodies were available for autopsy for the same time period.

Hospital death rate The number of inpatient deaths for a given period of time divided by the total number of live discharges and deaths for the same period of time.

Hospital inpatient A patient who has been admitted at least one night in the hospital.

Hospital outpatient A patient who either had surgery at a hospital or visited the emergency room, but is not admitted and does not spend the night there.

HTML A computer language that is the standard markup language for creating webpages.

Human resources A department in the healthcare facility that manages the needs of all employees and ensures the enforcement of all federal worker laws.

Hybrid health record A patient health record that is made up of paper and electronic elements.

Hyperlink Transfer Protocol (HTTP) A protocol used by the World Wide Web (www) that transfers HTML files across the Internet.

ICD-10-CM A medical code set that is used to report diagnosis for all healthcare encounters.

ICD-10-PCS A medical code set that is used to report only inpatient procedures; can be used for procedures that occur in ambulatory surgery centers and inpatient hospitals.

ICD-O-3 Also known as the International Classification of Disease for Oncology, a medical coding set that identifies the classifications of neoplasms.

Immunization registry A nationwide registry of patients who have been immunized for various deadly diseases; the registry allows for providers to access the information even though they did not administer the vaccine themselves.

Implementation A stage of the health information technology in which the planned and designed application is put into practice in the healthcare facility.

Implied consent Permission for healthcare treatment that is assumed by the provider and the caregiver because the patient is not conscious to give consent.

Incidence rate A computation that compares the number of new cases of a specific disease over a given time period to the population at risk for the disease during the same time period.

Incident report A quality tool used to report a breach of health information and/or an occurrence in which a patient was injured because quality health care was not delivered.

Income statement A financial report used to identify income and expenses for a healthcare facility.

Independent variable The factor used to manipulate an experimental study to obtain credible results.

Index An organized table that includes specific data related to the subject, such as disease, physician, etc.

Indian Health Service (IHS) A government payer that provides health insurance coverage to American Indians and Alaska natives.

Infant mortality rate The number of deaths of individuals younger than 1 year of age during a given time period divided by the number of live births recorded for that same time period.

Inferential statistics Statistics that are used to make conclusions about a larger population by reviewing trends from a sample of data.

Information governance (IG) A strategic information-management approach to maximizing a value while mitigating the risks associated with creating, using, and sharing enterprise information.

Informed consent A legal term referring to the patient's right to make their own treatment decisions based on the knowledge of the risks and benefits.

Injury One of four elements used in a negligence lawsuit, which may be economic (hospital expenses and loss of wages) or non-economic (pain and suffering), that must be proved to be successful.

Inpatient bed occupancy rate (percentage of occupancy) The total number of inpatient service days for a given time period divided by the total number of inpatient bed count days for the same time period.

Inpatient discharge The termination of hospitalization through the formal release of an inpatient from a hospital.

Inpatient prospective payment system (IPPS) The prospective payment system classification that is used specifically for inpatient hospital insurance claims.

Inpatient Service Day (IPSD) A unit of measure equivalent to the services received by one inpatient for one 24-hour period.

Institutional Review Board (IRB) An ethical administrative body that provides review, oversight, guidance and approval for research projects carried out by employees serving as researchers; also, the responsibility for protecting the rights and welfare of the human subjects involved.

Insurance verification The process of contacting the patient's health insurance company to ensure coverage for the date of service and obtain a patient's benefits.

Integrated Delivery System (IDS) A healthcare delivery system that includes hospitals, providers, insurers, and a community's resources that work together to deliver care to patients.

Intentional tort A circumstance in which a healthcare provider purposely commits a wrongful act that results in injury to a patient.

Interchange The ability for computer systems to communicate information to each other.

Internal analysis An evaluation of the internal environment to determine strengths and weaknesses of a healthcare organization.

Internal customer A customer within an organization, such as employees.

Internal forces Forces from inside an organization that are identified as strengths and weaknesses.

Interoperability The ability for computer systems to interact with each other seamlessly.

IP address A numerical label assigned to each device connected to a computer network that uses the Internet Protocol for communication.

Java A general-purpose computer programming language that is object oriented.

Job description A detailed list of job duties and responsibilities, reporting relationships, and working conditions per job title.

Joint Commission A private, not-for-profit accrediting organization that evaluates and accredits hospitals and other healthcare organizations on the basis of predefined performance standards; formerly known as the Joint Commission on Accreditation of Healthcare Organizations (JCAHO).

Jurisdiction The authority and power of the court to hear and decide specific types of cases.

Justice An ethical principle that recognizes the importance of treating all people fairly and applying all standards consistently despite the situation.

Key indicator A quantifiable measure used over a specific time that is used to determine whether some structure, process, or outcome supports high-quality performance measured against best practice criteria.

Laissez-faire leadership A leadership style in which the leader takes a hands-off approach to management;

the team performs the work, and the leader maintains the title.

Leadership The actions of a leader.

Leading by example A leadership style in which the leader acts as a role model for team members to follow and emulate.

Lean A process improvement methodology that is focused on reducing and eliminating waste and improving the flow of work processes.

Lean Six Sigma A quality improvement methodology that illustrates the elimination of waste from Lean and critical process quality characteristics from Six Sigma.

Legal health record Documents and data elements that comprise a record of the patient's healthcare encounter that is complete so it can be used in a court of law.

Length of stay (LOS) The total number of patient days for an inpatient episode, calculated by subtracting the date of admission from the date of discharge.

Liabilities Economic costs an individual, corporation, or country has with the expectation that it will reduce the value of assets; often reported on a balance sheet.

Licensure The legal authority from government authorities to perform certain activities as long as they fall within the standards and regulations already established.

Line chart A graphical representation that illustrates the relationship between continuous measurements.

Litigation A civil lawsuit or contest in court.

Local Coverage Determinations (LCD) A decision established by a Medicare Administrative Contractor (MAC) as to whether a delivered medical service was reasonable and necessary based on a geographical area.

Logical Observations, Identifiers, Names and Codes (LOINC) A database protocol developed by the Regenstrief Institute for Health Care aimed at standardizing laboratory and clinical codes for use in clinical care, outcomes management, and research; used by nurses.

Maintenance A stage of the health information technology implementation in which the implemented technology is maintained.

Malfeasance An ethical principle that recognizes a wrong or improper act.

Malware Software designed to invade another person's or facility's computer system with malicious intent.

Managed Care Organization (MCO) A type of insurance organization model that is focused on reducing the costs of health care while maintaining the quality of care delivered.

Management information system (MIS) Health information systems designed to support management operations in the healthcare facility.

Master patient index (MPI) A database created and maintained by the healthcare facility that includes admitting data for each patient and is never destroyed.

Maternal death rate (hospital-based) The total number of maternal deaths directly related to pregnancy in a hospital for a given time period divided by the total number of obstetrical discharges for the same time period.

Maternal mortality rate (community-based) The total number of deaths attributed to maternal conditions in the community during a given time period in a specific geographic area divided by the total number of live births for the same time period and area.

Mean A measure of central tendency that is determined by calculating the arithmetic average of the observations in a frequency distribution.

Meaningful Use (MU) Standards of electronic data and information use in a healthcare facility established by the HITECH Act.

Measures of central tendency Measures of location that indicate the typical value of a frequency distribution.

Median A measure of central tendency that shows the midpoint of a frequency distribution when the observations have been arranged in order from lowest to highest.

Medicaid A government payor that provides health insurance coverage to lower-income citizens; although the federal government pays for the program, each state manages its own Medicaid plan.

Medical examiner An appointed physician specializing in forensic medicine who performs autopsies to determine cause of death.

Medical identity theft Occurs when an individual's health information is misrepresented and used by an unauthorized individual to obtain healthcare goods, services, or money to which they are neither eligible nor entitled.

Medical Literature, Analysis, and Retrieval System Online (MEDLINE) An expert system sponsored by the U.S. National Library of Medicine (NLM) that includes over 19 million references to journal articles in life science, with a concentration on biomedicine.

Medical necessity A reimbursement term used to refer to a health insurance company's determination that services rendered were not medically necessary and thus not covered by patient's benefits.

Medical peer review A component of medical research that adds significance and value when reviewed by expert peers in the same industry.

Medical record number A unique numeric or alphanumeric identifier assigned to each patient's record upon admission to a healthcare facility.

Medicare A government payor that provides health insurance coverage to citizens older than 65, patients with permanent disabilities, and patients who have end stage renal disease (ESRD); the federal government sponsors and administers Medicare, and coverage does not change from state to state.

Medicare Administrative Contractors (MACs) Third-party Medicare administrators established by the Medicare Prescription Drug Improvement and Modernization Act of 2003 to assist with controlling healthcare costs of Medicare beneficiaries.

Medicare Advantage A plan available to Medicare beneficiaries that combines Part A, Part B, and Part D in which benefits are paid by the Medicare administrator; also known as Medicare Part C.

Medicare Part A The Medicare plan that covers inpatient hospital care; guaranteed to all Americans who qualify for Medicare.

Medicare Part B The Medicare plan that covers physicians' services and some other services such as labs and radiology; Medicare Part A participants must pay a monthly premium for Medicare Part B coverages.

Medicare Part D The Medicare plan that covers drugs and pharmaceuticals; Medicare Part A participants must pay a monthly premium for coverage.

Medicare Provider Analysis and Review File (MPAR) A database that stores information submitted by fiscal intermediaries that is used by the Office of the Inspector General (OIG) to identify suspicious reimbursement practices.

Medicare severity diagnosis-related groups (MS-DRG) The U.S. government's 2007 revision of the DRG system; the MS-DRG system better accounts for severity of illness and resource consumption.

Medication record reconciliation A medical record present in every inpatient hospital patient record that reconciles all medications from admission to discharge.

Medigap The secondary insurance that covers the 20% deductible for Medicare patients; patients pay a separate monthly premium for coverage.

Meeting minutes Detailed notes recorded by a meeting secretary that documents the issues and decisions made during the meeting.

Metadata Descriptive data that characterizes data to develop a clearer understanding and meaning to achieve greater reliability and quality of information.

Middle management The management level in the healthcare facilities that implements the strategic planning goals established by executive management.

Minimum Data Set Version 3.0 (MDS 3.0) A federally mandated standard data set that Medicare- and/or Medicaid-certified nursing facilities must use to collect demographic and clinical data on nursing home residents.

Minimum necessary standard A stipulation of the HIPAA Privacy Rule that requires healthcare facilities and other covered entities to make reasonable efforts to limit the patient-identifiable information they disclose to the least amount required to accomplish the intended purpose for which the information was requested.

Mission statement A written statement that defines the goals and objectives of a healthcare organization's operations and functions.

Mixed methods A research methodology that incorporates qualitative and quantitative research.

Mode A measure of central tendency that consists of the most frequent observation in a frequency distribution.

Movement diagram A project management tool used to display the movement of activities and actions through the project completion process.

Multi-voting technique A decision-making technique that allows team members to determine the prioritization of issues.

National Cancer Registrars Association (NCRA) A not-for-profit association that represents cancer registrars and certifies registrars as certified tumor registrars (CTRs).

National Committee for Quality Assurance (NCQA) A private, not-for-profit accreditation organization whose mission is to evaluate and report on the quality of managed care organizations in the United States.

National Correct Coding Initiative (NCCI) Coding edits published by Medicare used to promote national correct coding methodologies and to control improper coding leading to inappropriate payment in Part B claims.

National coverage determinations (NCD) A decision established by a Medicare Administrative Contractor (MAC) as to whether a delivered medical service is reasonable and necessary based on nationwide trends.

National Drug Codes (NDC) A medical code set that organizes product identifiers for human drugs.

National Provider Database (NPDB) A nationwide database of healthcare providers with the primary goals of improving healthcare quality, protecting the public, and reducing healthcare fraud and abuse in the United States.

National Vital Statistics System (NVSS) The national database of birth and death certificates.

Natural language processing A field of computer science and linguistics concerned with the interactions between computers and human (natural) languages that converts information from computer databases into readable human language.

Need-to-know principle A principle used in the release of information process to establish the minimal necessary standard.

Negligence An ethical and legal term that refers to the result of an action by an individual who does not act the way a reasonably prudent person would act under the same circumstances.

Neonatal mortality rate The ratio of stillbirth deaths compared to all births.

Net autopsy rate The ratio of inpatient autopsies compared to inpatient deaths calculated by dividing the total number of inpatient autopsies performed by the hospital pathologist for a given time period by the total number of inpatient deaths minus un-autopsied coroners' or medical examiners' cases for the same time period.

Net death rate The total number of inpatient deaths minus the number of deaths that occurred less then 48 hours after admission for a given period of time divided by the total number of inpatient discharges minus the number of deaths that occurred less than 48 hours after admission for the same time period.

Network controls A method of protecting electronic data from unauthorized change and corruption during transmission among information systems.

Newborn (NB) An inpatient who was born in the hospital at the beginning of the current inpatient hospitalization.

Newborn autopsy rate The number of autopsies performed on newborns who died during a given time period divided by the total number of newborns who died during the same time period.

Newborn death rate The ratio of newborn deaths compared to all births.

Nomenclature An accepted system of terms that follow established naming conventions.

Nominal group technique A decision-making technique that includes silent listing and rank ordering to prioritize projects and activities.

Nominal-level data Data that falls into mutually exclusive groups or categories with no specific order (for example, patient demographics such as third-party payer, race, and sex); also called categorical data.

Normal distribution A measure of central tendency that uses continuous frequency distributions characterized by a symmetric bell-shaped curve, with an equal mean, median, and mode, any standard deviation, and with half of the observations above the mean and half below it.

North American Association of Central Cancer Registrars (NAACCR) An accreditation organization that supports certification programs for state population-based registries.

Notice of Privacy Practices A statement (mandated by the HITECH) issued by a healthcare organization that informs individuals of the uses and disclosures of patient-identifiable health information that may be made by the organization, as well as the individual's rights and the organization's legal duties with respect to that information.

Notifiable disease A disease and/or condition that must be reported to a government agency (CDC) so that regular, frequent, and timely information on individual cases can be used to prevent and control future cases of the disease.

Object-oriented database A type of database that contains objects organized by rows and columns.

Occupational Safety and Health Act (OSHA) The federal legislation that establishes comprehensive safety and health guidelines for all work environments in the United States.

Office of the Inspector General (OIG) The office of federal oversight assigned to protect the integrity of the Department of Health and Human Services through national audits, investigations, and inspections.

Office of the National Coordinator (ONC) The office of federal oversight assigned to coordinate national efforts to implement the meaningful use of health information technology throughout the country.

Operating budget The amount allocated for healthcare facility day-to-day operations.

Operation index An index of all the surgical procedures, including ICD-10-PCS and CPT codes, if applicable, and including the line charges per procedure.

Operational planning The day-to-day tasks performed to keep a healthcare facility operating.

Opportunity An external force evaluated to determine potential revenue-generating sources.

Ordinal-level data Data with inherent order and with higher numbers usually associated with higher values; also called ordinal data or ranked data.

Organization chart A chart used to visually display the relationships of positions, departments, and employees in a healthcare organization.

Organization mergers The process of combining two or more healthcare organizations operationally, financially, and executively.

Orientation The initial training provided to new healthcare facility employees to ensure they follow the organization mission, standards of conduct, and HIPAA compliance.

Out-of-pocket expense A patient's financial responsibility after the health insurance has paid a health insurance claim; includes deductible, coinsurance, and copayment.

Outcome and Effectiveness Research (OER) Federally sponsored studies on the effectiveness of delivered therapeutic care.

Outcome indicator An indicator that evaluates the results of delivered patient care.

Outcomes and Assessment Information Set (OASIS) A standard core assessment data tool developed to measure the outcomes of adult patients receiving home health services under the Medicare and Medicaid programs.

Outlier cases Healthcare cases in which delivered care expense is exponentially higher due to unexpected complications.

Outpatient Prospective Payment System (OPPS) The prospective payment system classification used specifically for outpatient hospital insurance claims.

Overcoding The regular practice of assigning additional codes in order to increase reimbursements; a fraudulent practice.

Paired t test A statistical calculation used to determine whether the difference between two sets of observations is zero.

Palliative care A type of health care delivered to relieve the patient's pain and suffering without attempting to cure the underlying disease.

Pareto chart A bar graph in which the bars are arranged in order of descending size to display projects with a higher priority.

Participating provider A healthcare provider who is approved to provide services to patients of the health insurer; the provider must complete the credentialing process to qualify.

Passwords A unique series of characters, including alpha, numerical, and symbols, that must be entered to authenticate a user's identity to gain access to a secured site.

Patient account number A number assigned by a healthcare facility for billing purposes that is unique to a particular episode of care; a new account number is assigned each time the patient receives care or services at the facility.

Patient Assessment Instrument (PAI) A standardized quality management tool used to evaluate the patient's condition after admission to, and at discharge from, a healthcare facility.

Patient Centered Outcomes Research Institute (PCORI) A government-sponsored organization responsible to research the relative effectiveness of health care delivered.

Patient identifiable data Data found in the patient's electronic health record that can be linked specifically to them, including the patient name, age, date of birth, gender, and address.

Patient portals Online portals that provide a patient access to their health information.

Pay-for-performance A financial incentive offered by a government insurance payor that is issued based on the improvement of clinical data using the electronic health record.

Pearson correlation coefficient A statistical calculation that measures the strength of the linear relationship between two variables.

Penalties Financial consequences issued when a healthcare provider is convicted of fraudulent reimbursement practices.

Per diem A contract with additional workers that is based on the census of the healthcare facility.

Performance improvement The continuous improvement and process improvement adaptations to contribute to a healthcare facility's efficiency and quality.

Performance indicator An indicator that evaluates the quality, effectiveness, and efficiency of services rendered.

Performance management An ongoing process focused on improving productivity and quality.

Personal health record (PHR) An electronic record of health-related information on an individual that is managed by the patient.

Physical safeguards Security measures used by the HIM department, such as locking doors to safeguard data and software systems to prevent unauthorized access.

Physician Index An index of all of the approved providers in a healthcare facility.

Physician query A tool used by coders to clarify medical documentation to determine the most accurate code.

Picture archiving and communication systems (PACS) A medical imaging technology that cost-effectively stores images in an electronic health record.

Pie chart A chart used to visually display different categories by percentage.

Plaintiff The party that brings a case against someone or another party. In a civil case, the civil complaint is made against the plaintiff; in a criminal case, it is the party that accuses the defendant.

Planning The first step of the health information system implementation process that asks what is needed for the project.

Point of care (POC) The physical location to which the healthcare provider delivers therapeutic services to the patient.

Point of service plan (POS) A managed care model in which the beneficiaries select a primary care physician from the assigned network.

Policy holder The subscriber of the healthcare plan who pays the monthly premium.

Population-based statistics Statistics based on a defined population rather than on a sample drawn from the same population.

Portals Special web pages that offer secure access and entry of data upon authorization of the owner of the page.

Postoperative infection rate The number of infections that occur in clean surgical cases for a given time period divided by the total number of operations within the same time period.

Post-surgical activities Activities in the operative report that are included in the procedural code that occur after the procedure such as suture, completing anesthesia, and testing the operative area.

Power and influence theory A leadership theory that states leaders use authority and control to accomplish team tasks.

Preauthorization The process of verifying patient health insurance coverage before services are delivered.

Predictive analytics A branch of advanced analytics that uses data mining, statistics modeling, and artificial intelligence to make predictions about the future.

Preferred provider organization (PPO) A managed care model that allows the patient to choose any physician, either general or specialist, within the network of chosen physicians to access health care.

Premium The monthly payment made for health insurance coverage.

Prescriptive analytics A branch of analytics that uses descriptive and predictive analytics to make financial decisions.

Present on Admission (POA) An indicator on the CMB-1450 health insurance claim form for a patient condition that existed prior to admission.

Pre-surgical activities Activities in the operative report that are included in the procedural code and that occur before the procedure, such as prepping the surgical area, making the incision, identifying the surgical area.

Prevalence rate The proportion of people in a population that have a particular disease at a specific point in time or over a specified time period.

Primary data source Data in the health record that is used directly in patient care.

Privacy An essential element of HIPAA in which private health information is hidden and concealed from access.

Privacy officer A position in the healthcare organization that is responsible to keep health information concealed from unauthorized access.

Procedural statement The statement in the operative report that describes the procedure performed.

Program evaluation and review technique (PERT) A project management tool that presents a project's timeline in a diagram.

Project Management Professional (PMP) A certification offered to professionals that follow an established set of principles and procedures to accomplish projects efficiently.

Proportion A type of ratio in which the elements included in the numerator also must be included in the denominator.

Proportionate mortality rate (PMR) The total number of deaths due to a specific cause during a given time period divided by the total number of deaths due to all causes.

Prospective Payment System (PPS) A reimbursement system that uses preset payment levels established by the health insurance company instead of paying the physician or hospital charges in total.

Prospective review A review of the health record prior to admission to determine the medical necessity of therapeutic care recommended.

Prospective studies Studies designed to observe healthcare delivery outcomes.

Protected health information (PHI) Information in the patient health record that is identifiable, such as name, date of birth, age, gender, address, and contact information.

Proximal attributes Leadership traits that include problem-solving skills, expertise, and tacit knowledge that is gained from the leader's professional environment.

Purged records Patient health records that have been removed from the active file area because they have been inactive at least the minimum standard time.

Qualitative analysis A review of the health record in order to ensure that standards are met including the adequacy of the documentation of healthcare delivery.

Qualitative research A type of research design that focuses on perceptions, attributes, feelings, attitudes, and other qualitative characteristics.

Quality improvement A management approach undertaken to improve healthcare delivery that involves two principal steps: problem identification and process redesign.

Quality indicator An established indicator that represents the level of performance for the standard of care.

Quality Integrity Organizations (QIOs) Third-party organizations that use peer review for Medicare and Medicaid submitted health insurance claim forms to ensure accurate diagnosis, procedure, quality care, and appropriateness of care.

Quantitative analysis A type of research design that focuses on health record completeness and accuracy.

Quasi-experimental study A type of experimental study that has no manipulated independent variable and no control group.

Query A form of communication between the medical coder and the healthcare provider who documented the health record; used to ensure accurate coding.

Qui tam The whistleblower provision of the False Claims Act, which protects individuals who file a complaint.

Quid pro quo A legal term referring to a favor or exchange for something given.

Range A measure of variability between the smallest and the largest observations in a frequency distribution.

Rate A statistical measure used to compare an event over time; a comparison of the number of times an event did happen (numerator) with the number of times an event could have happened (denominator).

Ratio A mathematical calculation determined by dividing one quantity by the total number possible.

Ratio analysis A financial activity in which financial categories are compared to provide a clear picture of the financial health of a healthcare organization.

Ratio-level data Data defined by a unit of measure, a real zero point, and with equal intervals between successive values; also called ratio data.

Recovery audit contractor (RAC) A third-party organization whose goal is to identify overpaid or underpaid Medicare claims.

Referred patient A patient referred to a specialist from a general practitioner.

Registered Health Information Administrator (RHIA) A certification offered by AHIMA to accredited 4-year college degree HIM program candidates who pass the RHIA exam.

Registered Health Information Technician (RHIT) A certification offered by AHIMA to accredited 2-year college degree HIT program candidates who pass the RHIT exam.

Registration-admission-discharge-transfer system (R-ADT) A health information system used to store administrative information for a healthcare facility.

Registry A database of care information related to a specific disease, condition, or procedure that assists in health information analysis.

Reimbursement The process of submitting a health insurance claim for medical services rendered and receiving payment from the health insurance company.

Relational database A type of database that stores data in predefined rows and columns.

Release of information (ROI) The process of releasing protected health information to authorized individuals.

Remittance Advice (RA) An explanation of benefits issues by Medicare electronically for claims submitted.

Requisition A request from an authorized health record user to gain access to their medical record.

Resident Assessment Instrument (RAI) A uniform assessment instrument developed by the Centers for Medicare and Medicaid Services to standardize the collection of skilled nursing facility patient date; includes the Minimum Data Set 3.0, triggers, and resident assessment protocols.

Resource-based Relative Value Scale (RBRVS) A Medicare reimbursement system implemented in 1992 to compensate physicians according to a fee schedule predicated on weights assigned on the basis of the resources required to provide the services.

Resource Utilization Groups (RUGs) A case-mix-adjusted classification system based on minimum data set assessments and used by skilled nursing facilities.

Retention Storing and maintaining inactive health records for future use in compliance with state and federal minimum requirements.

Retrospective review The process of continually monitoring a patient's medical record after their hospital stay for medical necessity and the appropriateness of care delivered.

Revenue The total amount of income reported on the income statement financial report.

Risk analysis An assessment of possible security threats to an organization's data.

Risk management A comprehensive program of administrative activities intended to minimize the potential for injuries to occur in a facility and to anticipate and respond to ensuing liabilities for those injuries that do occur.

Risk of mortality score (ROM) An indicator that reports the risk of inpatient death.

Root-cause analysis An analytical tool used in performance improvement to determine the causes of problems.

Rules and regulations Facility operating documents that detail the rules and regulations under which a healthcare organization operates.

RxNorm A clinical drug nomenclature developed by the Food and Drug Administration, the Department of Veterans Affairs, and HL7 to provide standard names for clinical drugs and administered dose forms.

Scatter diagram A chart that displays the linear relationship between two variables visually.

Secondary data source Data in the health record that is deidentified and used for research and education.

Security An essential element of HIPAA in which private health information is secured from unauthorized access.

Security breach An event that is a violation of the policies or standards developed to ensure security.

Security threat An information breach that has the potential to open unauthorized access to private patient information in the EHR.

Sentinel event An event defined by the Joint Commission that involves an unexpected occurrence involving death or serious injury to the patient.

Serial numbering system A type of health record identification and filing system in which patients are assigned a different but unique numerical identifier for every admission.

Severity of illness documentation (SOI) EHR documentation that supports objective clinical indicators of patient illness to confirm diagnosis and to justify medical intervention.

Six Sigma A quality improvement methodology that is disciplined and data-driven for reducing deficiencies in healthcare delivery.

Skilled Nursing Facility Prospective Payment System (SNFPP) The prospective payment system classification used specifically for skilled nursing facilities.

SMART goals A performance improvement tool that develops goals that are specific, measurable, attainable, relevant, and time based.

SNOMED CT A clinical vocabulary used as a controlled vocabulary for health care, specifically in the background of the EHR.

Social Security Act The federal legislation that created the Medicare health insurance program.

Source systems The health information systems in which data was originally created.

Span of control A management term that refers to the specific subordinates managed by the supervisor.

Spearman correlation coefficient A statistical calculation that measures the strength and direction of association between two ranked variables.

Specialization A healthcare provider completing additional medical training to specialize care for specific body system conditions.

Speech recognition A health information system that converts dictation into narrated reports.

Staff recruitment The human resource management process of hiring for the different job openings in the healthcare facility.

Staff retention The human resource management function of keeping quality and effective employees for the healthcare organization.

Standard deviation A measure of variability that describes the deviation from the mean of a frequency distribution in the original units of measurement; the square root of the variance.

Standard Query Language (SQL) A computer programming language that is used for databases.

Stark Law A federal legislation that prohibits physicians promoting goods and services that they have a financial interest in.

Statement of Cash Flows A financial statement that represents the flow of cash through the healthcare organization during a defined period of time.

Statute of limitations An assigned time frame allowed by local, state, or federal law for bringing a litigation case.

Stem and leaf plots A visual chart that organizes data to show its shape and distribution, using two columns, with the stem in the left-hand column and all the leaves associated with that stem in the right-hand column; the "leaf" is the ones digit of the number, and the other digits form the "stem."

Strengths An internal force evaluated to determine a stronger position compared to other healthcare organizations in the market.

Strength-Weaknesses-Opportunities-Threats (SWOT) An organization assessment and analysis tool that identifies internal and external forces that affect the healthcare facility.

Structure indicator A type of indicator that measures the attributes of the healthcare facility setting.

Structured brainstorming A decision-making technique that allows team members to brainstorm for ideas to prioritize.

Subjective, Objective, Assessment, Plan (SOAP) A format healthcare providers use to document physician notes in the patient health record.

Subpoena ad testificandum A legal term that commands a person to appear, give testimony, and bring all documents, paper, books, and records described in the subpoena.

Supervisory management The management level in the healthcare facilities that manages the everyday operations of the healthcare facility.

Surgical package Activities included with each procedure code; includes preoperative, surgical, and post-operative activities.

Surveys Quality improvement tools that support the evaluation process of healthcare delivery.

Systems Development Life Cycle (SDLC) A model used to implement health information software and/or hardware upgrades; includes the following stages: planning, design, implementation, and evaluation and maintenance.

Taxonomy The practice and science of naming medical conditions.

Team charter A document that defines the role of team leader and includes the project deliverables and time frame.

Telecommuting A flex time work schedule that allows employees to work from their home computers.

Telehealth A telecommunications system that connects healthcare providers and patients from diverse geographic locations for medical consultation and treatment.

Terminal digit filing system A system of paper health record filing in which the last digits of the record number determines file placement.

Third-party payer A health insurance company that reimburses providers for healthcare services rendered.

Threats An external force evaluated to determine potential negative impacting forces.

Title VII of the Civil Rights Act A federal legislation that prohibits employment discrimination based on race, religion, sex, disability, or national origin.

Tort A legal action taken when one party believes that the other party caused harm through wrongful conduct and negligence, so they seek compensation.

Total length of stay (discharge days) The sum of the days of stay of any group of inpatients discharged during a specific period of time.

Trait theory A leadership theory that states leaders are born with traits and qualities that make them strong leaders.

Transactions The transmission of data or information between two healthcare entities for a financial or administrative purpose related to health care, according to HIPAA and HITECH legislation.

Transmission Control Protocol/Internet Protocol (TCP/IP) A collection of protocols used to connect network devices on the Internet.

Trauma registry A database that documents acute care delivered to patients hospitalized with traumatic injuries.

TRICARE The federal healthcare program that provides insurance coverage for dependents of armed forces personnel and for retirees receiving care outside military treatment facilities.

Unbundling A fraudulent medical coding practice of assigning multiple codes to bill for the presurgical and postsurgical steps of a surgical procedure.

Unified Medical Language System (UMLS) A program developed by the National Library of Medicine to build an intelligent, automated system that can understand biomedical concepts, words, and expressions and their interrelationships.

Uniform Ambulatory Care Data Set (UACDS) A data set that collects information about the delivery of ambulatory care; collected through the CMB1500 form.

Uniform Hospital Discharge Data Set (UHDDS) A data set that collects information about the delivery of hospital inpatient care; collected through the CMB1450 form.

Unit numbering system A health paper record identification system in which the record is assigned a unique medical record number at the time of the first encounter that is used for all subsequent encounters.

Unity of command An organizational structure principle in that all subordinate members report to a single leader.

Unstructured data Free text, readable data.

Upcoding A fraudulent medical coding practice of assigning a higher specified code representing higher reimbursement when the documentation does not support it.

Usual, customary, and reasonable charges (UCR) A type of retrospective fee-for-service payment method in which the third-party payer reimburses for fees that are usual, customary, and reasonable.

Utilization management (UM) The management of resources for the healthcare facility to ensure that facilities and resources are used maximally and that use is consistent with patient care needs.

Utilization review The review process initiated by case management to examine whether the medical care delivered is necessary according to preestablished objective screening criteria at time frames specified in the organization's utilization management plan.

Variability The spreading of measures around the population mean.

Variance A measure of variability that gives the average of the squared deviations from the mean.

Virtual private network An encrypted transmission channel through the Internet to ensure a private and secure transmission of data.

Vision statement A statement determined by the board of directors or executive management that provides a road map and direction the healthcare organization would like to go.

Vital statistics Data collected from birth and death statistics, marriage statistics, and fetal deaths.

Voice recognition technology A health information technology that encodes speech signals that do not require speaker pauses (but uses pauses when they are present) and of interpreting at least some of the signals' content as words or the intent of the speaker.

Waste The overutilization of services and misuse of resources.

Weaknesses An internal force evaluated to determine a weaker position compared to other healthcare organizations in the market.

Whistleblower Protection Act A federal law that protects federal whistleblowers who work for the government and report the possible existence of an activity constituting a violation of law, rules, or regulations, or mismanagement.

Workers' Compensation A health insurance plan that covers employees injured while at work.

Workflow analysis A performance improvement tool used to study the flow of work in the healthcare facility.

Workforce planning A study of national trends including social and economic data as well as required staffing regulations to determine the organization's staffing needs.

World Health Organization (WHO) An organization sponsored by the United Nation that focuses on improving the health of populations all over the world.

Index

Note: Page numbers followed by *t* indicate material in tables.